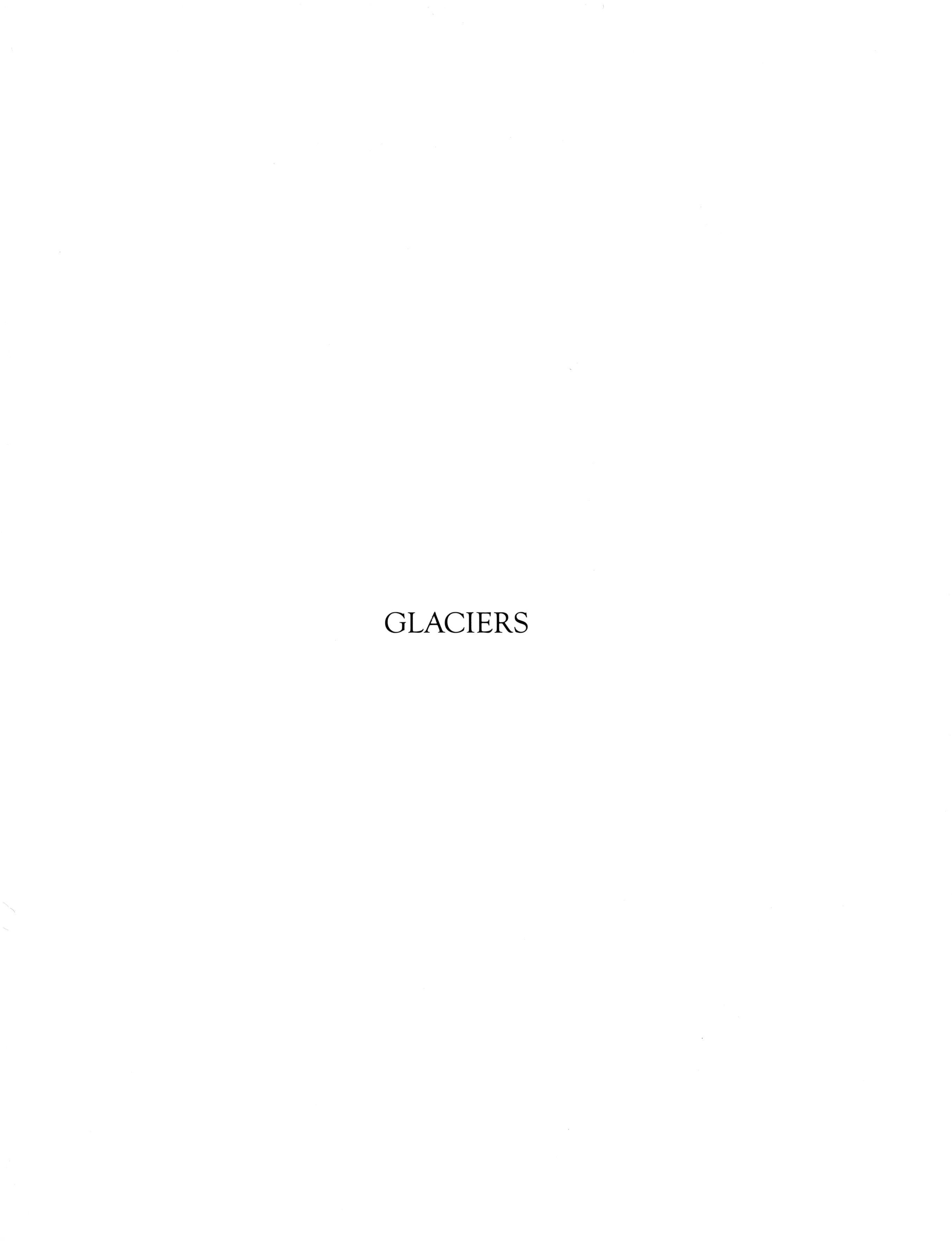

GLACIERS

SEBASTIÃO SALGADO

GLACIERS

Edited by Lélia Wanick Salgado

Prestel

Munich • London • New York

The Glacier

We stopped, ventured a glance
Down the sad green jaws,
And the strength in our breasts dissolved
Like lost hope. Within him a sad strength sleeps,
And when at night, in the silence
of the moon, he sometimes shrieks and roars,
It is because, in his stone bed,
Huge sluggish dreamer,
He is struggling to turn over and cannot.

Primo Levi
Avigliana, 15 March 1946

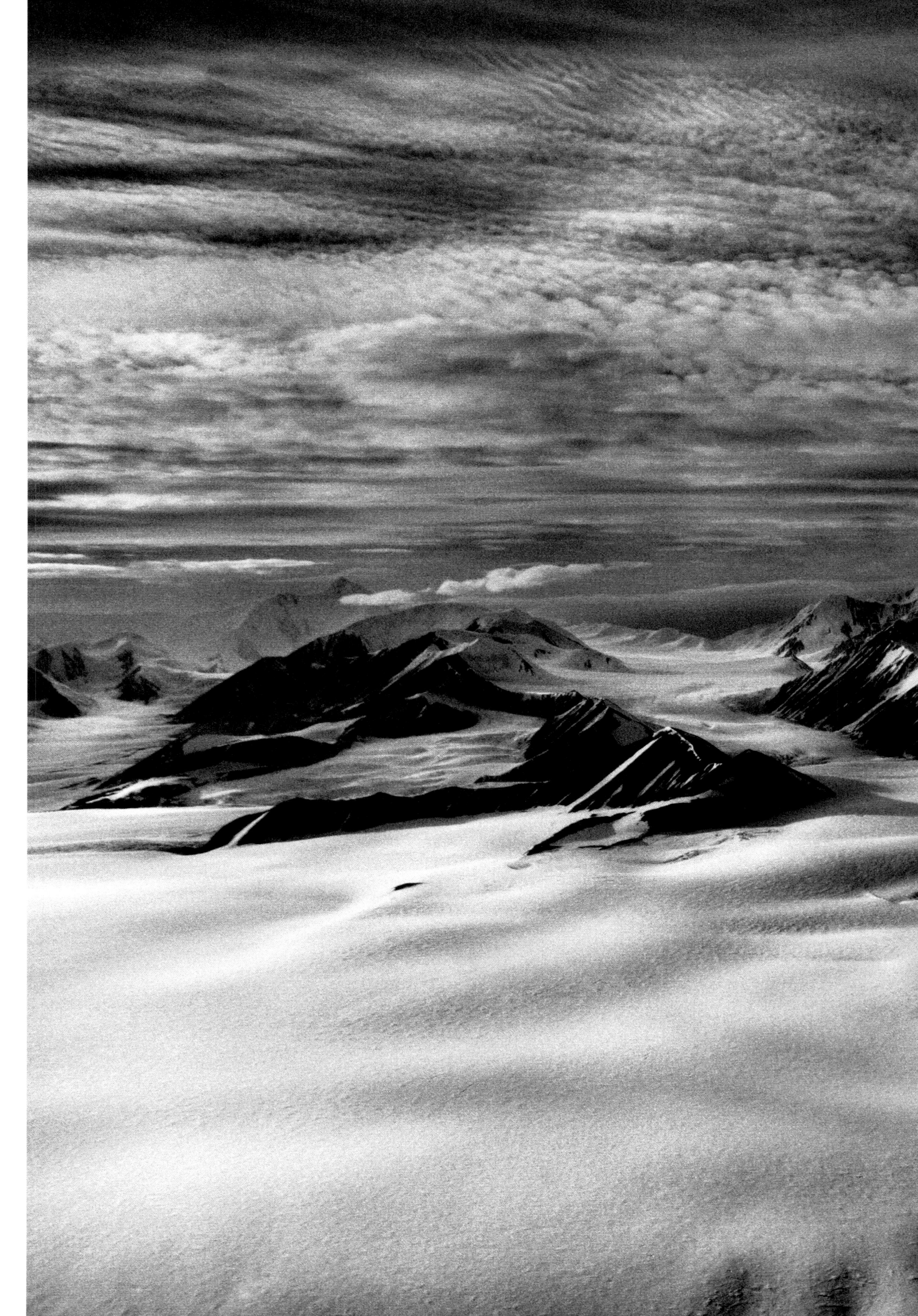

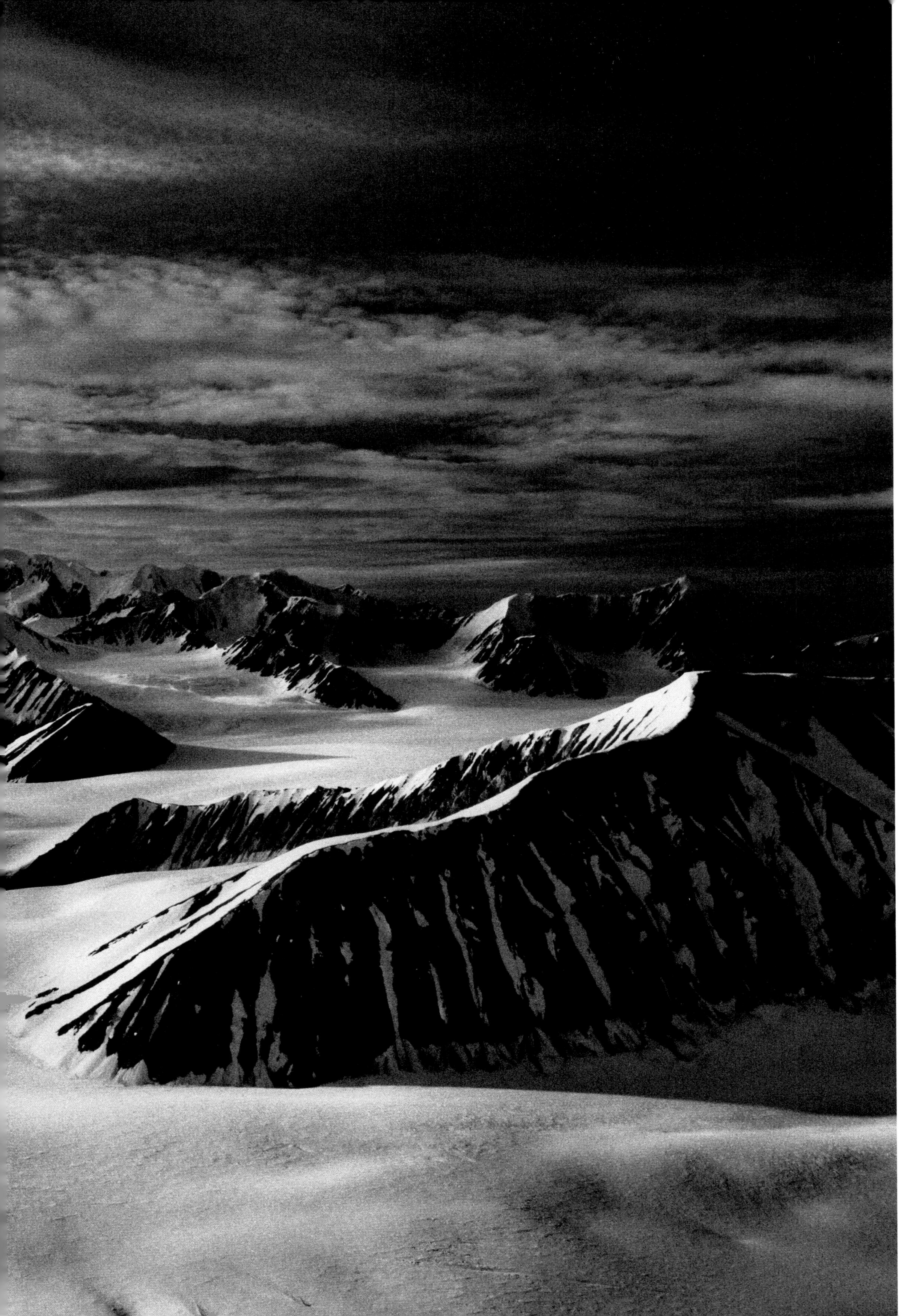

Glaciers: Natural Sensors of the Changing Climate

Elisa Palazzi

Glaciers form where soft, light snow that accumulates during the cold, wet winter does not melt completely when the weather turns warm and dry, instead undergoing a series of transformations as the years go by. At first, it accumulates, layer upon layer, gradually growing denser, after which it is transformed into an older, granular, highly compacted form of snow called "firn" and ultimately becomes glacial ice. These processes unfold at high altitude in the mountains in what is known as the glacier's accumulation zone; from there, the ice begins its slow progression towards lower altitudes, moving into what is called the ablation zone, where it can melt. A glacier in motion – slowly flowing from the accumulation to the ablation zone, driven by the force of its weight – is a glacier that is alive. It is alive because it is moving. The transition from the accumulation zone to the ablation zone corresponds to an imaginary line, the equilibrium line; at this point the glacier's mass balance, in other words the relationship between the amount of ice accumulated at higher altitudes and its loss lower down the mountain, is zero.

If a glacier shrinks excessively, for example in this era of global warming, it no longer has the strength to move, to flow, and this often sounds its death knell even before it becomes completely ice-free (different terminology is used to refer to the residual ice, which is known as a glacieret, a transitional form between firn [névé] and a glacier). That is precisely what happened, for example, to the Icelandic glacier Okjökull, whose funeral was held on 18 August 2019. A small patch of ice at the top of the Ok volcano, just 7 per cent of the extent of the ice cover a hundred years earlier, was all that remained of Okjökull in 2019. However, the glacier had already been officially pronounced dead a few years earlier, in 2014, when it had dwindled so dramatically that it was unable to move. At that point the ice no longer had sufficient mass to nourish the glacier's dynamics. Another parameter that indicates a glacier's health is a change in equilibrium-line altitude. That line moves up to higher altitudes in a warmer climate, which means that the overall area where glaciers can grow, nourished by snowfall in the cold season, is becoming smaller.

Let us stop for a moment and consider why glaciers are important, for the climate and for human beings. First of all, they play a significant role in regulating Earth's climate. Thanks to their highly effective reflection of solar radiation, they help ensure that the planet's surface does not grow too hot. They also serve as something akin to water towers for lowland regions: drinking water supplies for two billion people and two-thirds of the world's agriculture under irrigation depend on glaciers. A third, very important aspect, especially for climate scientists like myself, is that glaciers are extremely valuable climate archives. They allow us to reconstruct how the climate evolved in the past, even hundreds of thousands of years ago. If a cylinder of ice – one of those renowned cores – is extracted from a site with abundant ice, such as Antarctica, layers can be identified, corresponding to the accumulation of snow and its compaction year after year. When snow is transformed into ice, air bubbles, organic substances (pollen, plant fragments, insects), and inorganic substances (dust, soot, pollutants) are entrapped within the ice. Years later – even hundreds of thousands of years later – these serve as valuable tools for identifying climate traits from the past. Bubbles, for example, are analysed to determine the concentration of greenhouse gases in fossil air, using specialised dating methods and techniques. These traces of a history of which we can have no other memory make it possible to (re)read today's climate by putting it into perspective and help us understand its specific details, while at the same time serving as a data source to improve the models that underpin projections about future developments.

Glaciers, like the other elements in the cryosphere (everywhere on the planet where water is present in a solid state) are sentinels of climate change. The rapid pace at which glaciers have been melting recently bears witness to the unprecedented rate at which the planet is heating up.[1] A 2021 study showed that the cryosphere has lost around 87,000 square kilometres (an area the size of Portugal) per annum since the 1980s as a consequence of global warming.[2] Large expanses of sea ice have disappeared, along with the ice cover on lakes and rivers, while snow cover has also dwindled

1 Intergovernmental Panel on Climate Change (IPCC), *Climate Change 2021 – The Physical Science Basis: Working Group I Contribution to the Sixth Assessment Report of the Intergovernmental Panel on Climate Change* (Cambridge and New York, 2023), available online at https://bit. ly/43vHeb5.

2 Peng Xiaoqing, Zhang Tingjun, Oliver W. Frauenfeld, Ran Du, Haodong Jin, and Cuicui Mu, 'A Holistic Assessment of 1979–2016 Global Cryospheric Extent', *Earth's Future* 9, no. 8 (2021), available online at https://bit.ly/4bCF8Iy.

dramatically. Snow is likewise a natural sensor of the changing climate. A warmer world is tantamount to a world with less snow, in which the duration, extent, and thickness of snow cover decreases. If mountain soil is not covered by snow, which acts as a thermal insulator, it is at risk of freezing, leading to an alteration in the nutrient cycle that persists until summer, with knock-on effects for the ecosystem. If there is no snow in the mountains in winter, there is no guaranteed reserve of frozen water that will melt in spring and feed into rivers and streams, bringing water downstream. If there is no snow in winter, glaciers do not have a protective layer over their surface, which helps stop them from melting in the warmer seasons. Studies show that in the Alps the snow water equivalent (SWE: a parameter that indicates the snow's thickness and density and is a helpful measure to determine how much snow has fallen and its water content, potentially available for future use) will fall by between 80 and 90 per cent at around 1,500 metres by late 2100; at higher altitudes the reduction will be smaller, around 10%.[3] A 2020 study published in 2020 addresses the development in the equilibrium line of glaciers in the Alps over a two-century time span, from 1901 to 2100.[4] By 2100, this line could rise by at least 100 metres and at most 600 to 700 metres depending on the greenhouse gas emission scenario, which means that, in the best-case scenario, 69 per cent of the Alpine glaciers that still exist could disappear or, in the worst-case scenario, 92 per cent.

In light of current climate trends, seeking to reduce greenhouse gas emissions through mitigation strategies is only part of the answer. Ingrained mindsets must be abandoned to promote new ways of using and enjoying the mountains, taking the interests of all stakeholders into account and fostering a healthy attitude of respect for this high-altitude realm. This should not happen at the expense of the local populace and should respect the ecosystem of the mountains, in which the world of the glaciers plays such a vital role.

3 Silvia Terzago, Jost von Hardenberg, Elisa Palazzi, and Antonello Provenzale, 'Snow Water Equivalent in the Alps as Seen by Gridded Data Sets, CMIP5 and CORDEX Climate Models', *The Cryosphere* 11, no. 4 (2017), pp. 1625–45, available online at https:// bit.ly/3FhXBhD.

4 Manja Žebre, Renato R. Colucci, Filippo Giorgi, Neil F. Glasser, Adina E. Racoviteanu, and Costanza Del Gobbo, '200 Years of Equilibrium-Line Altitude Variability Across the European Alps (1901–2100)', *Clim Dyn*, no. 56 (2020) pp. 1183–1201, available online at https://bit.ly/4ihltQP.

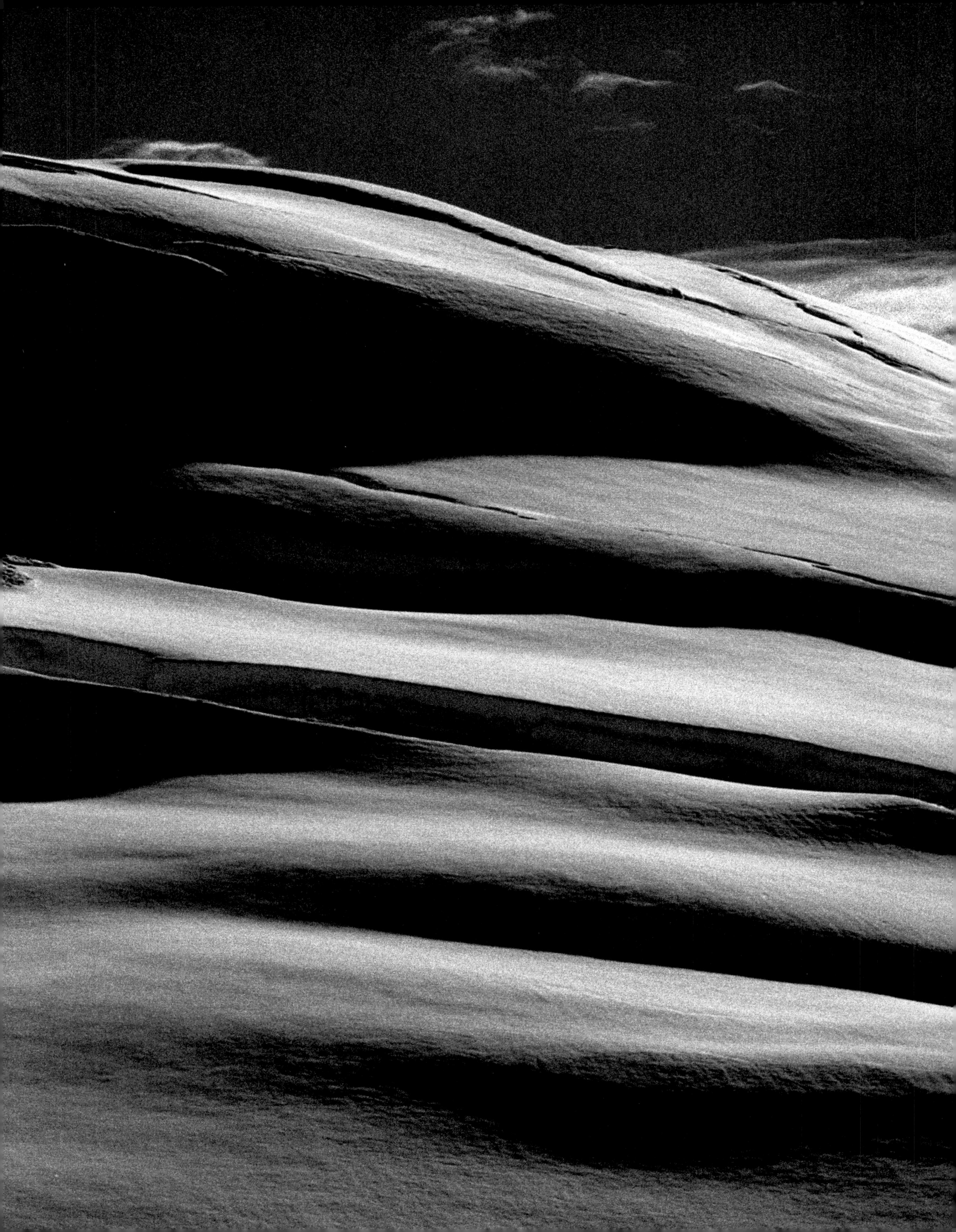

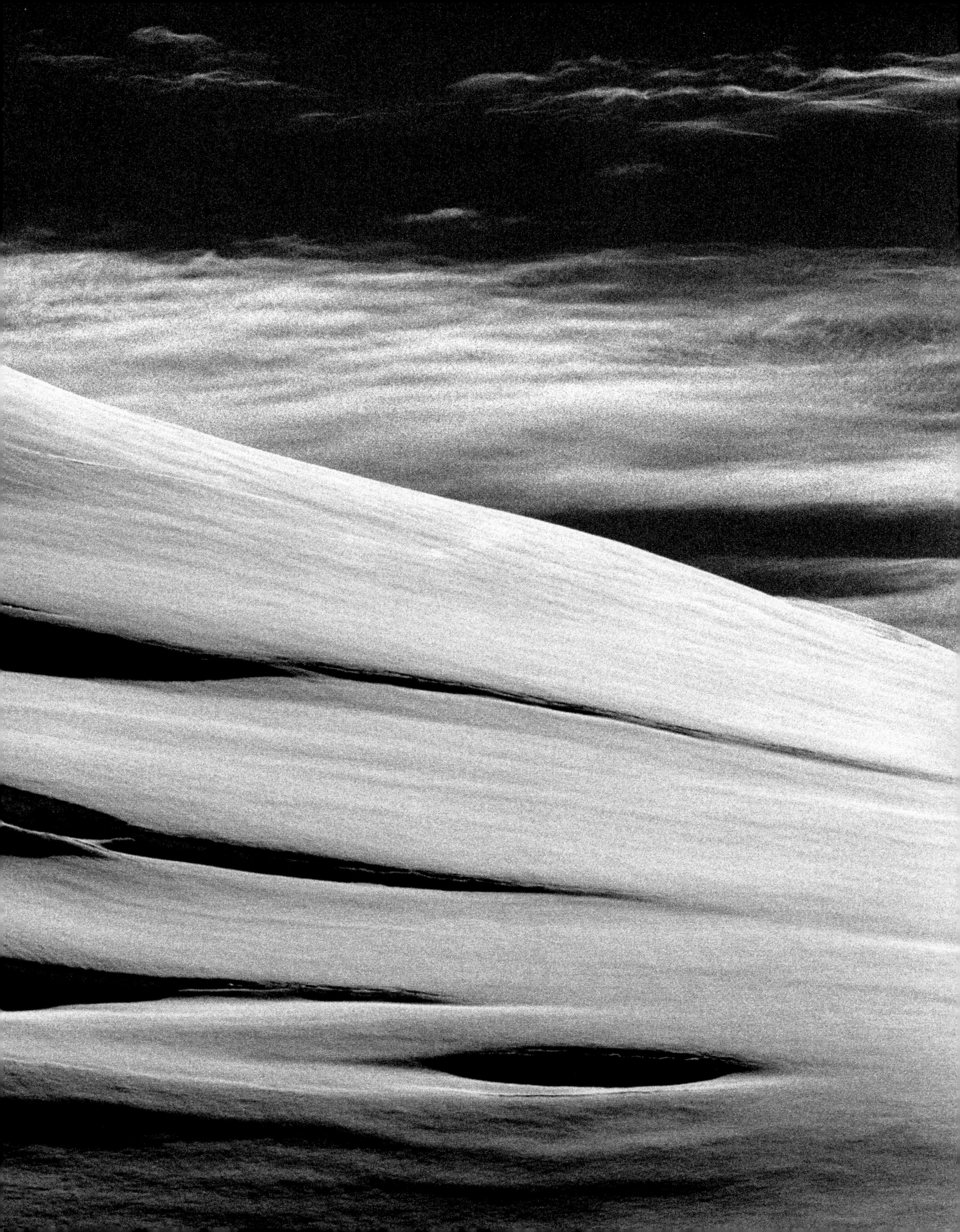

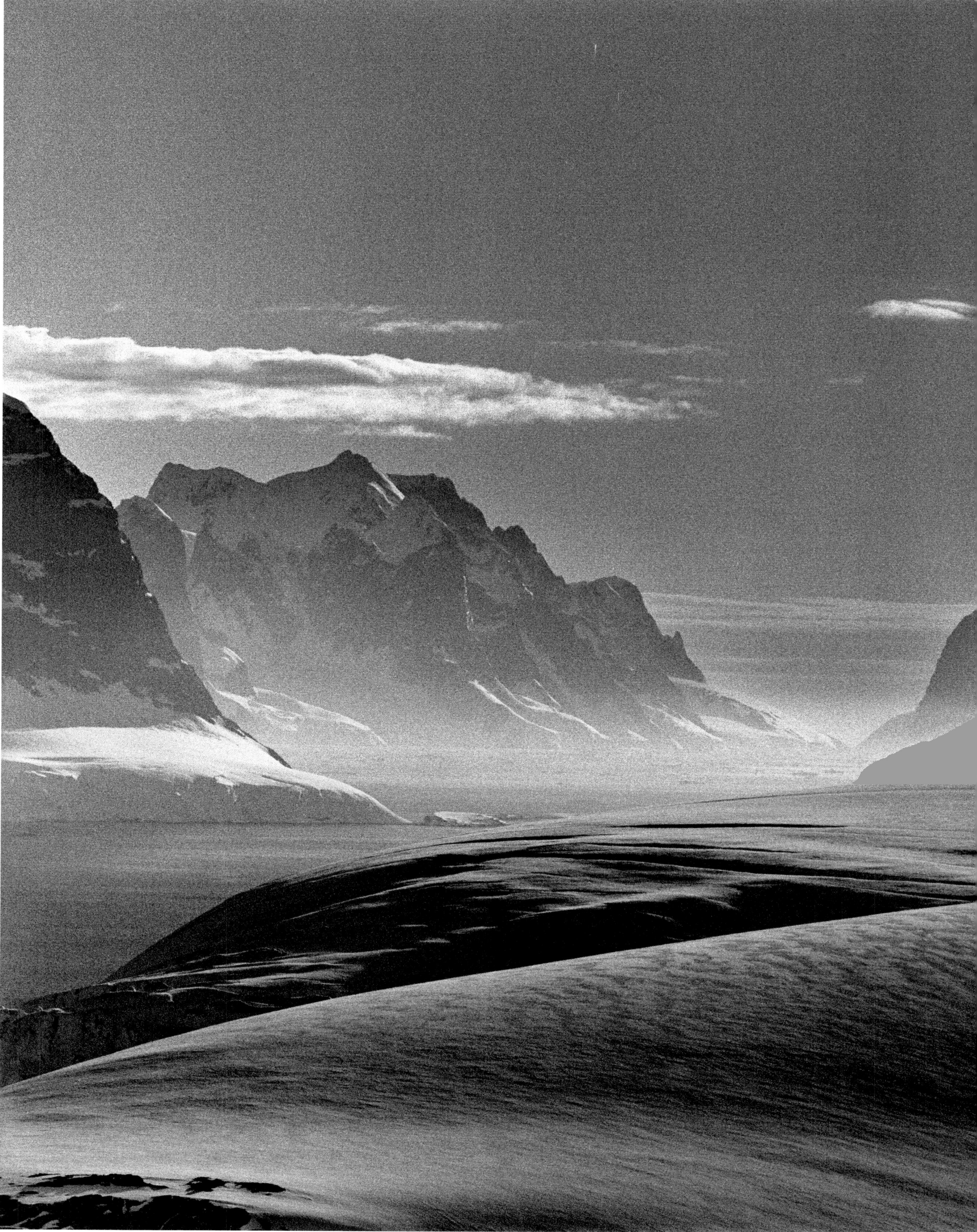

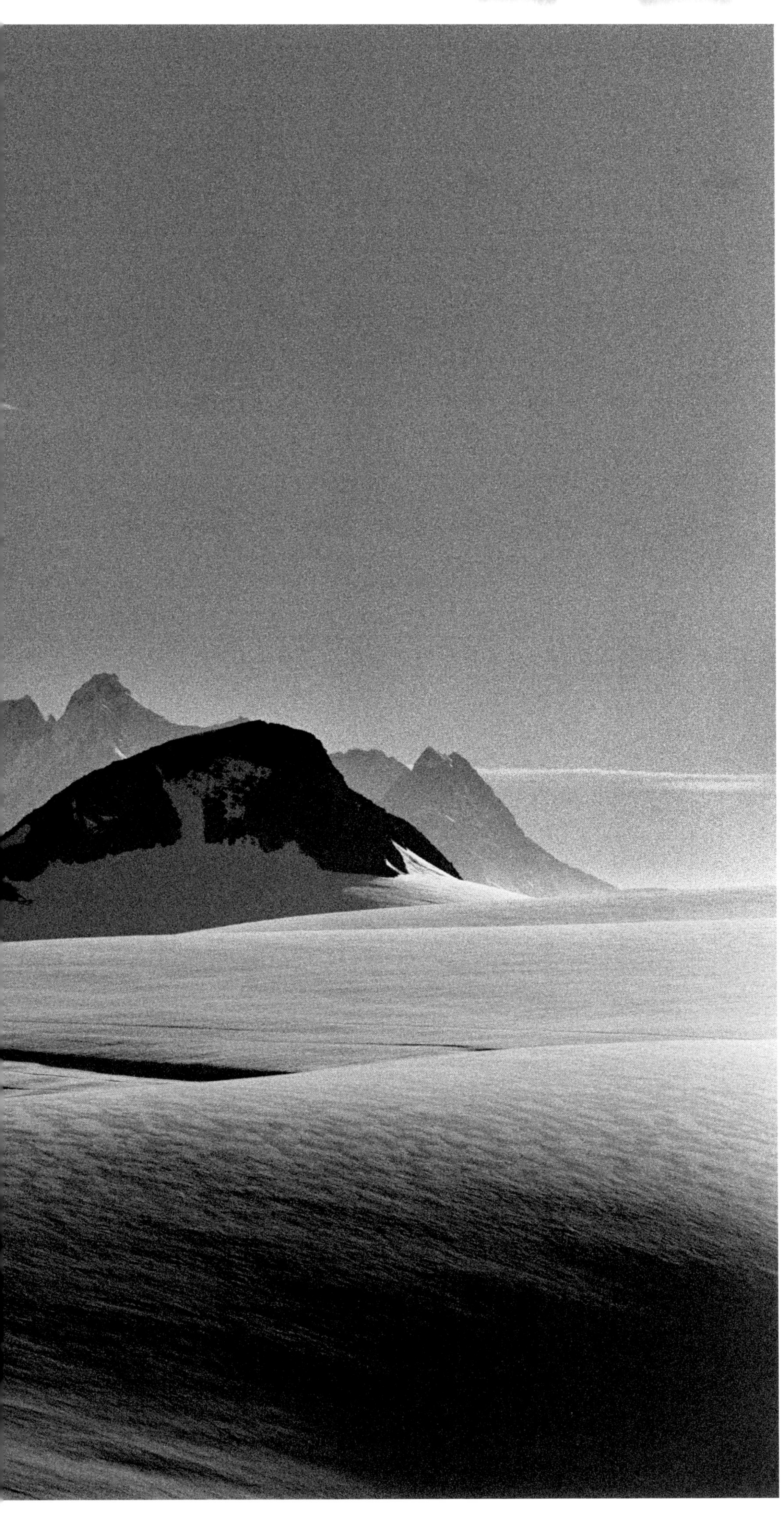

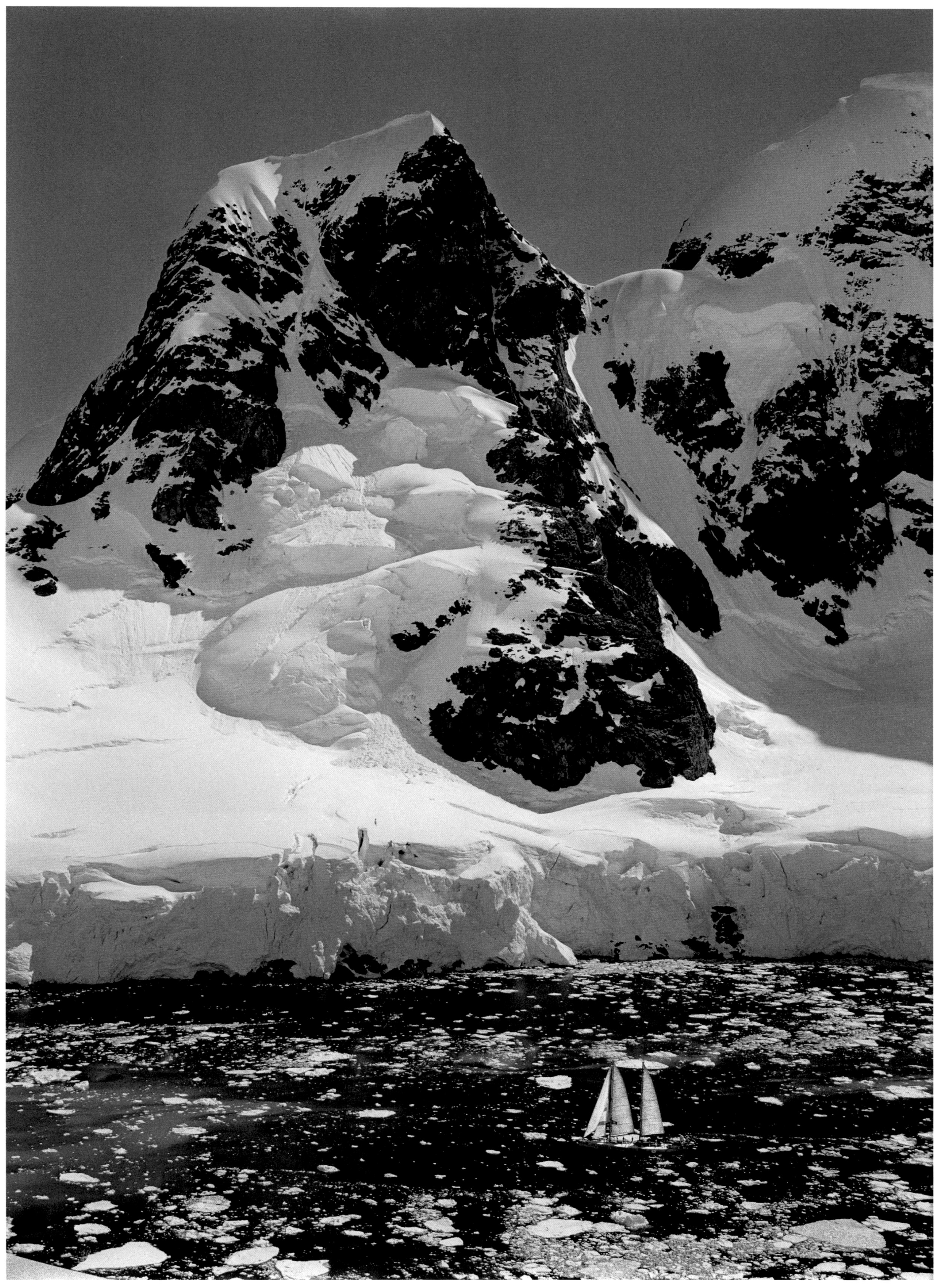

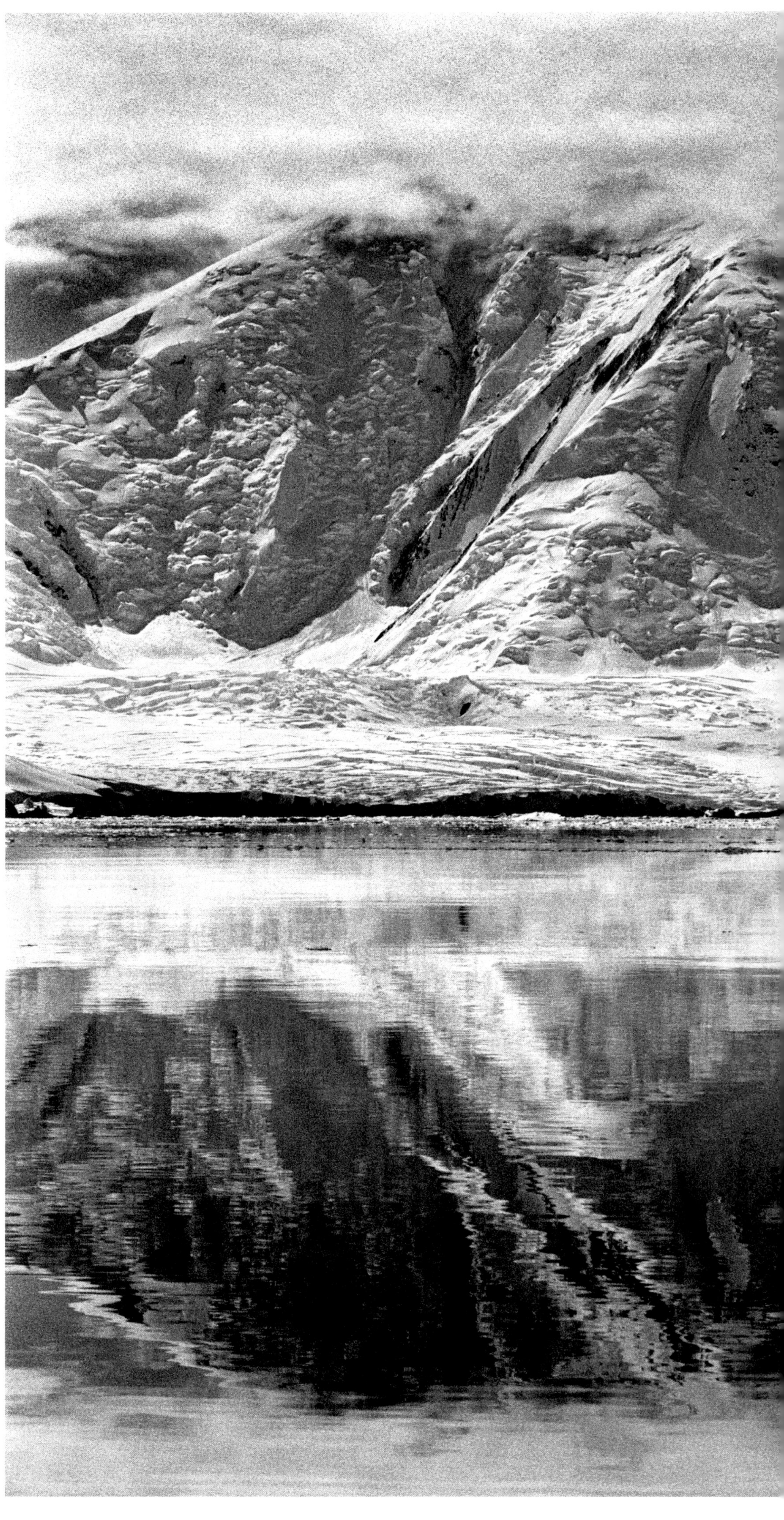

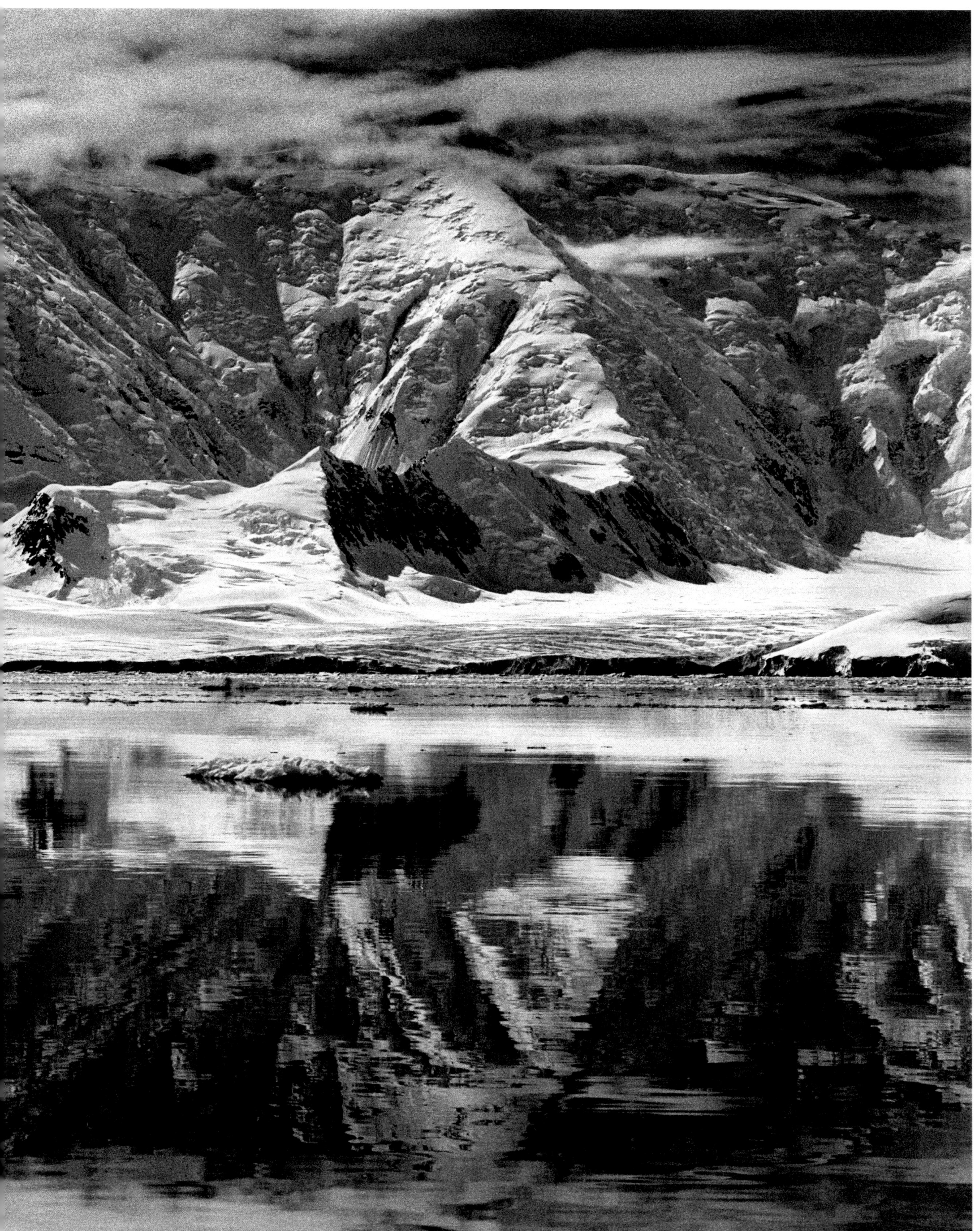

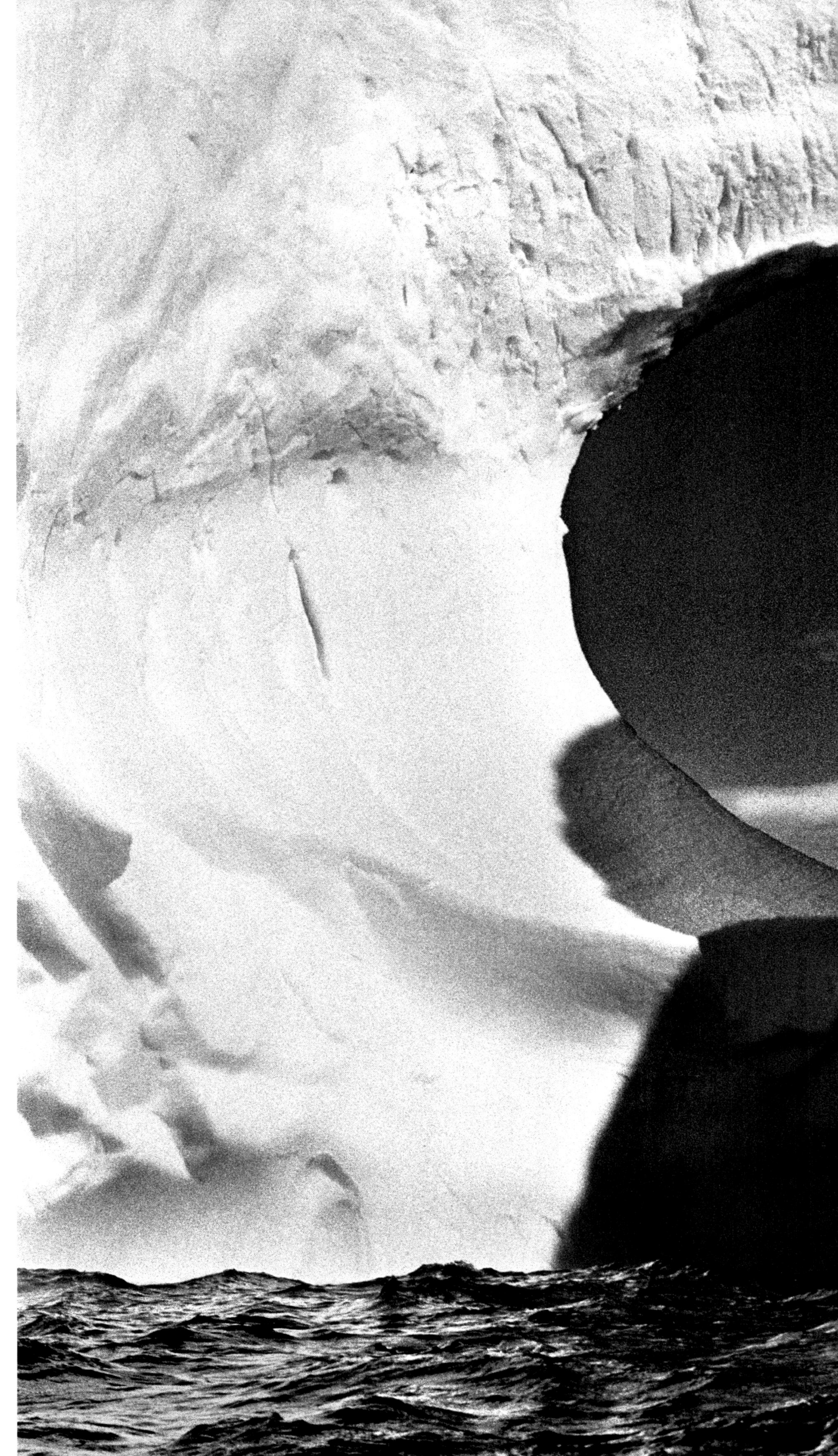

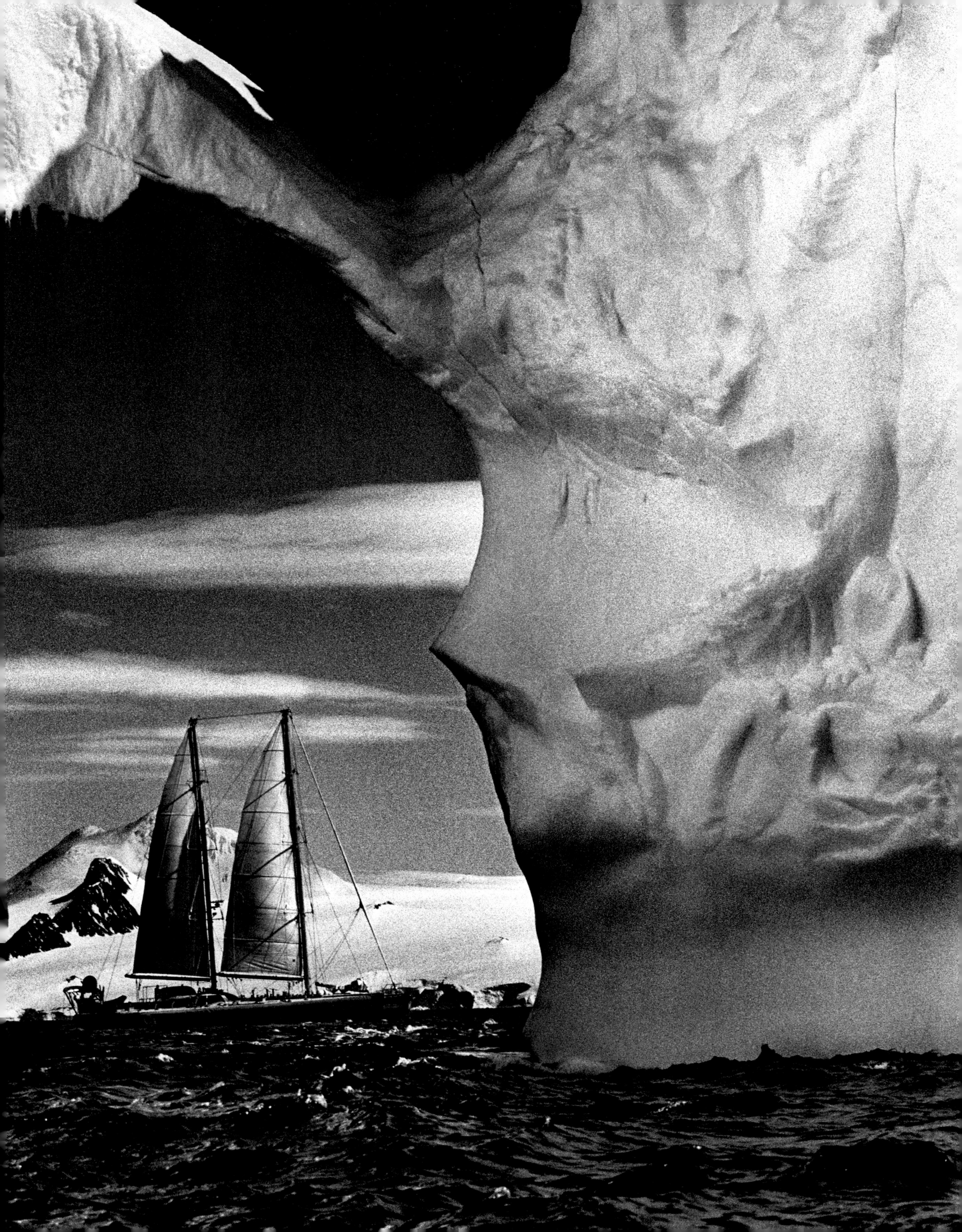

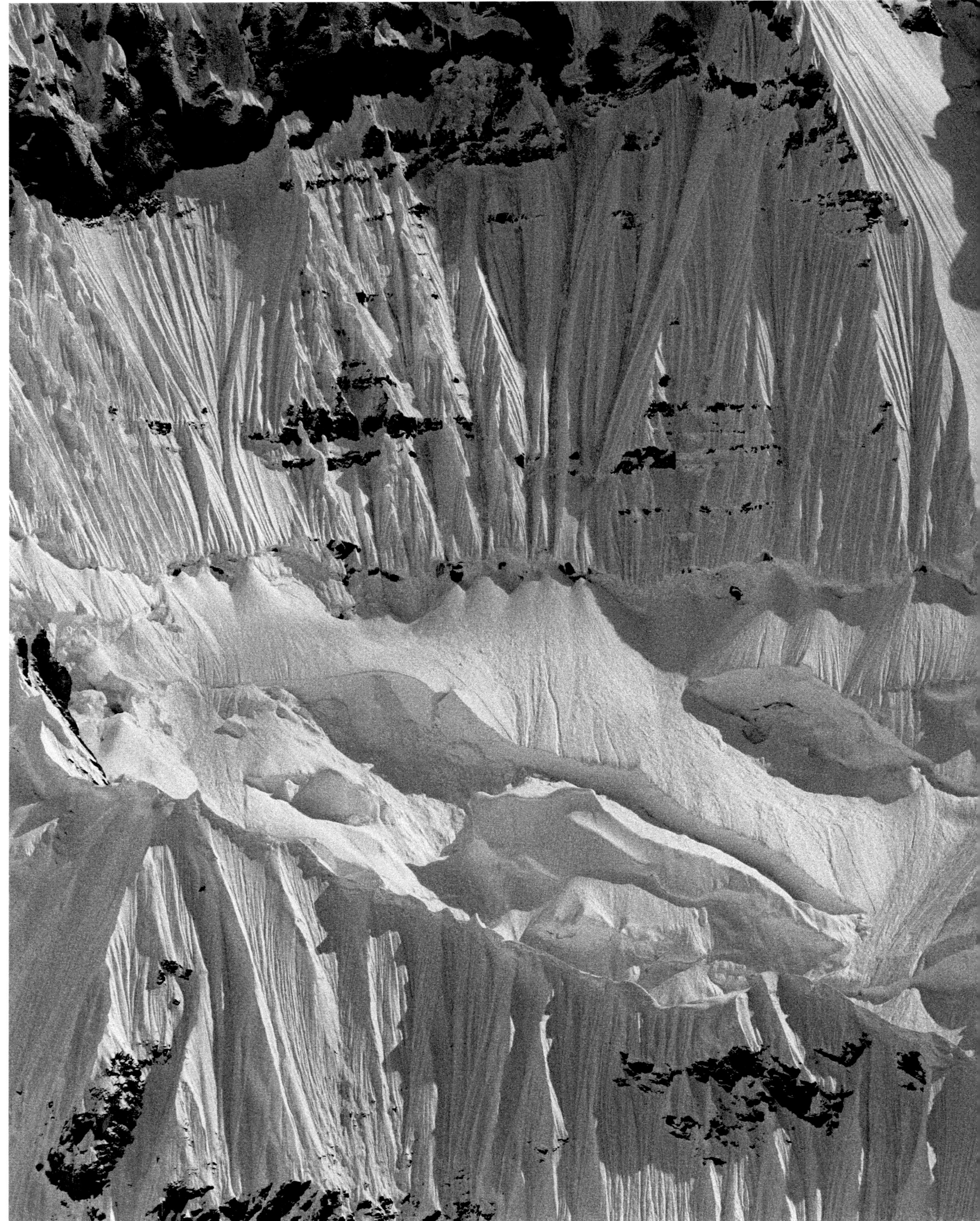

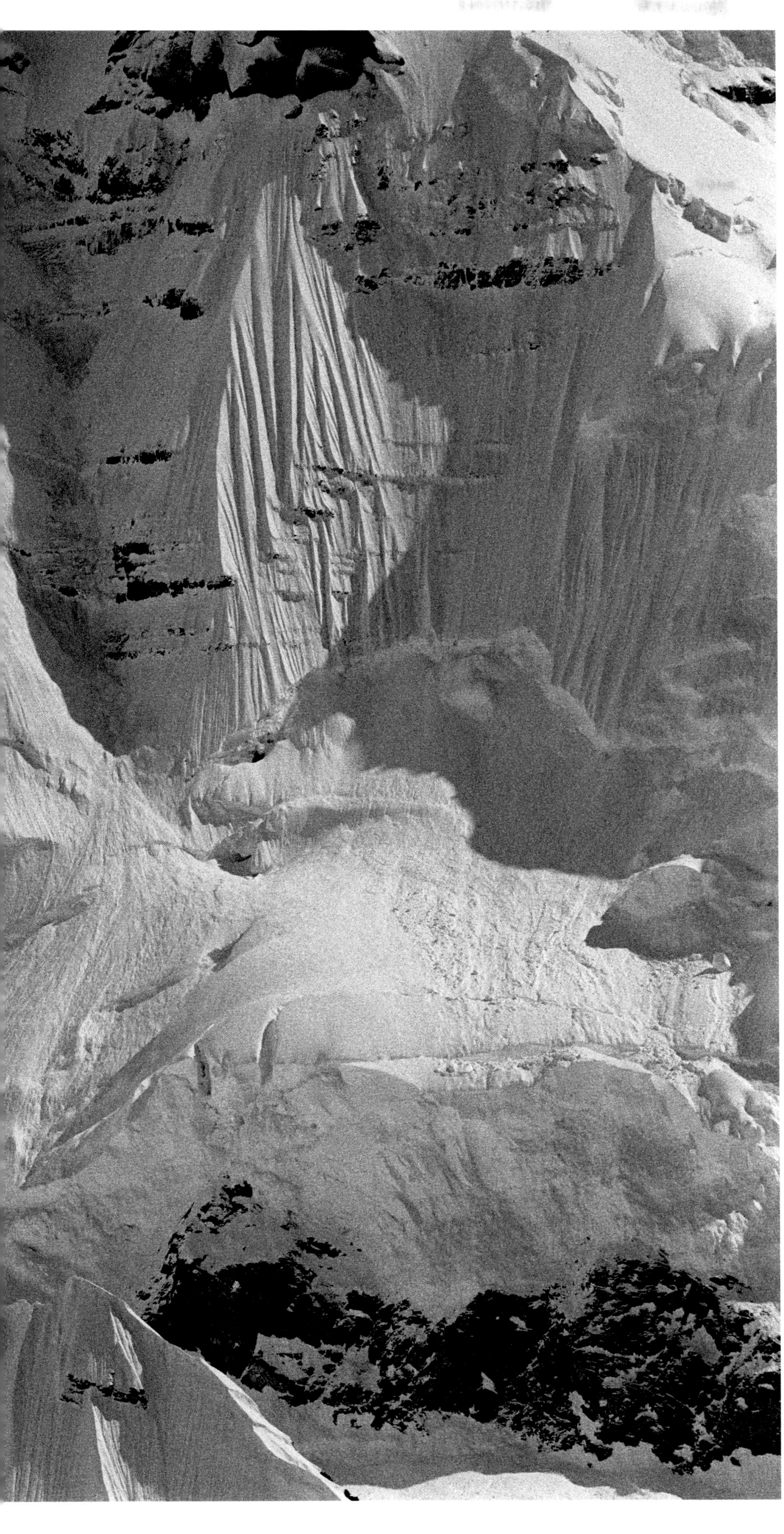

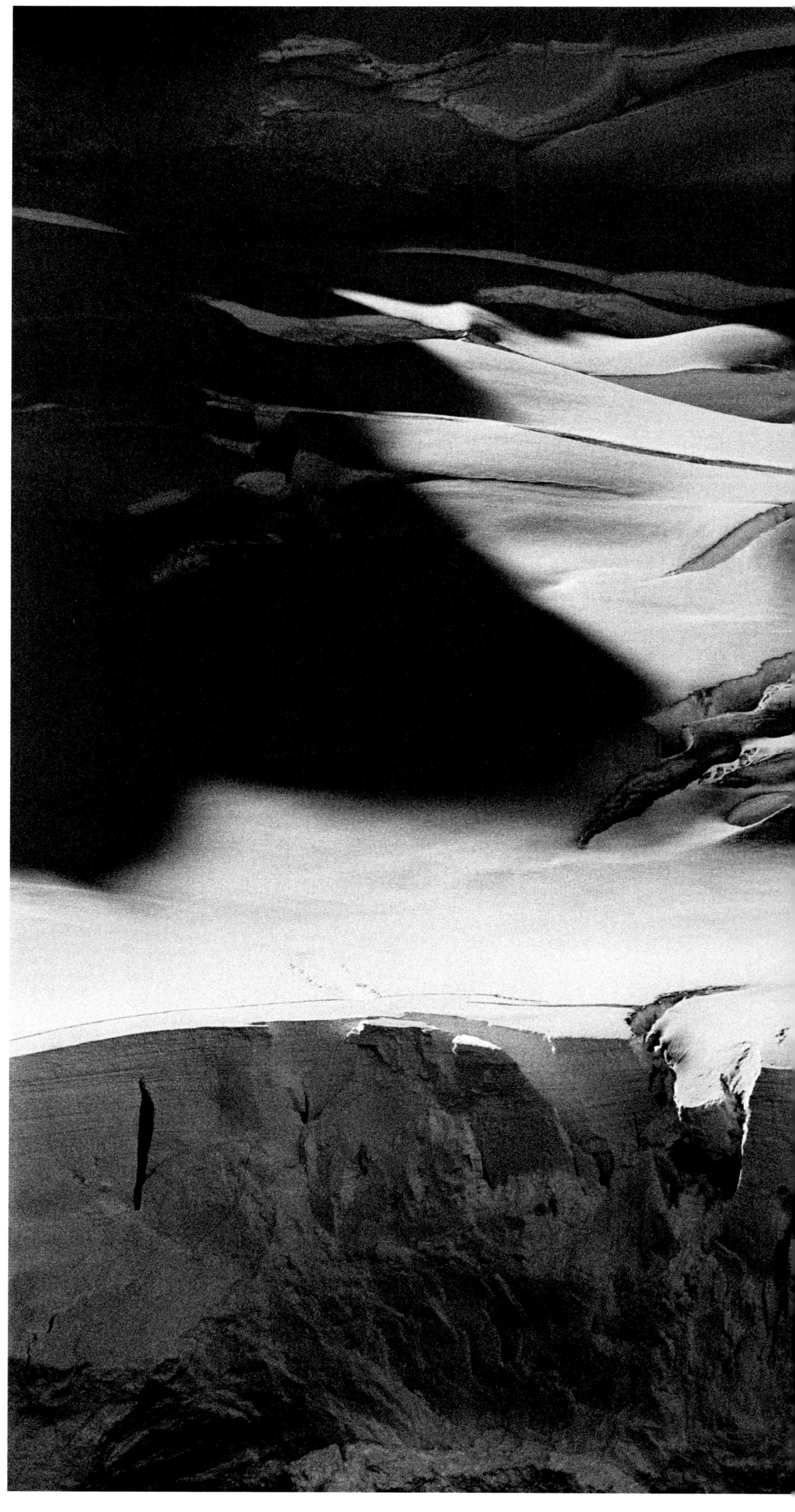

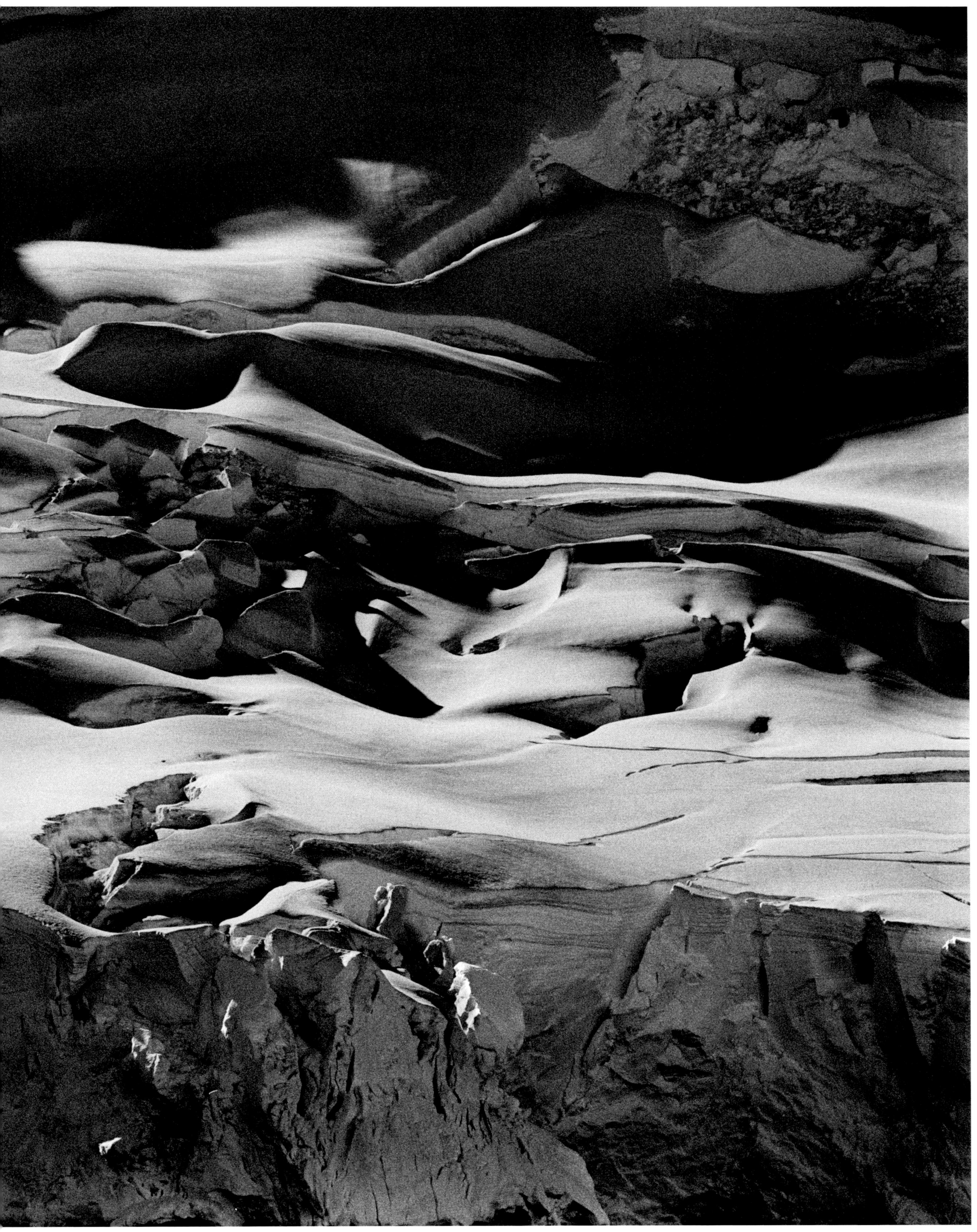

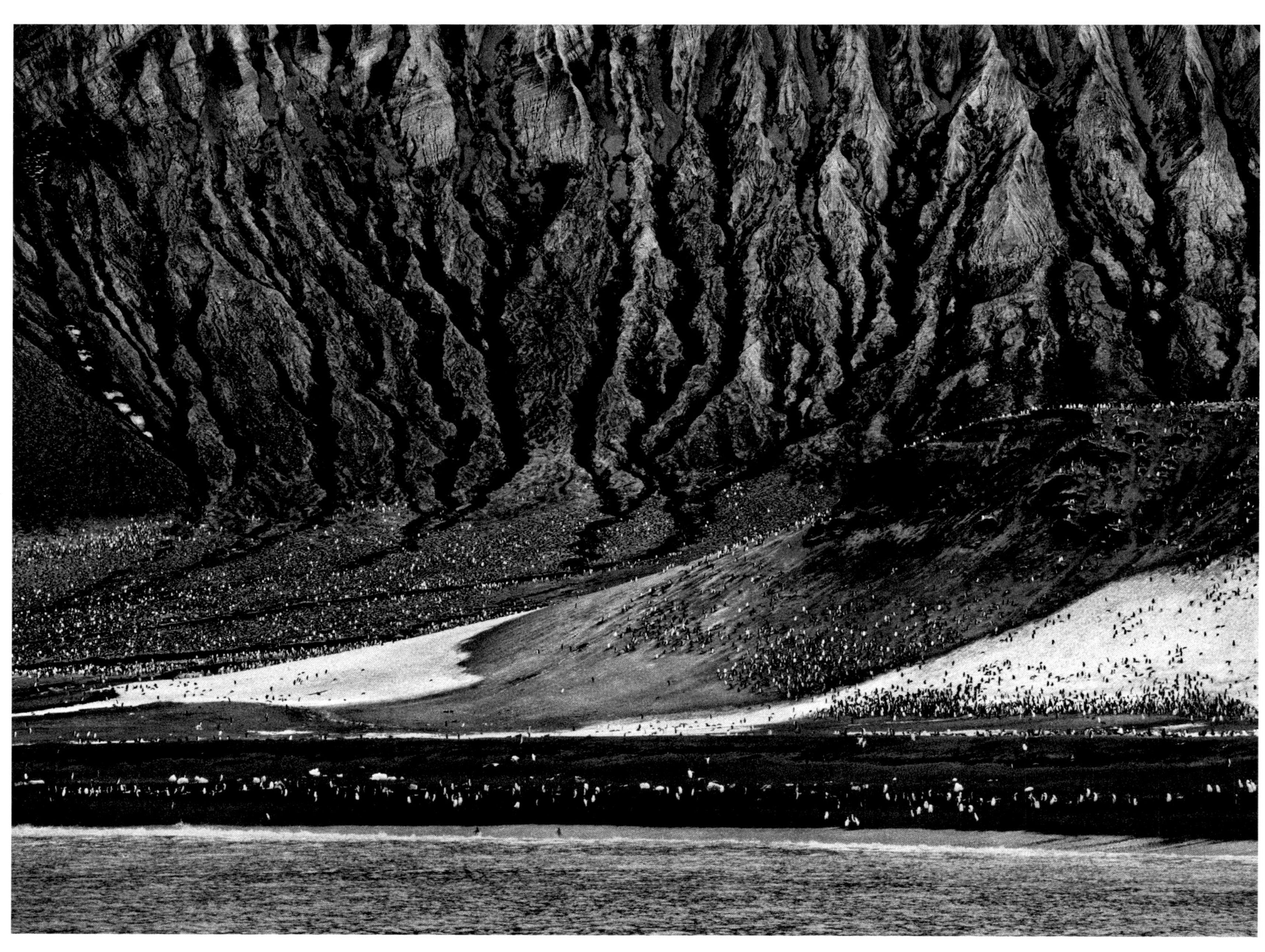

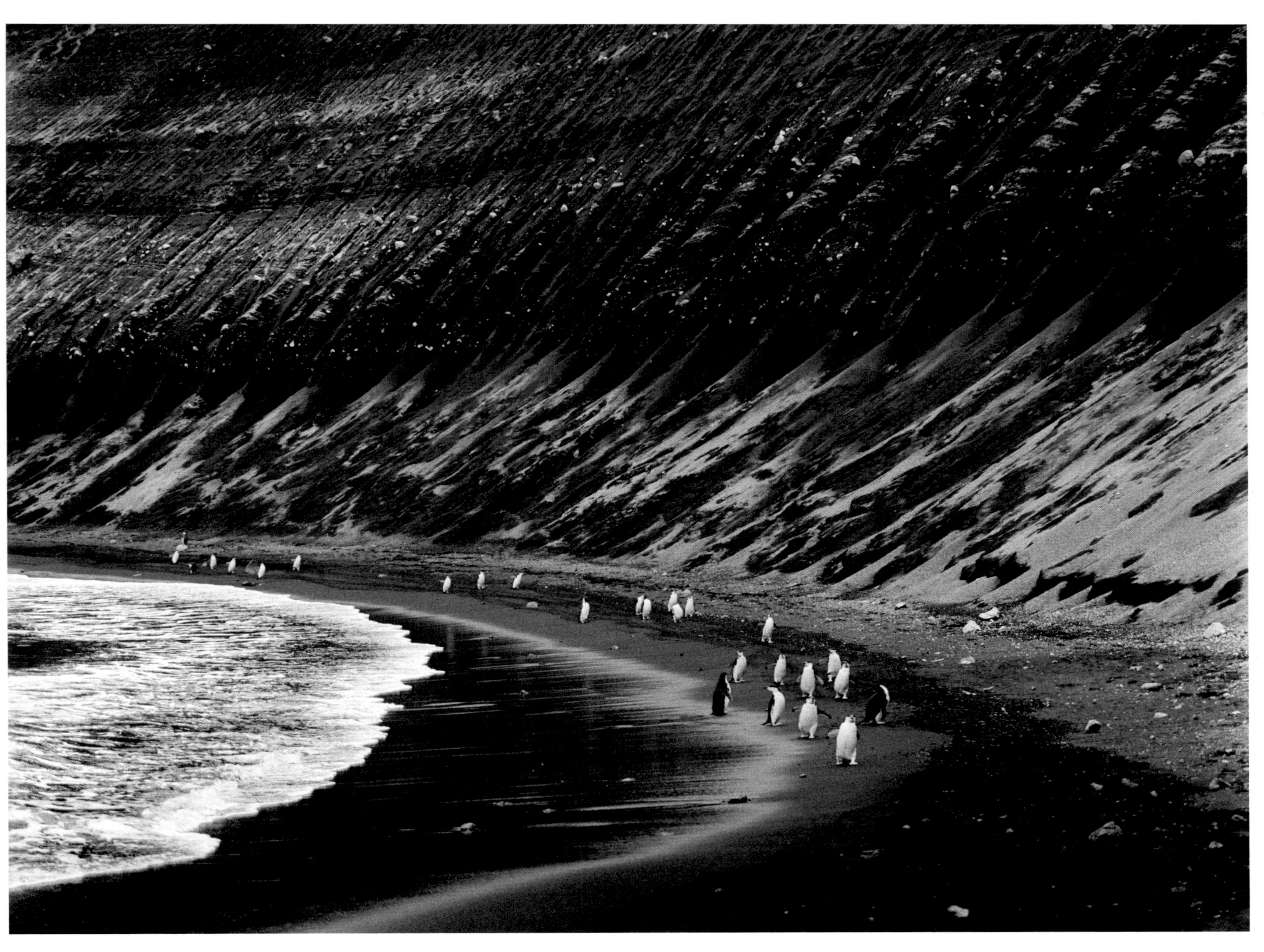

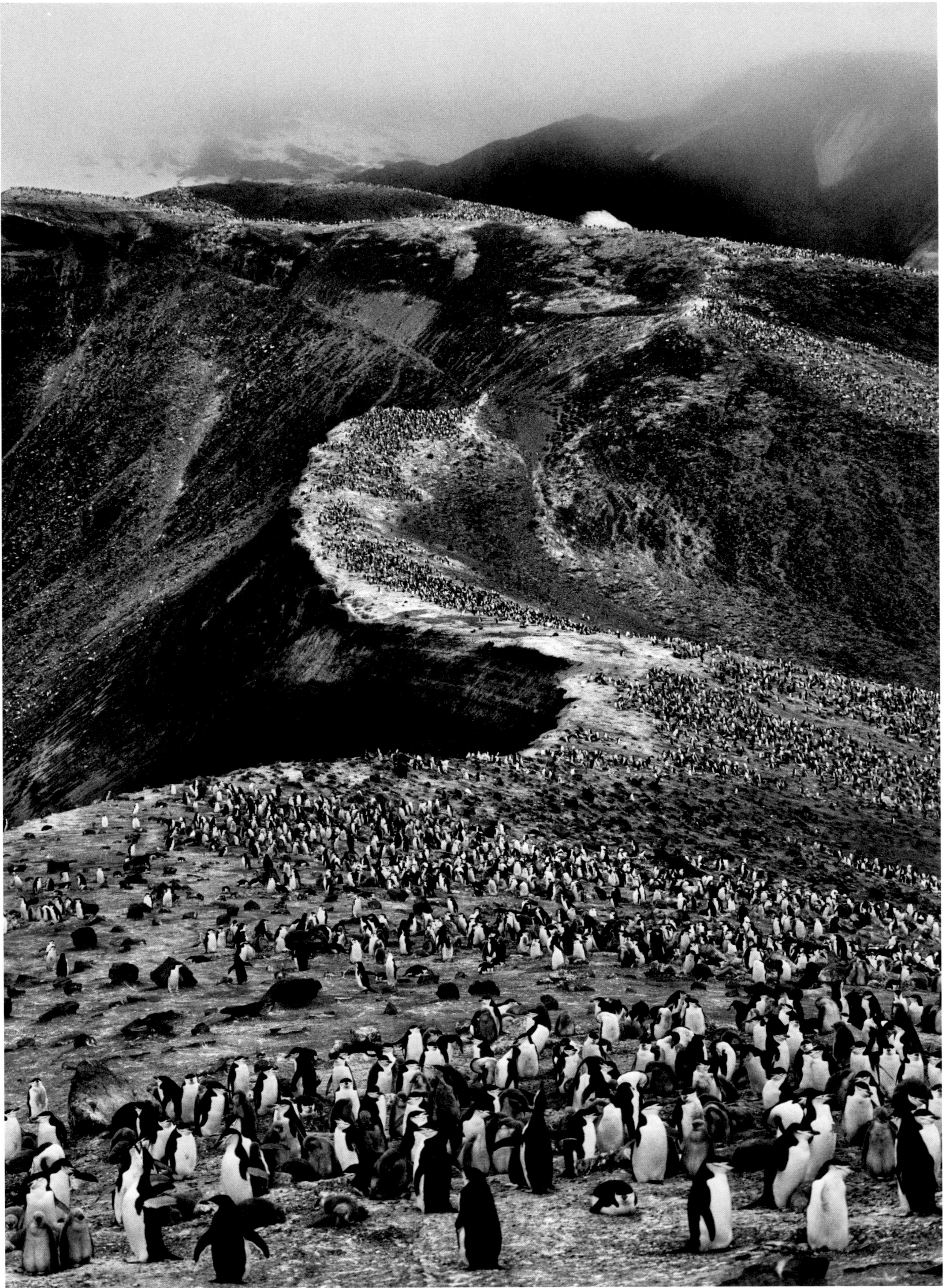

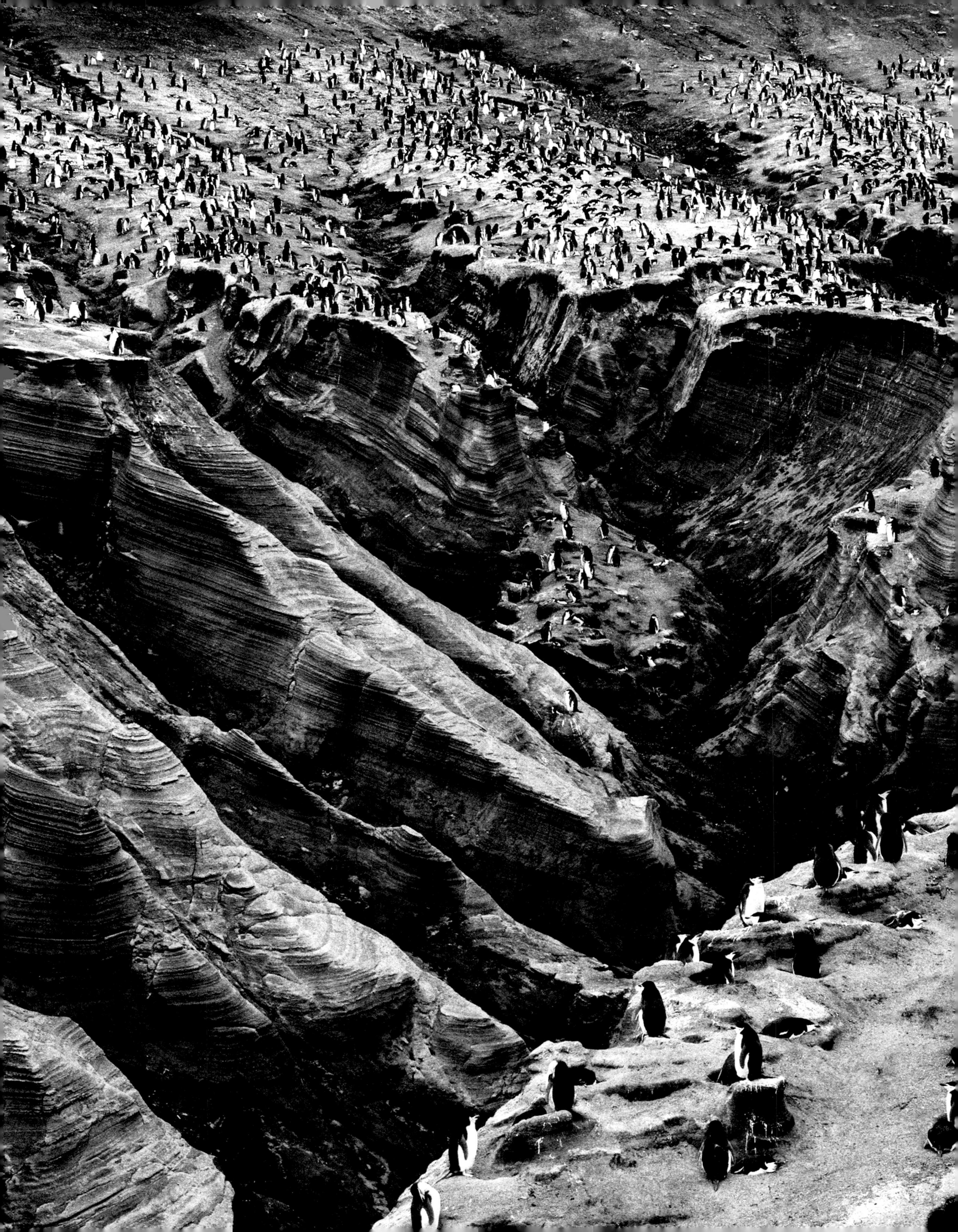

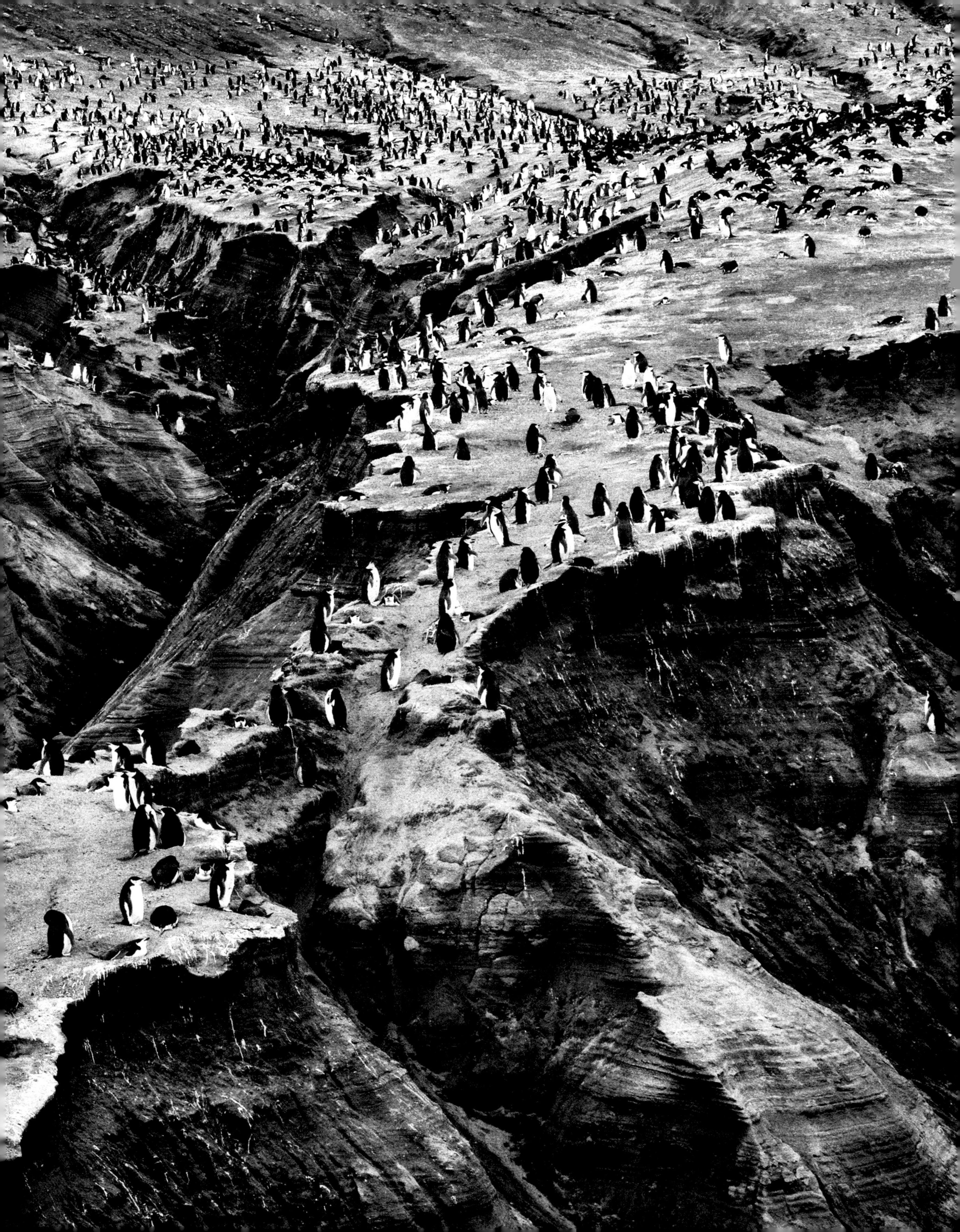

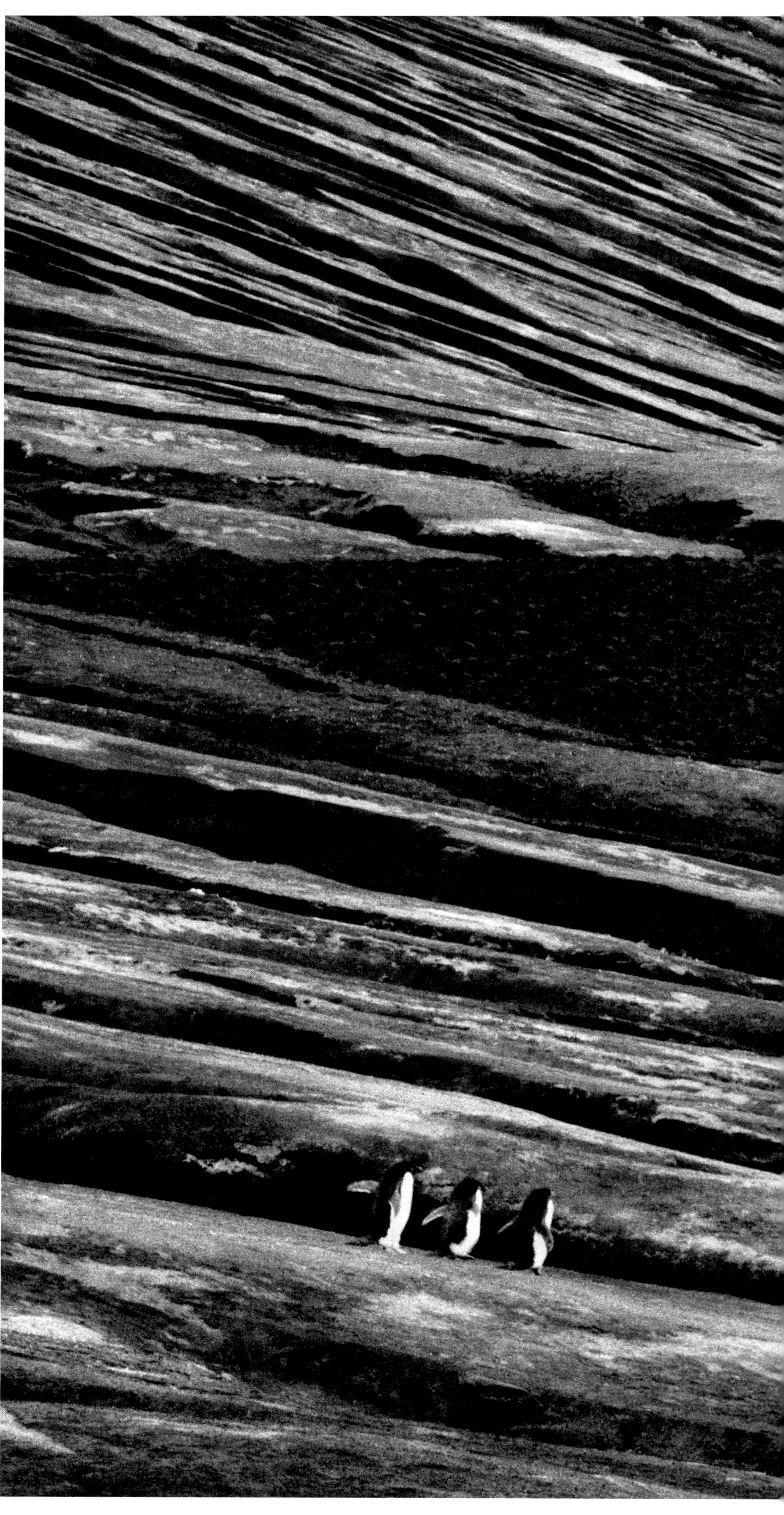

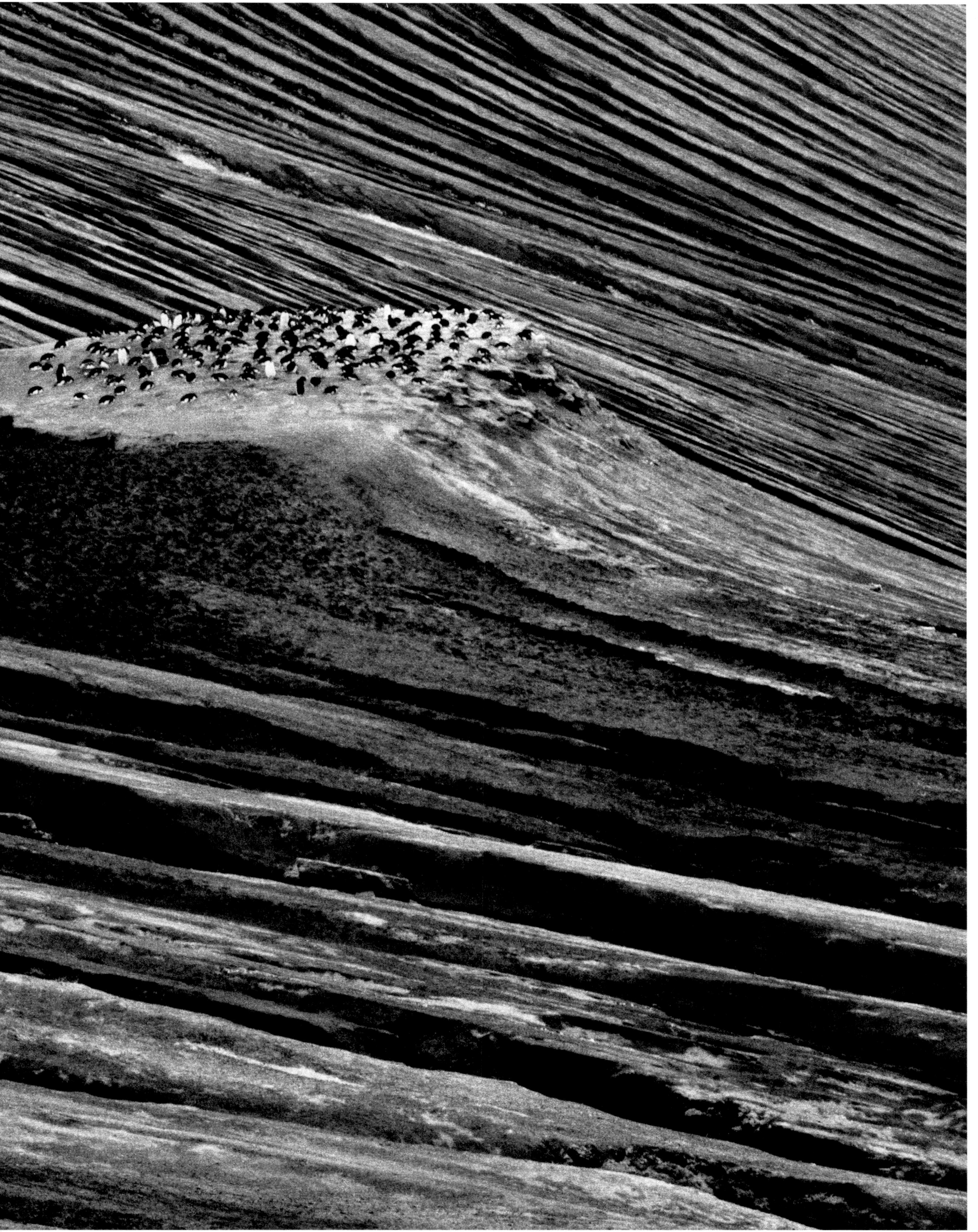

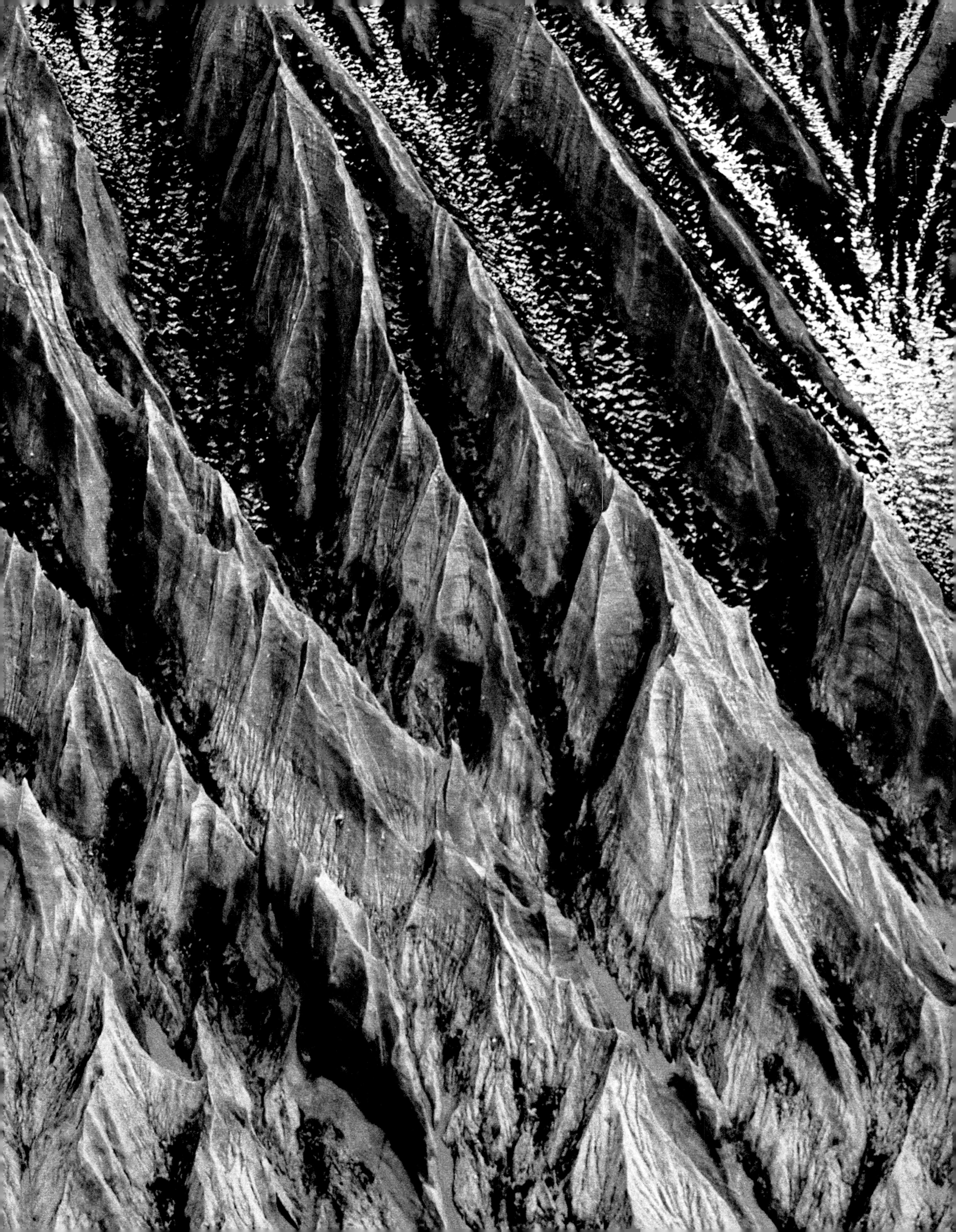

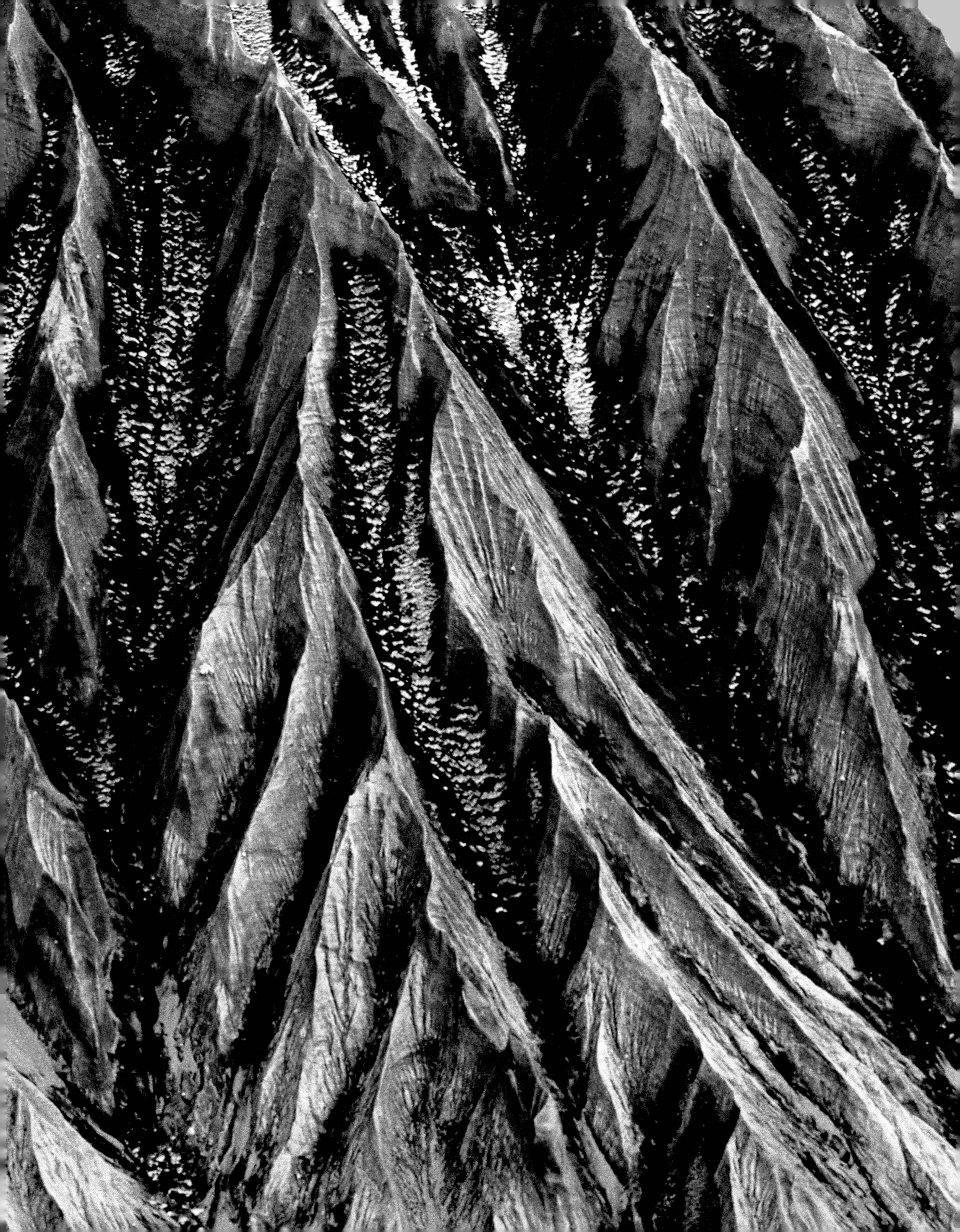

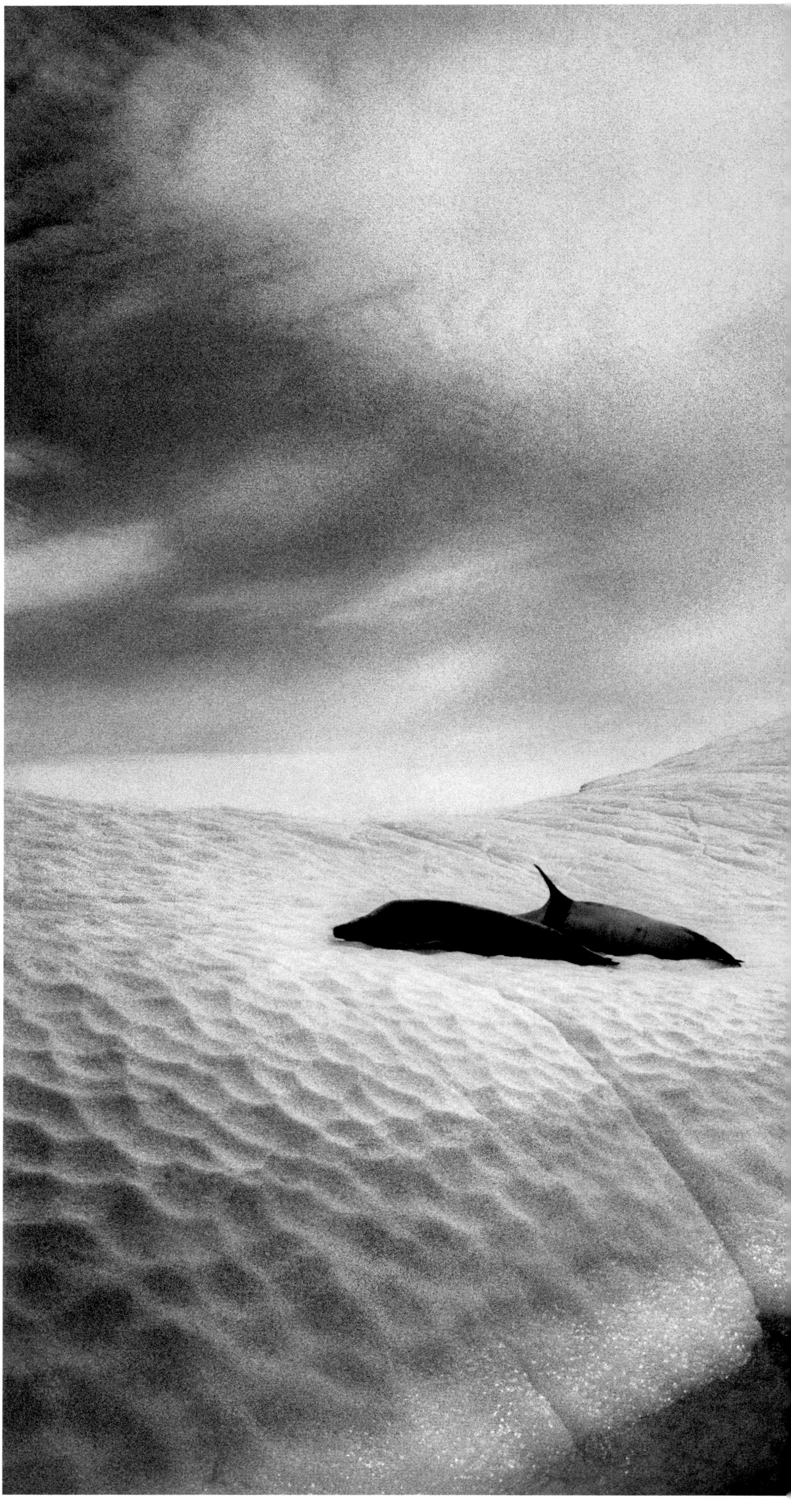

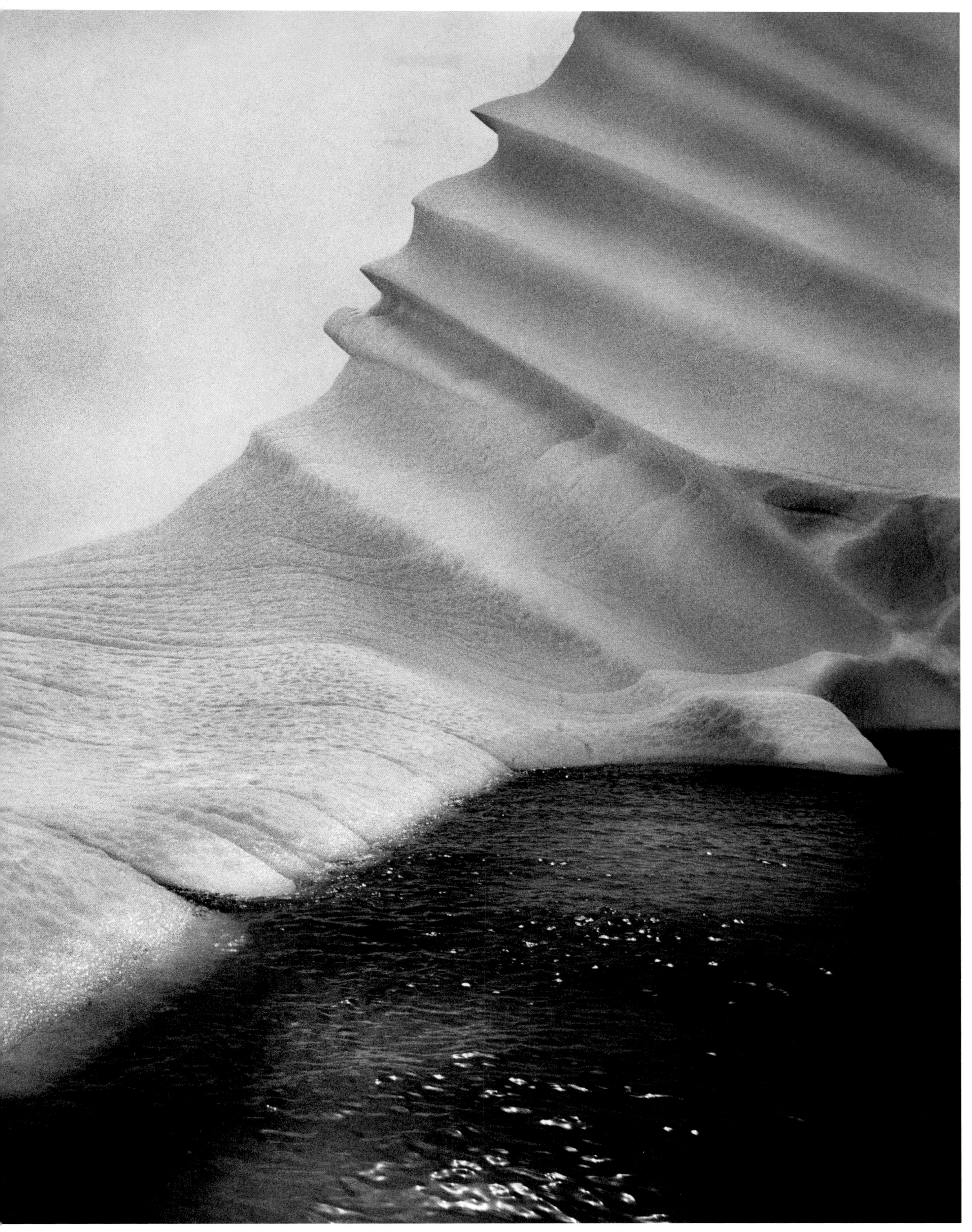

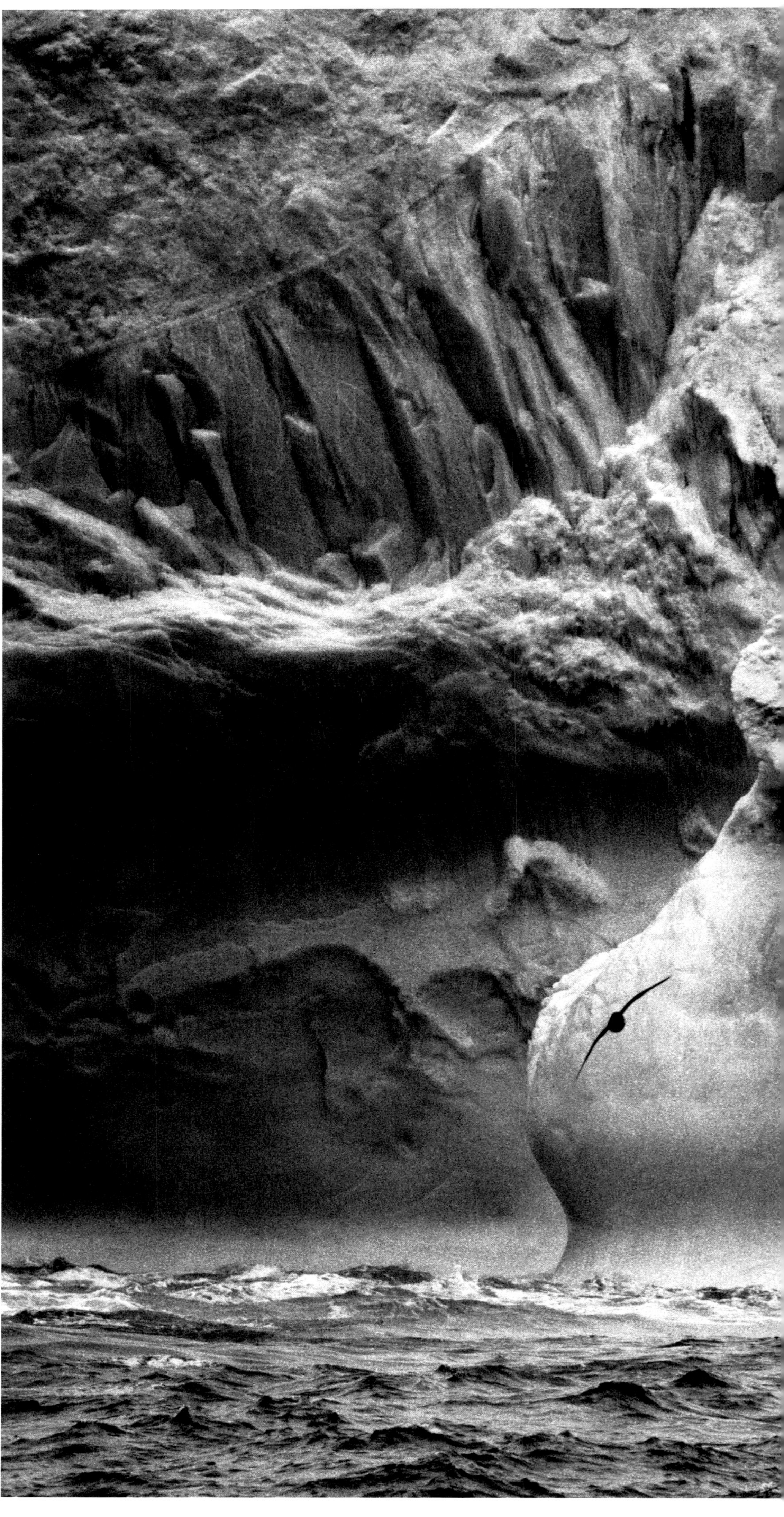

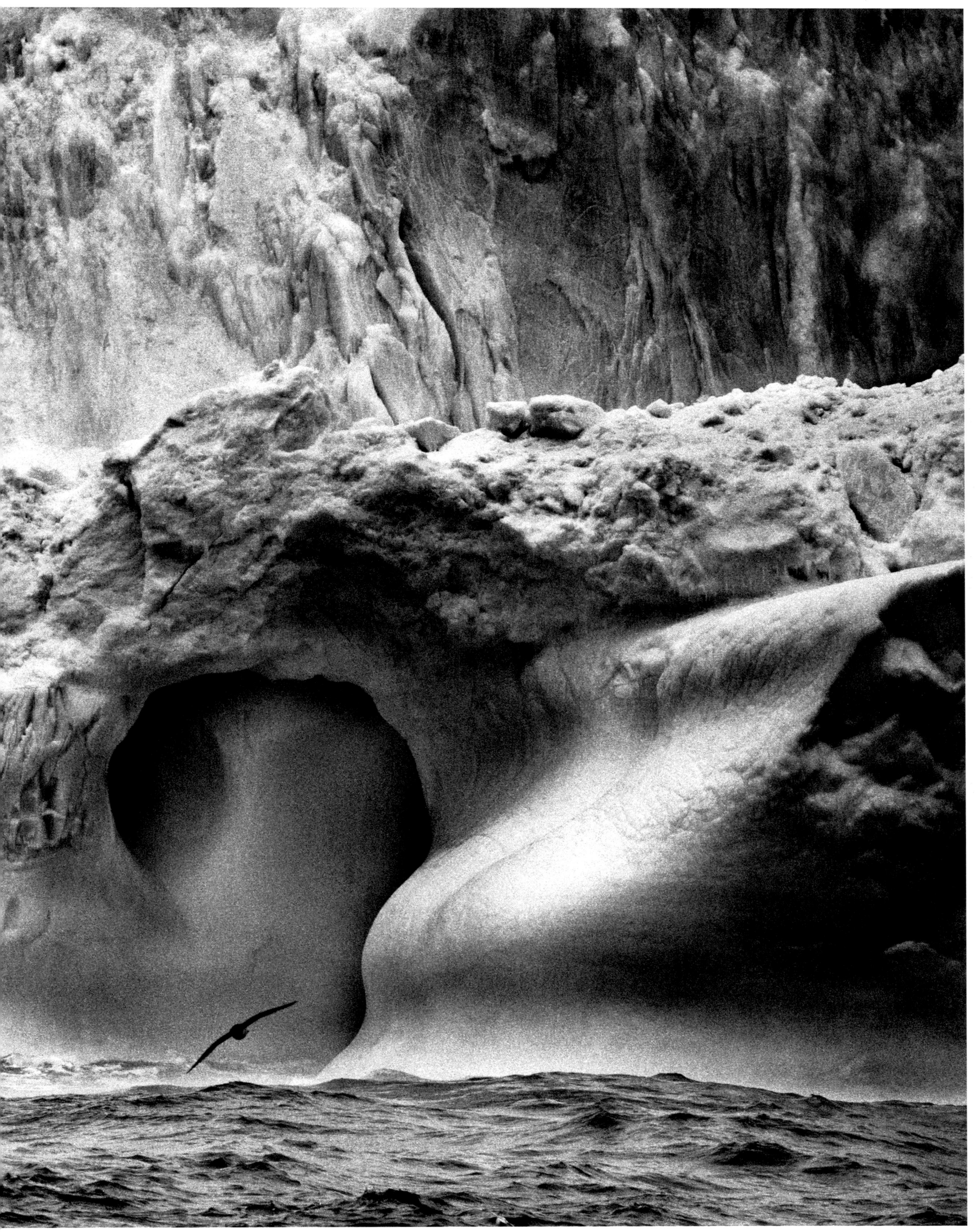

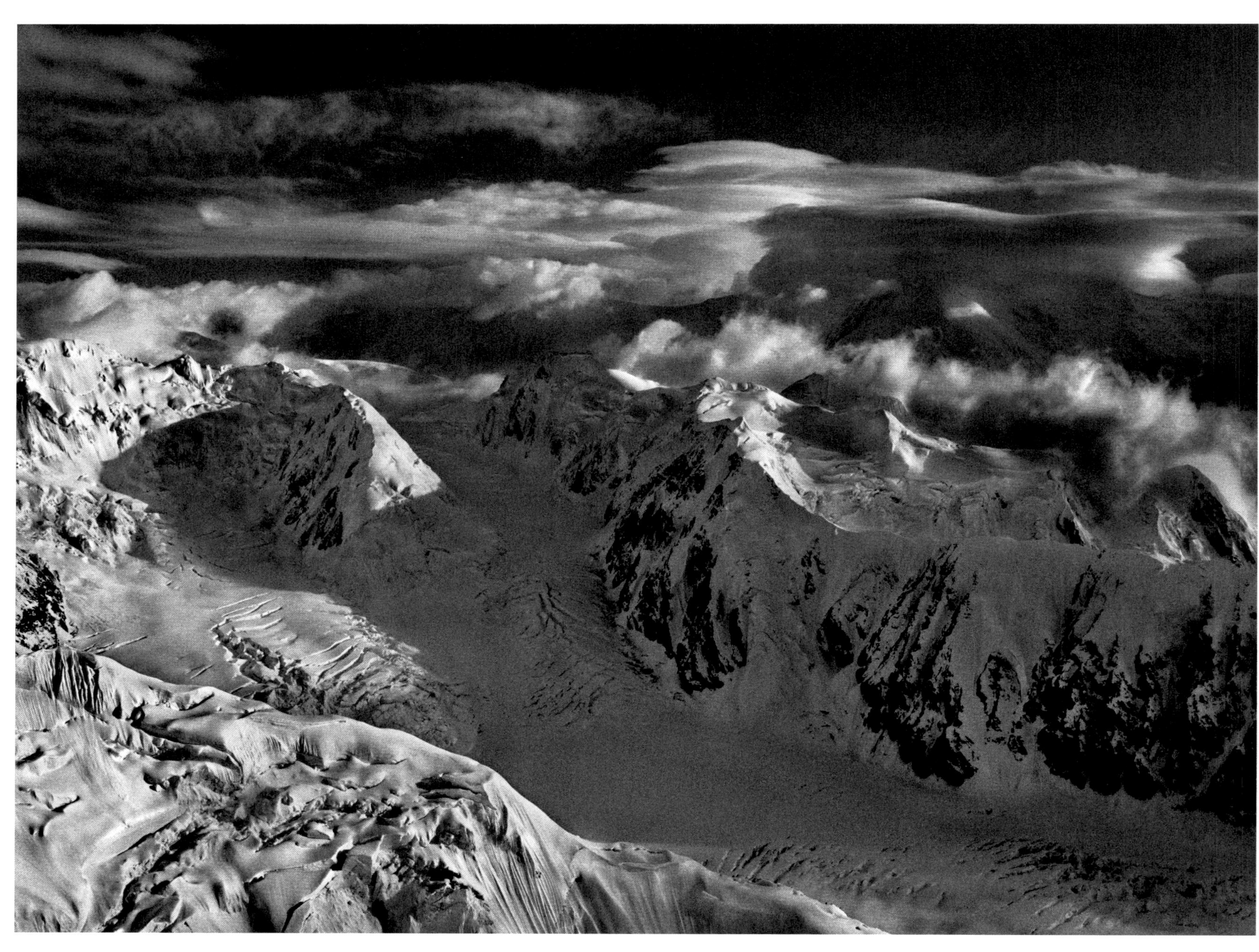

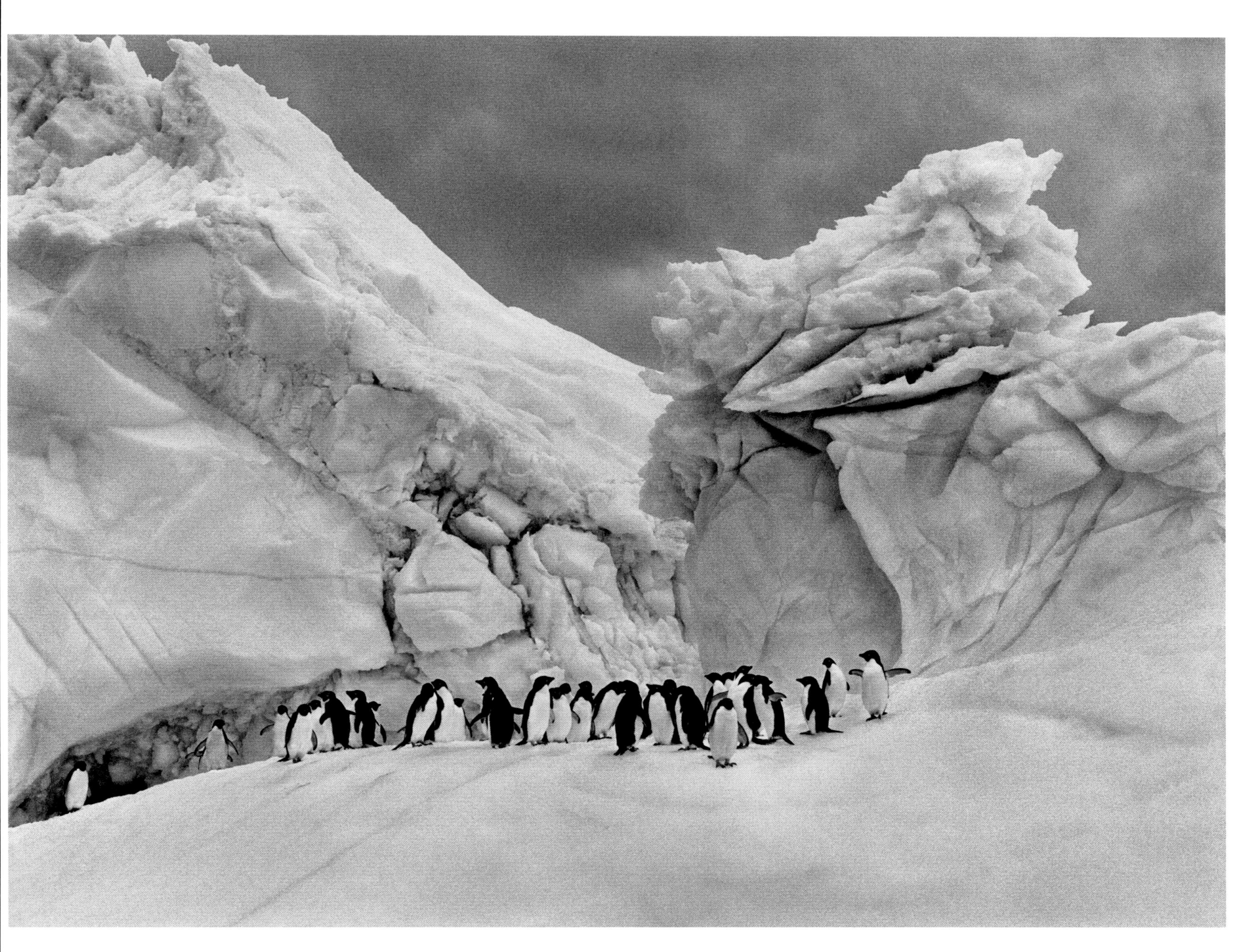

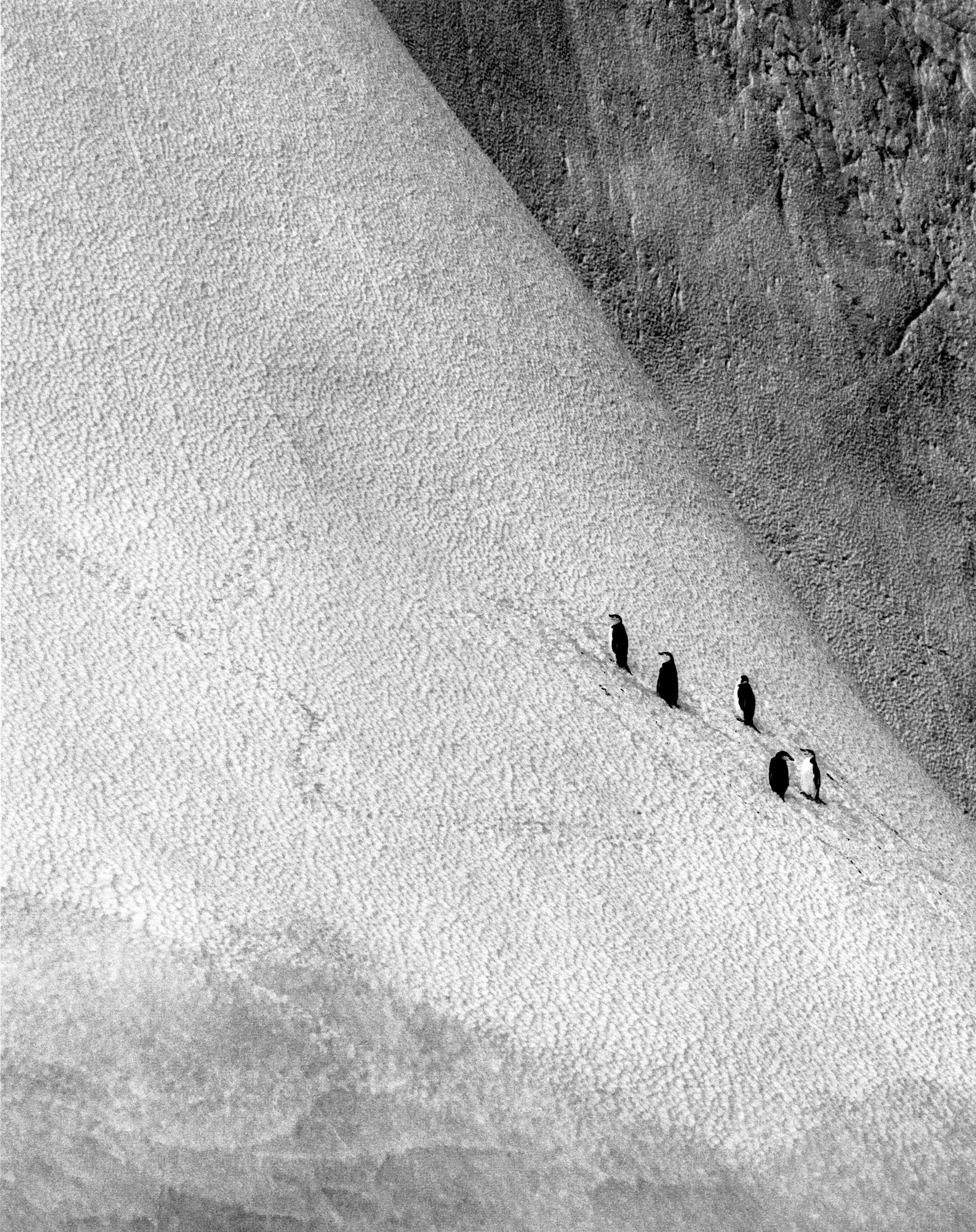

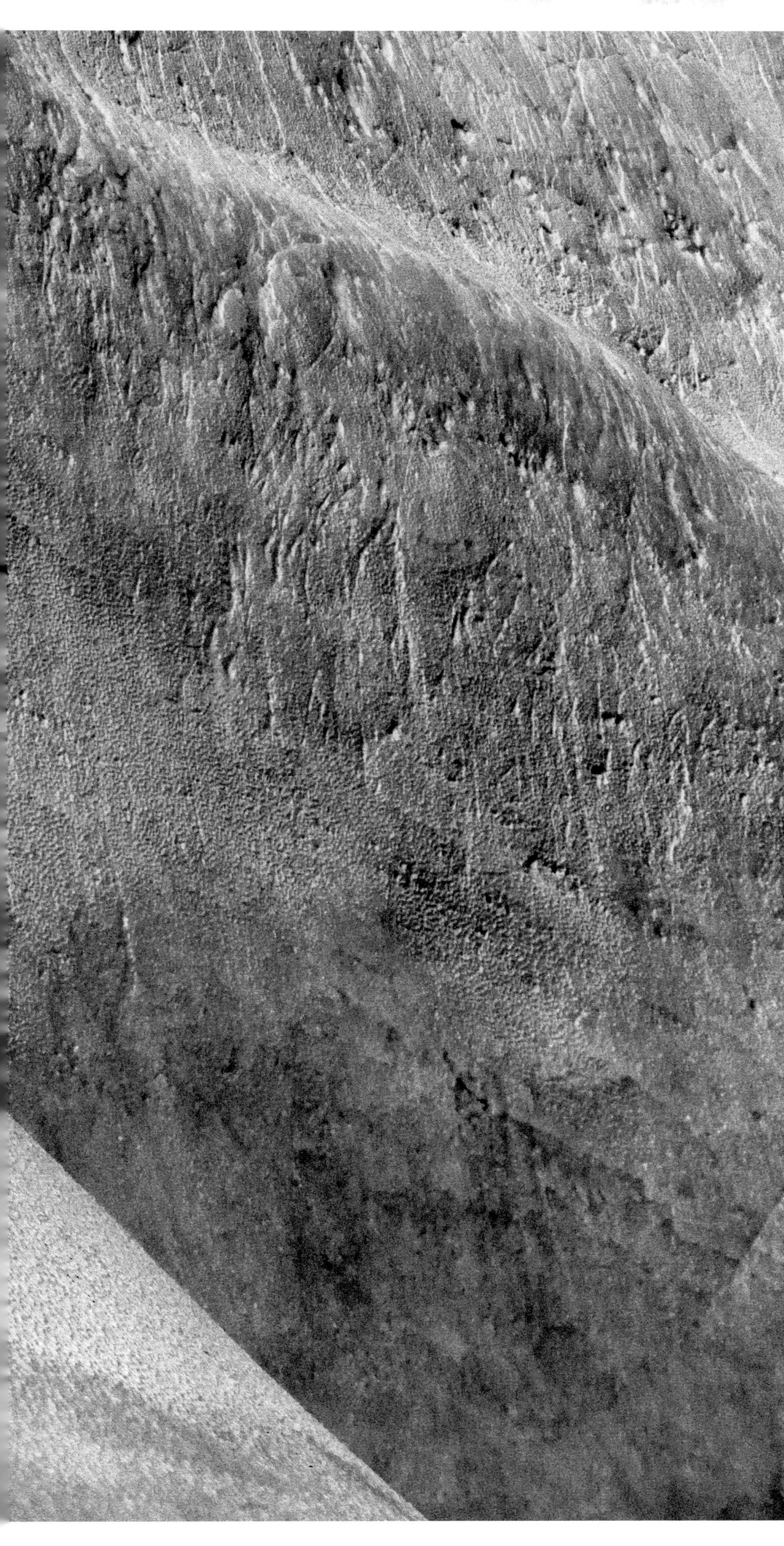

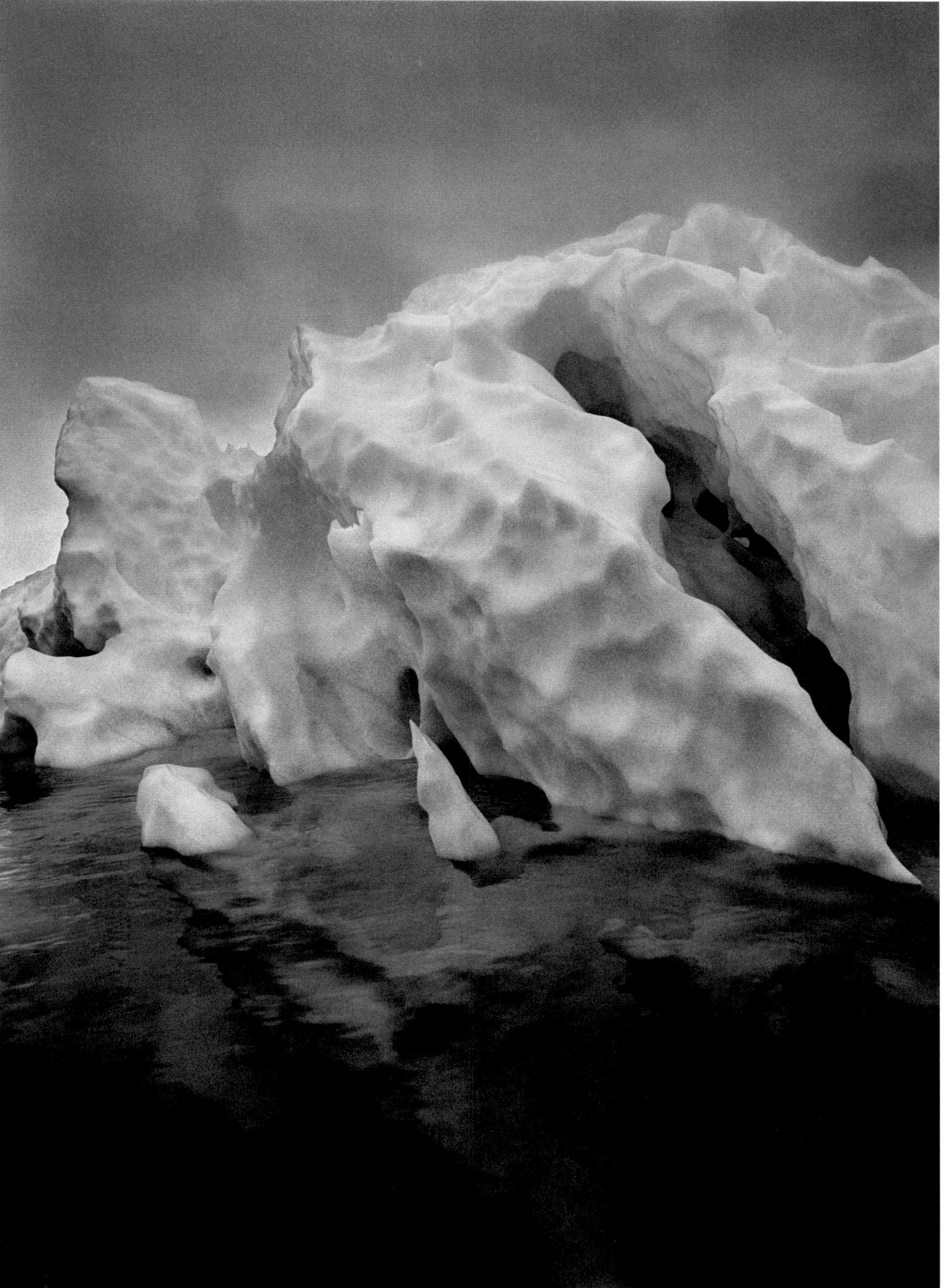

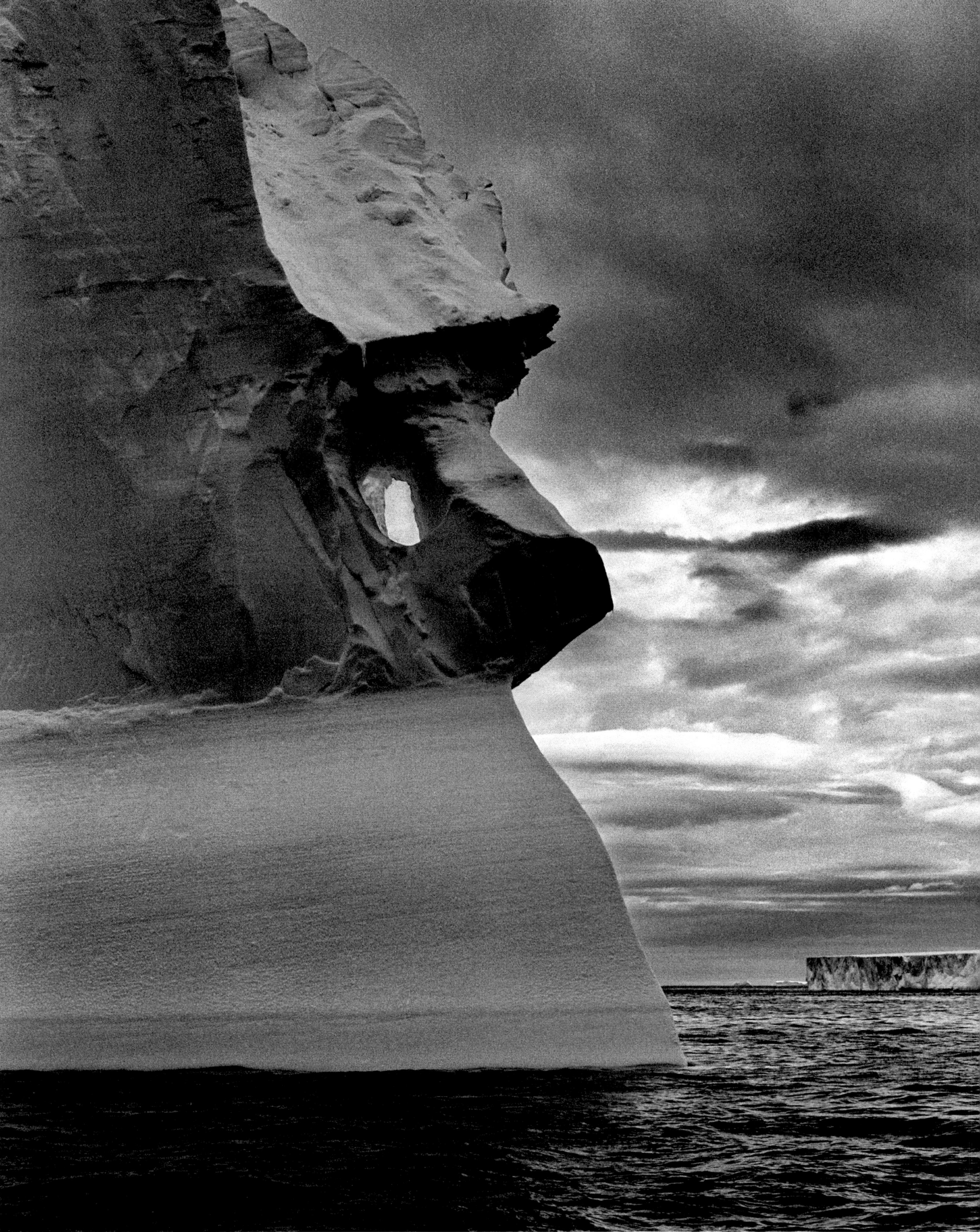

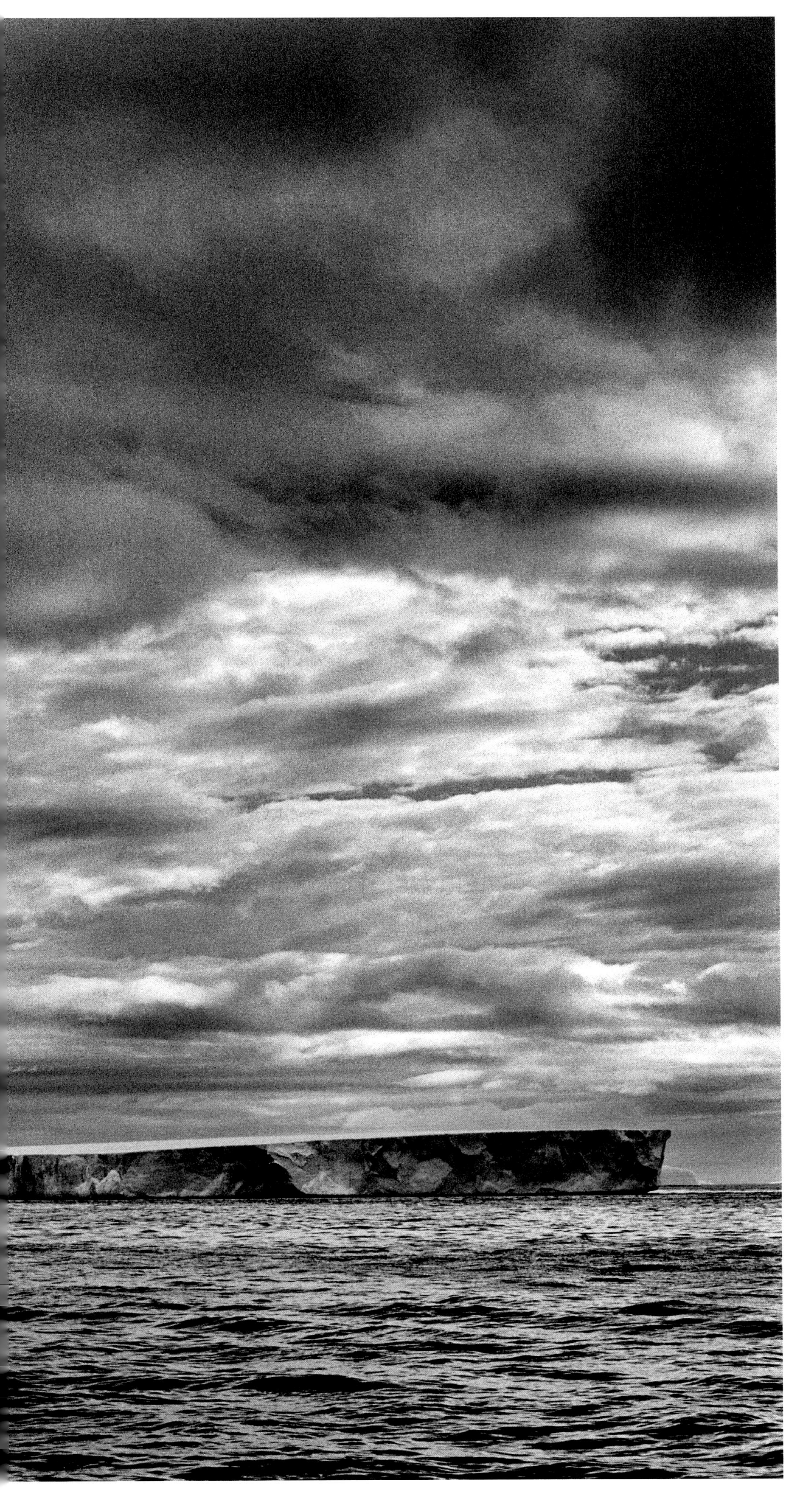

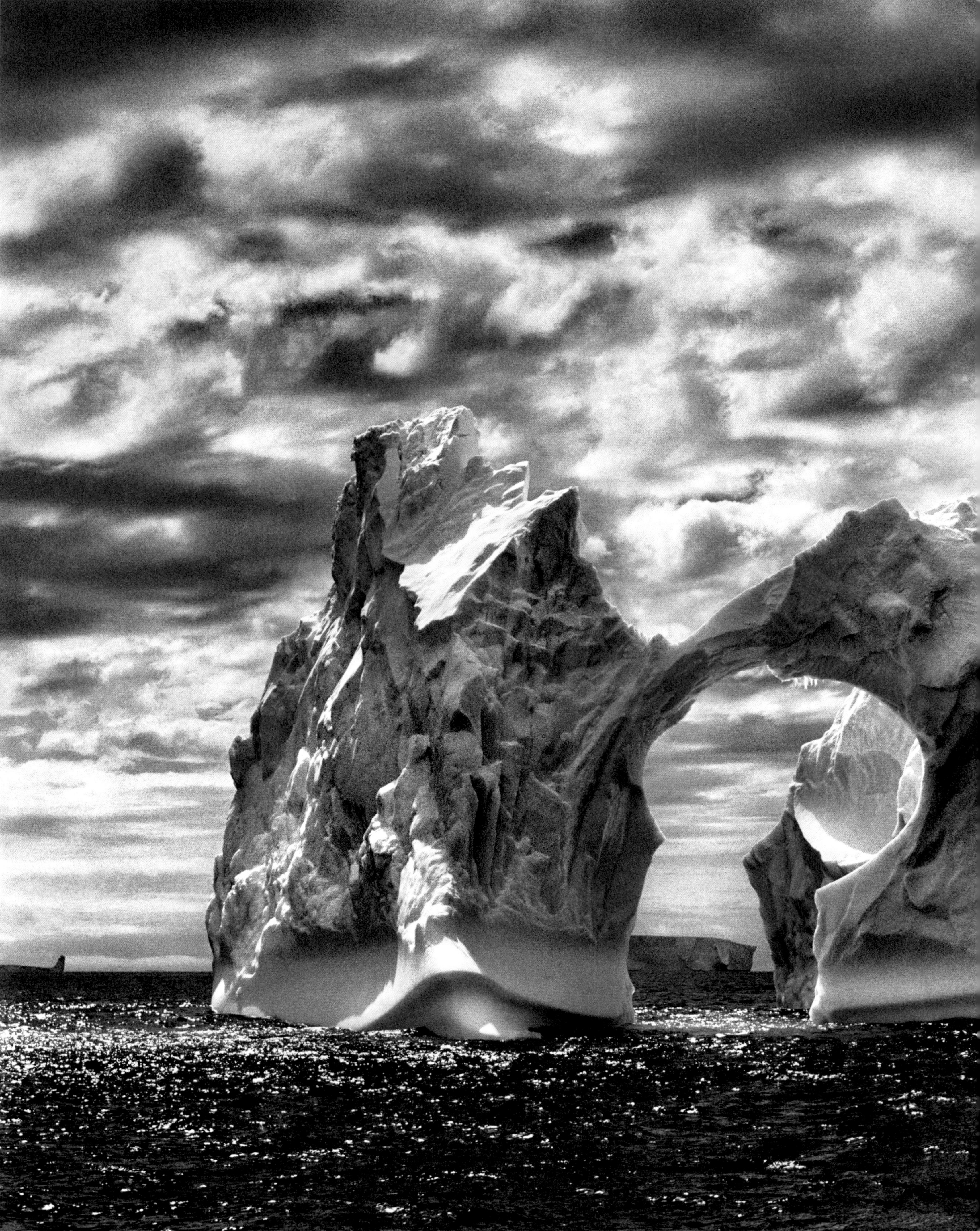

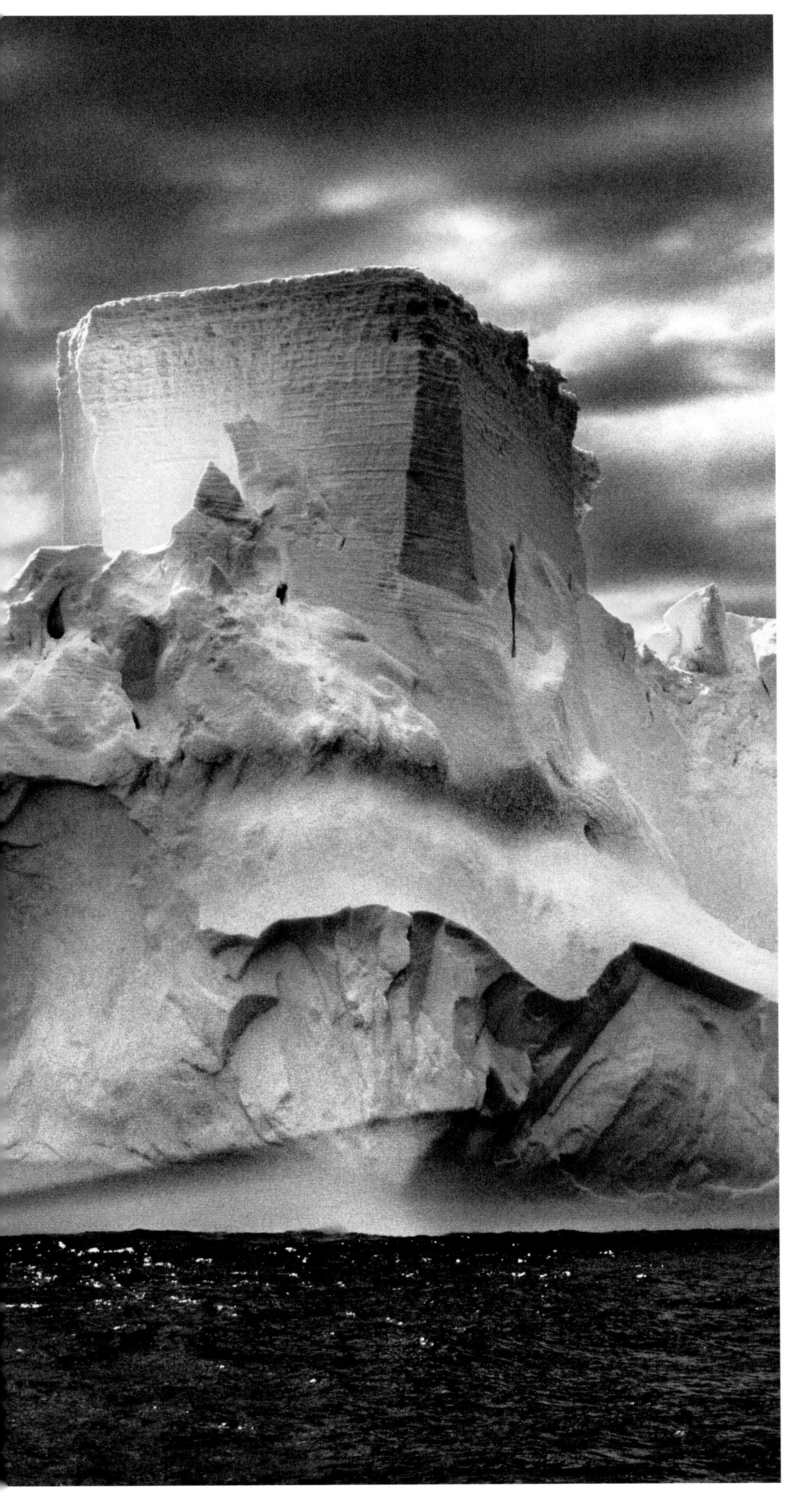

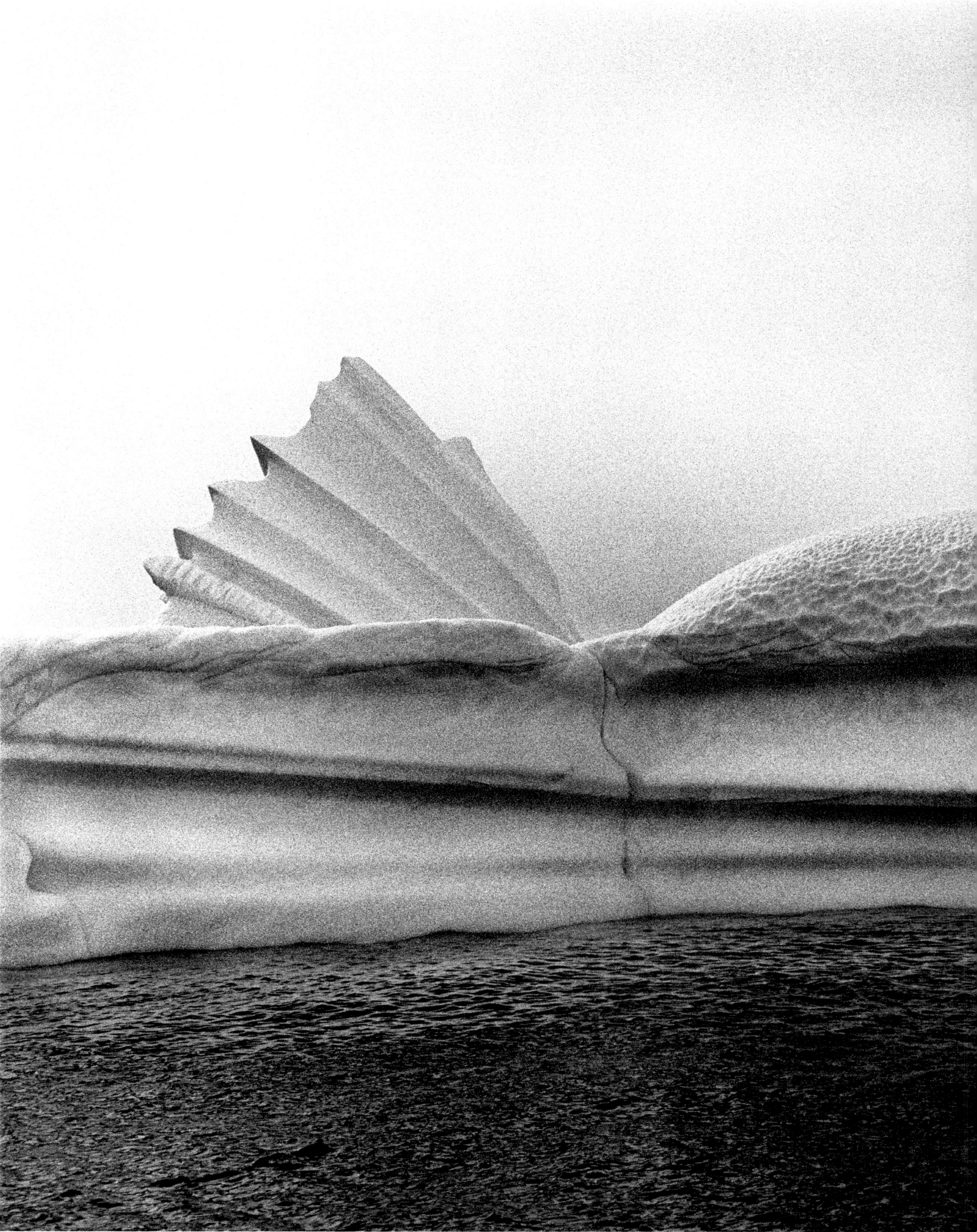

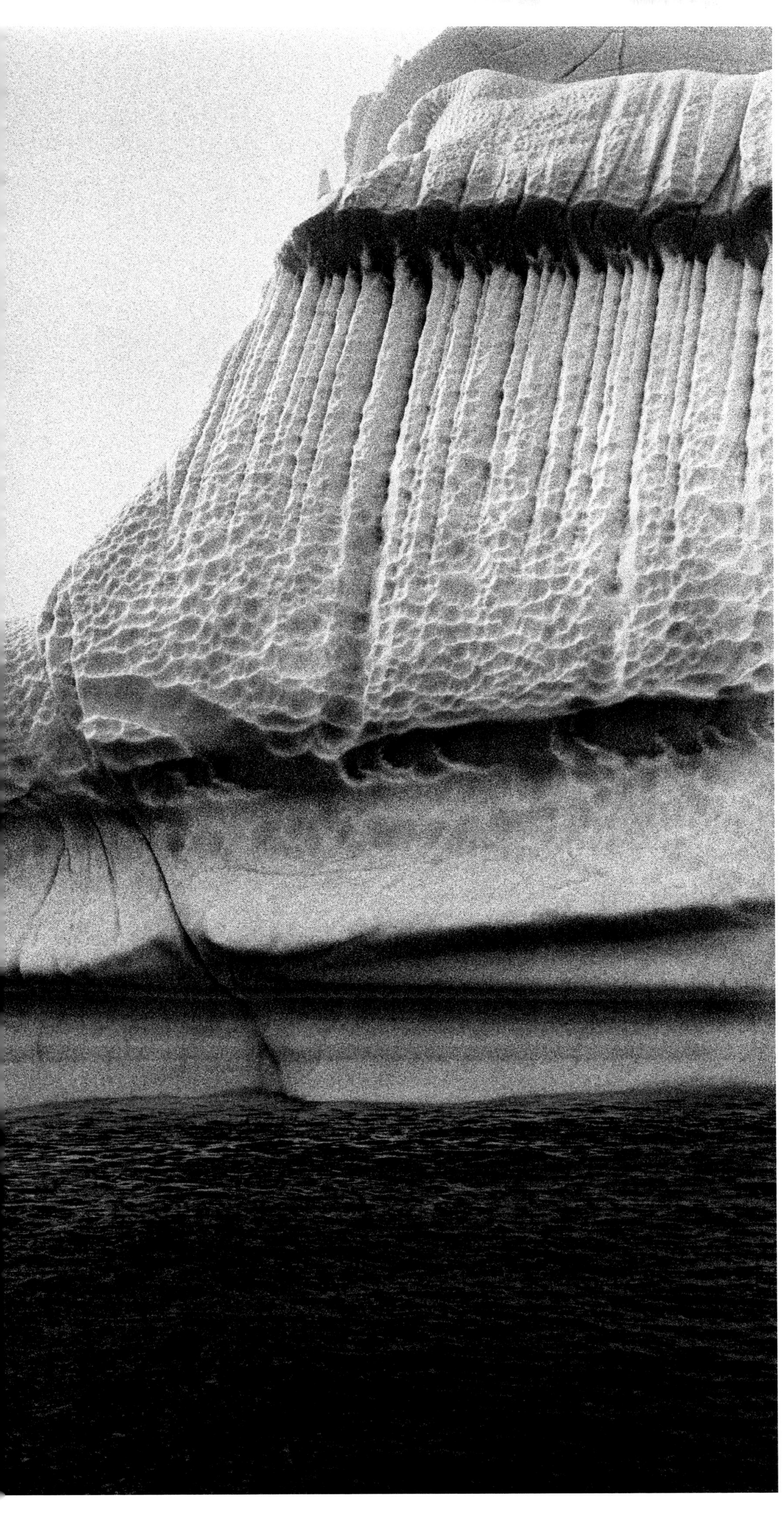

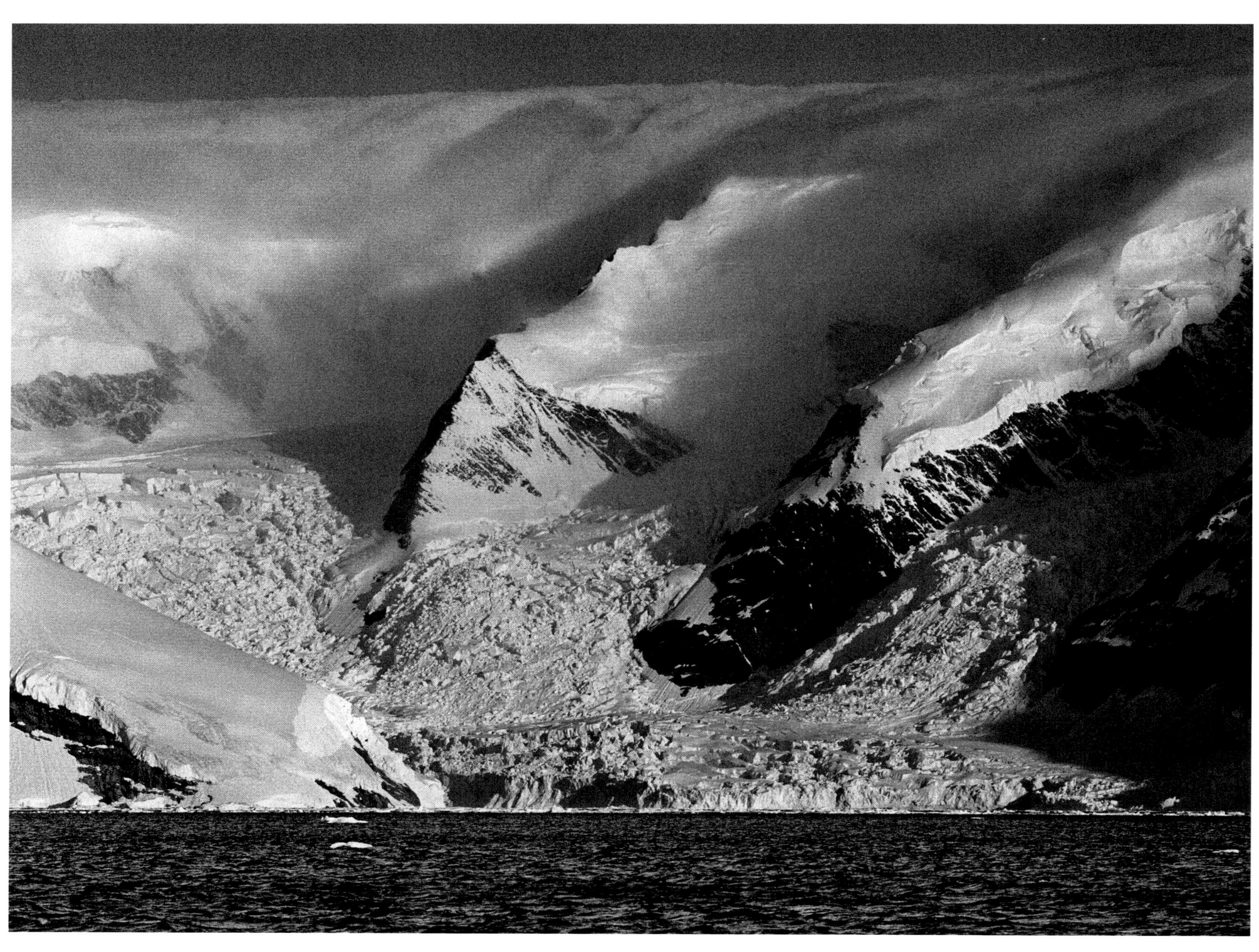

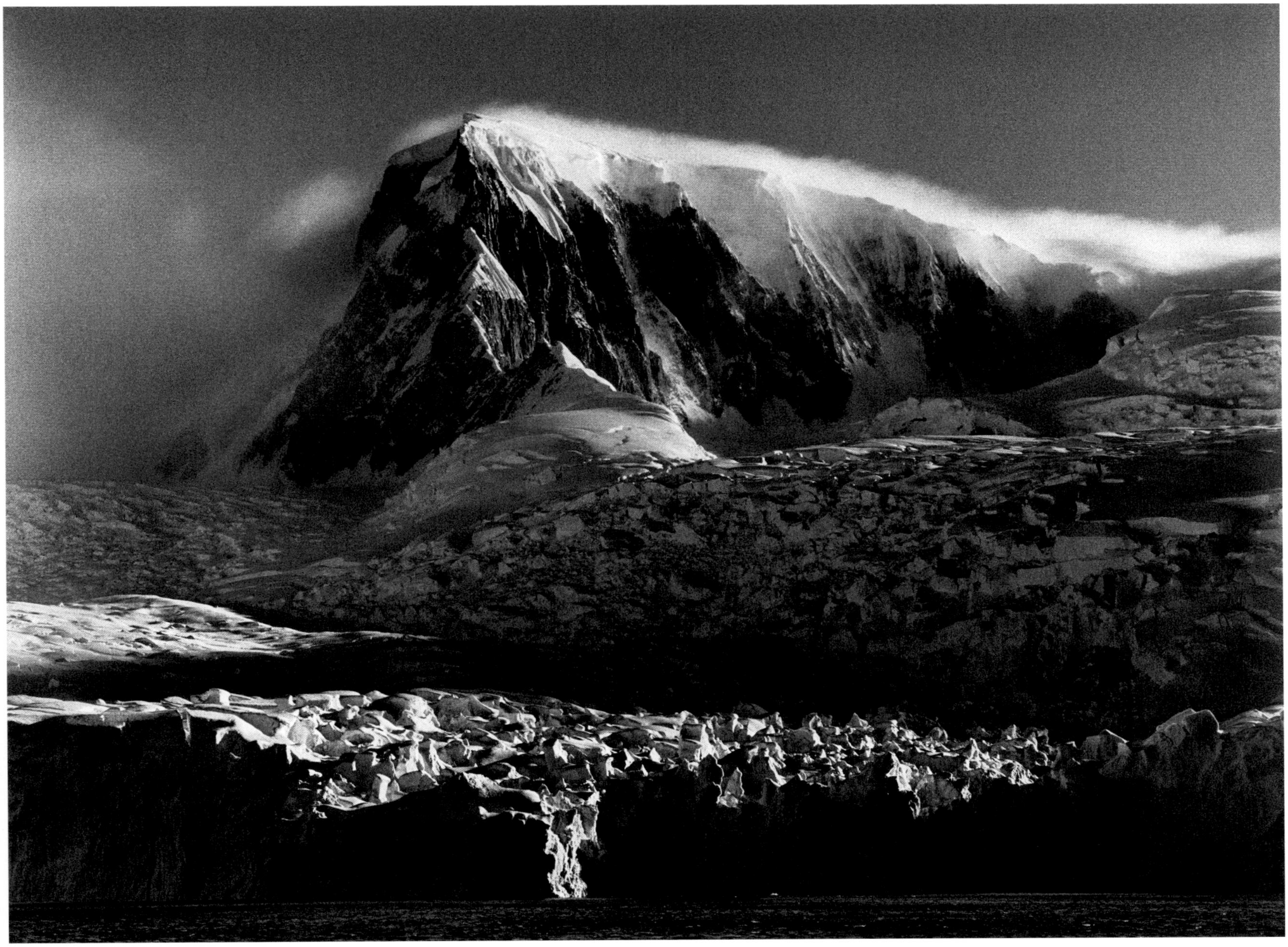

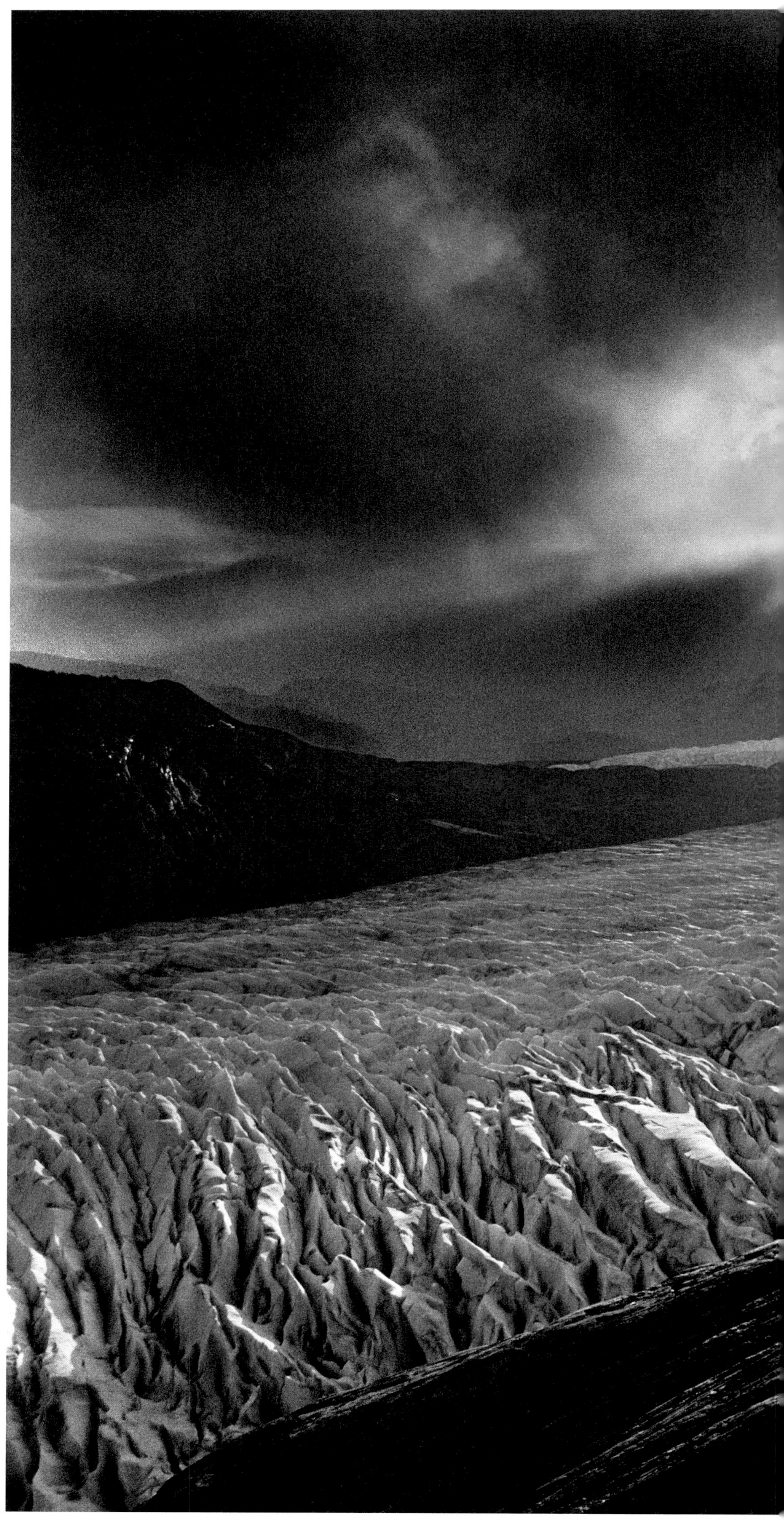

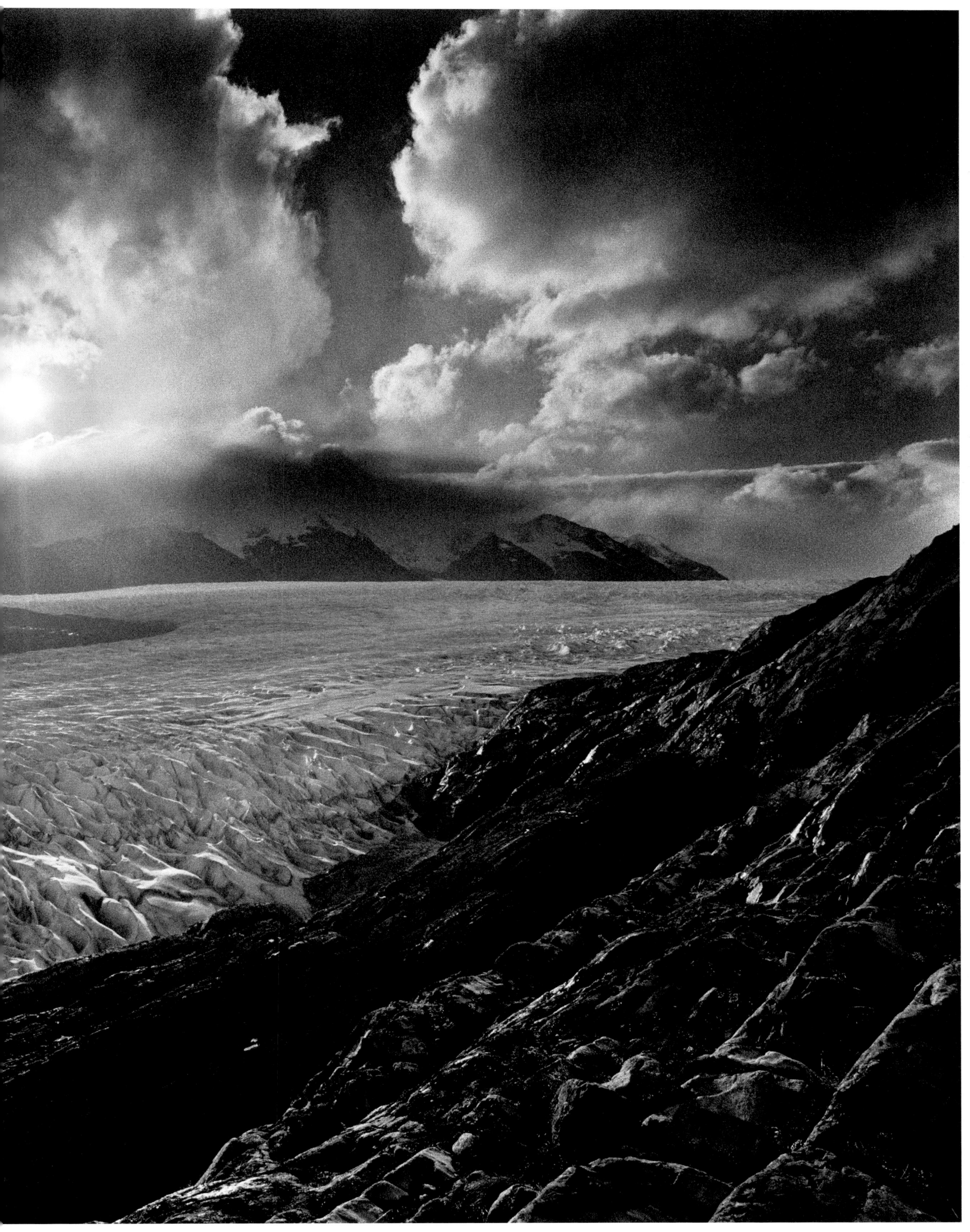

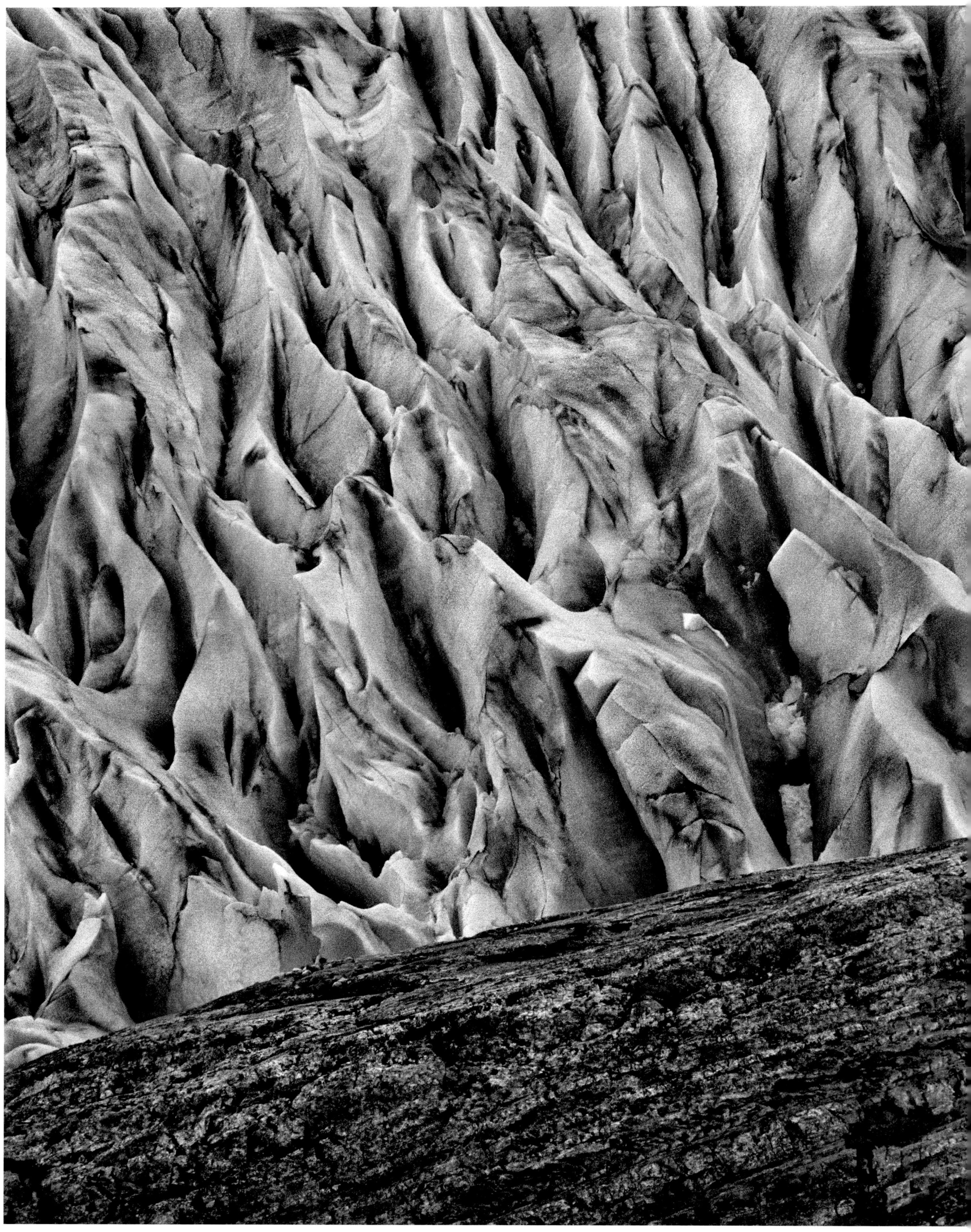

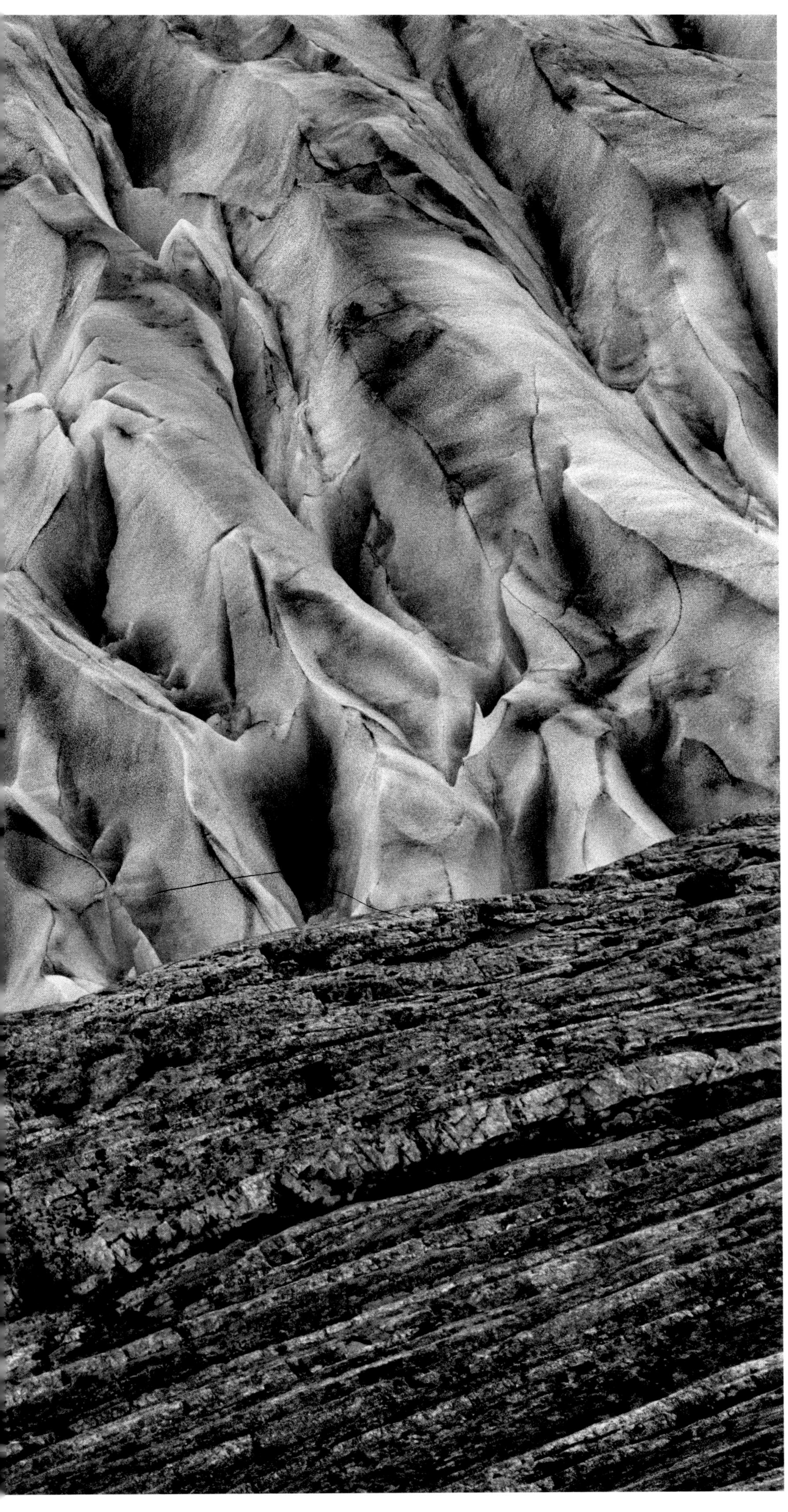

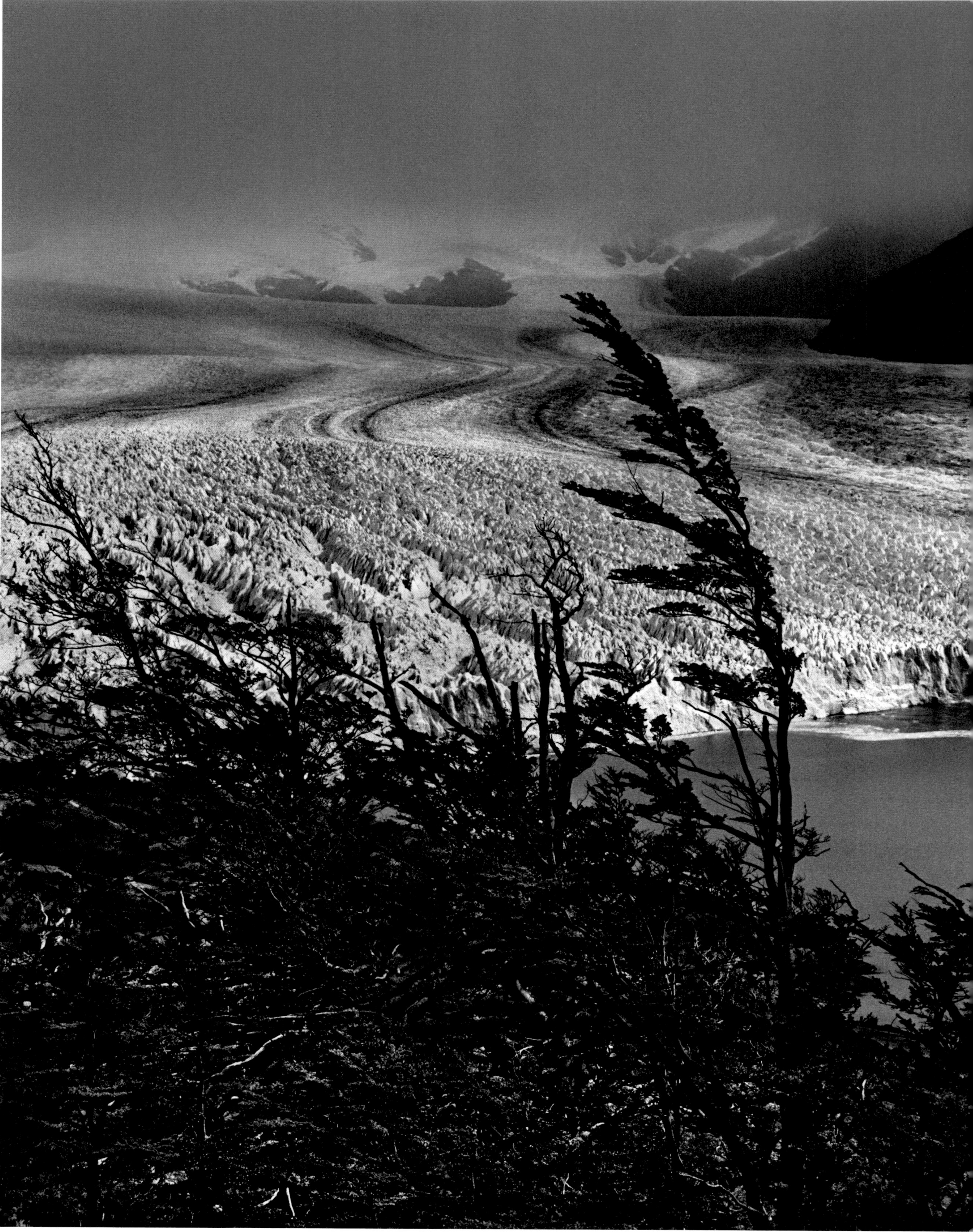

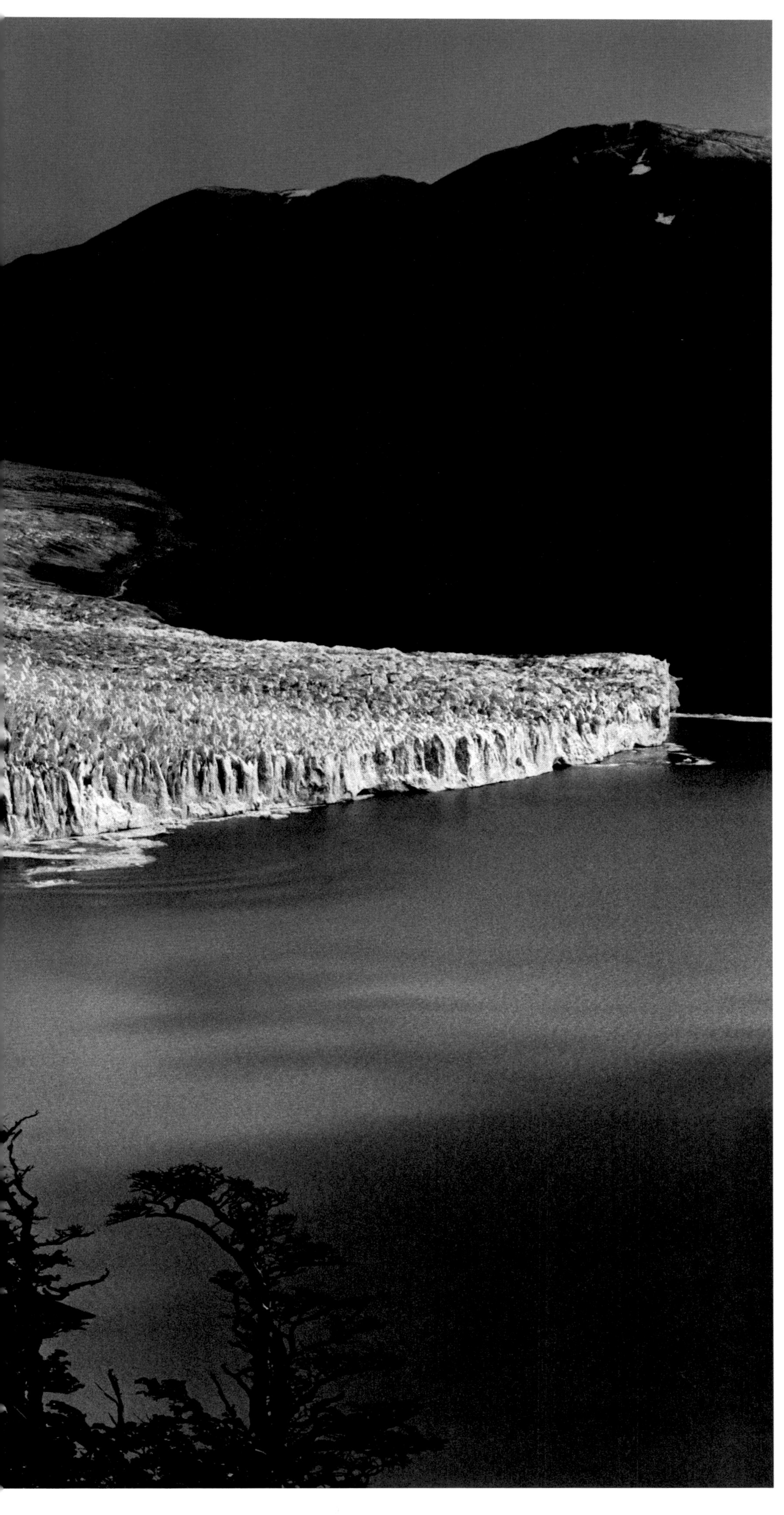

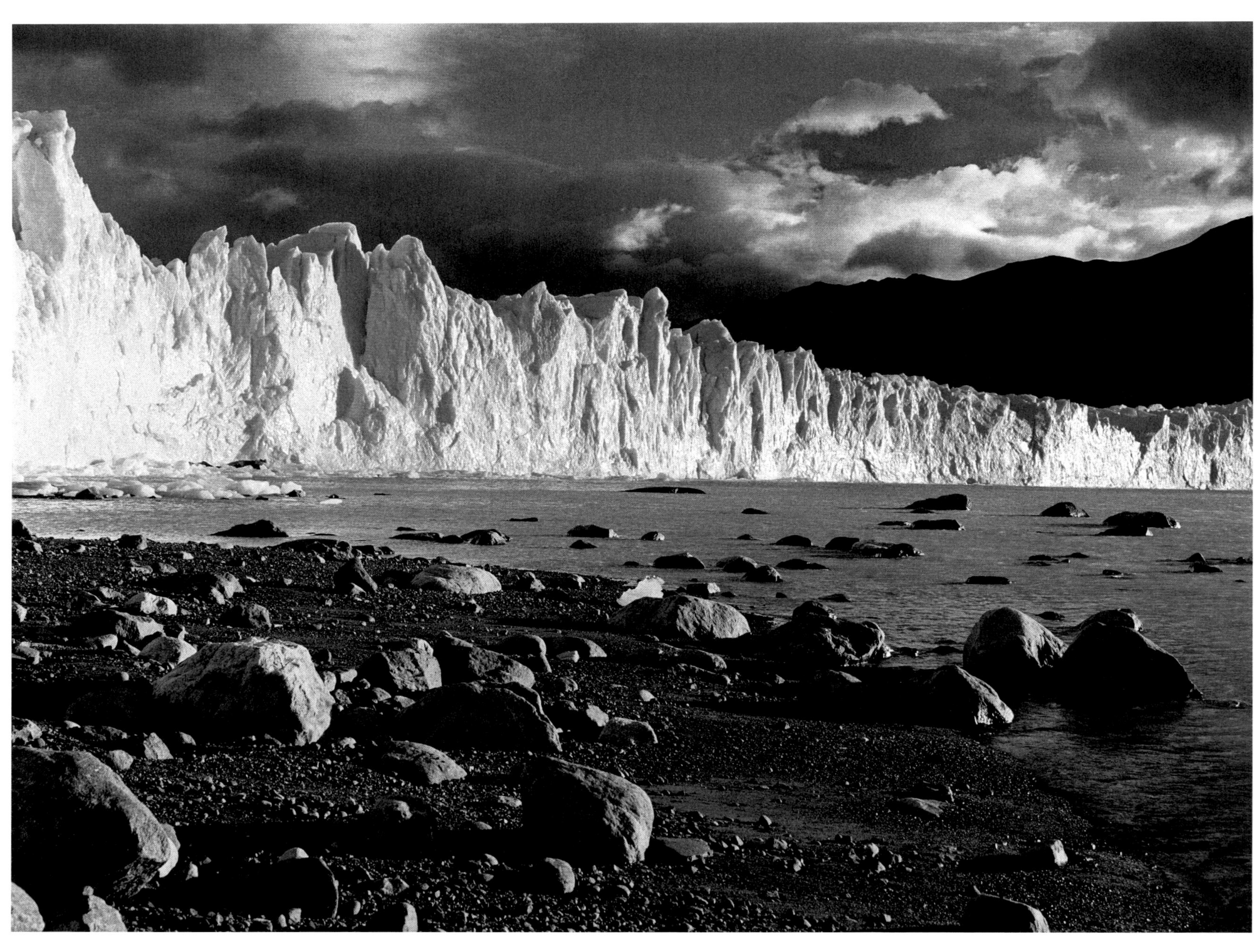

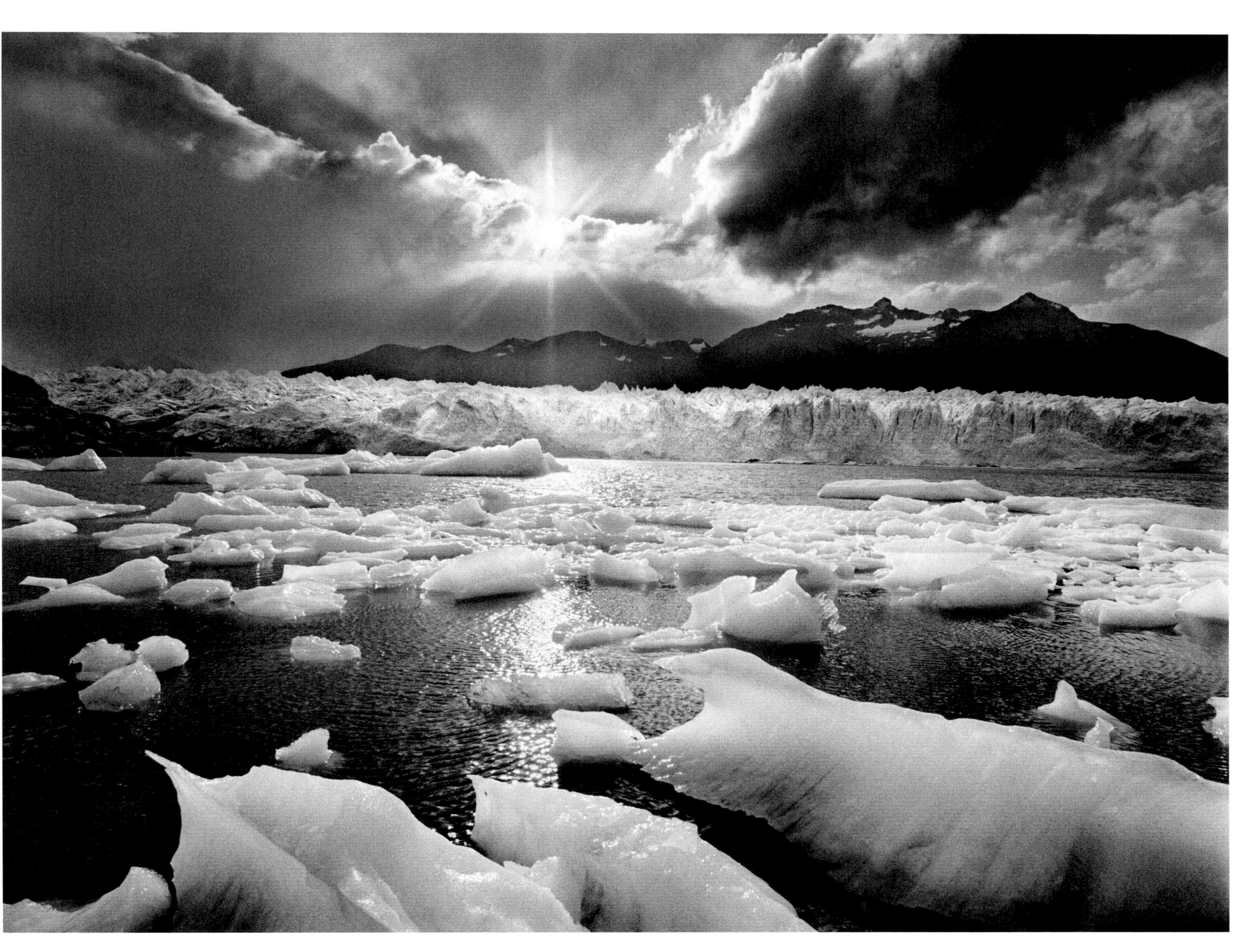

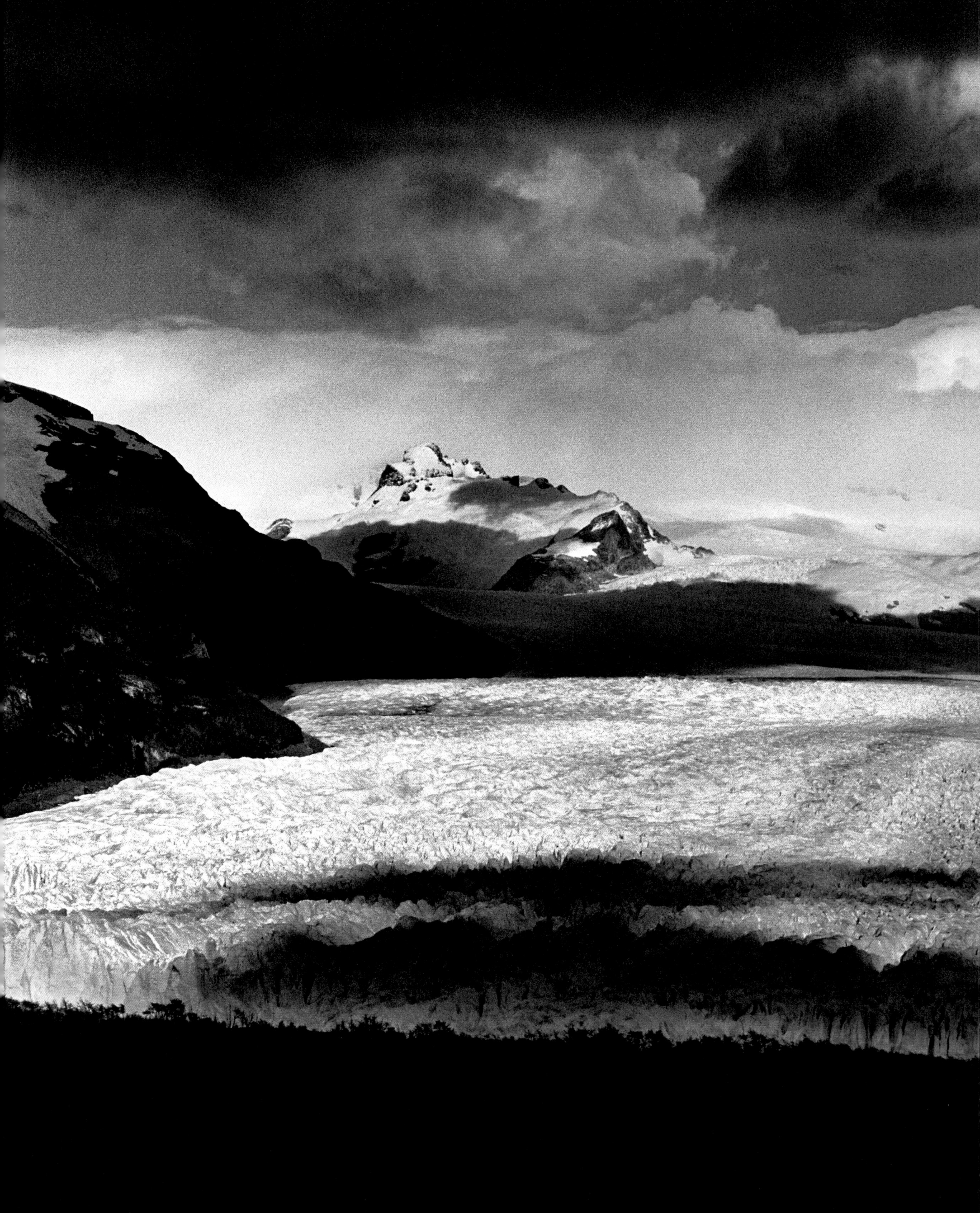

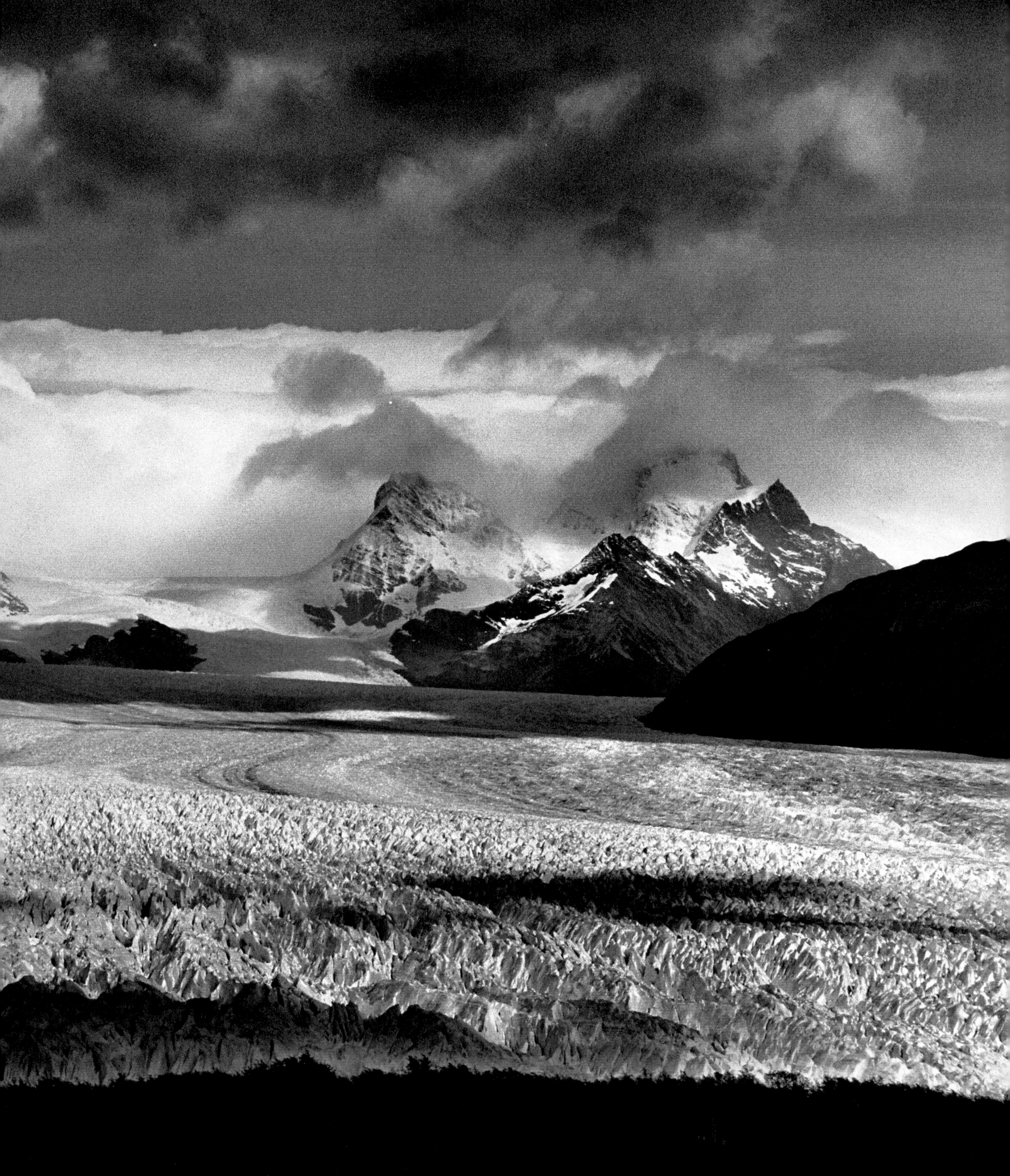

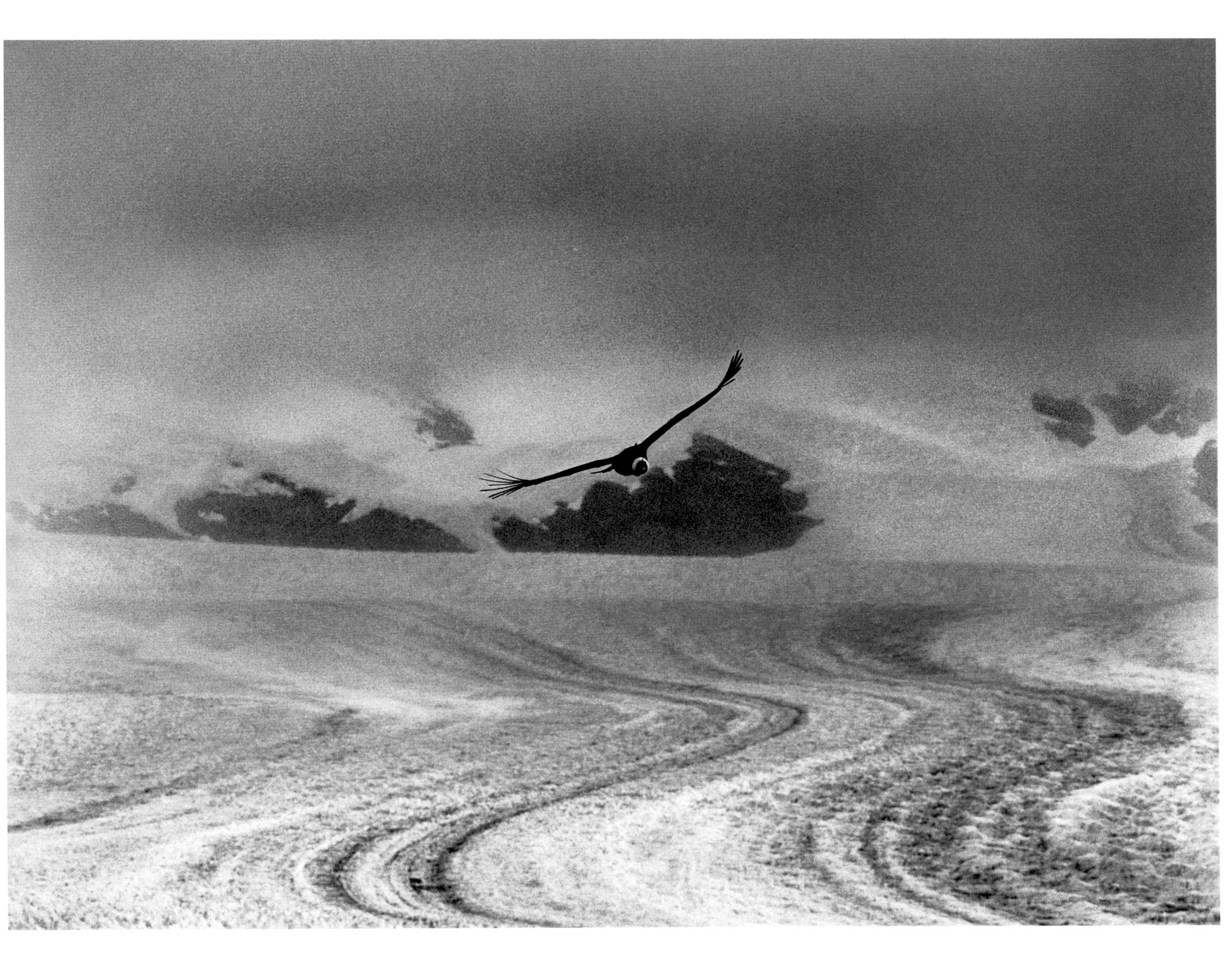

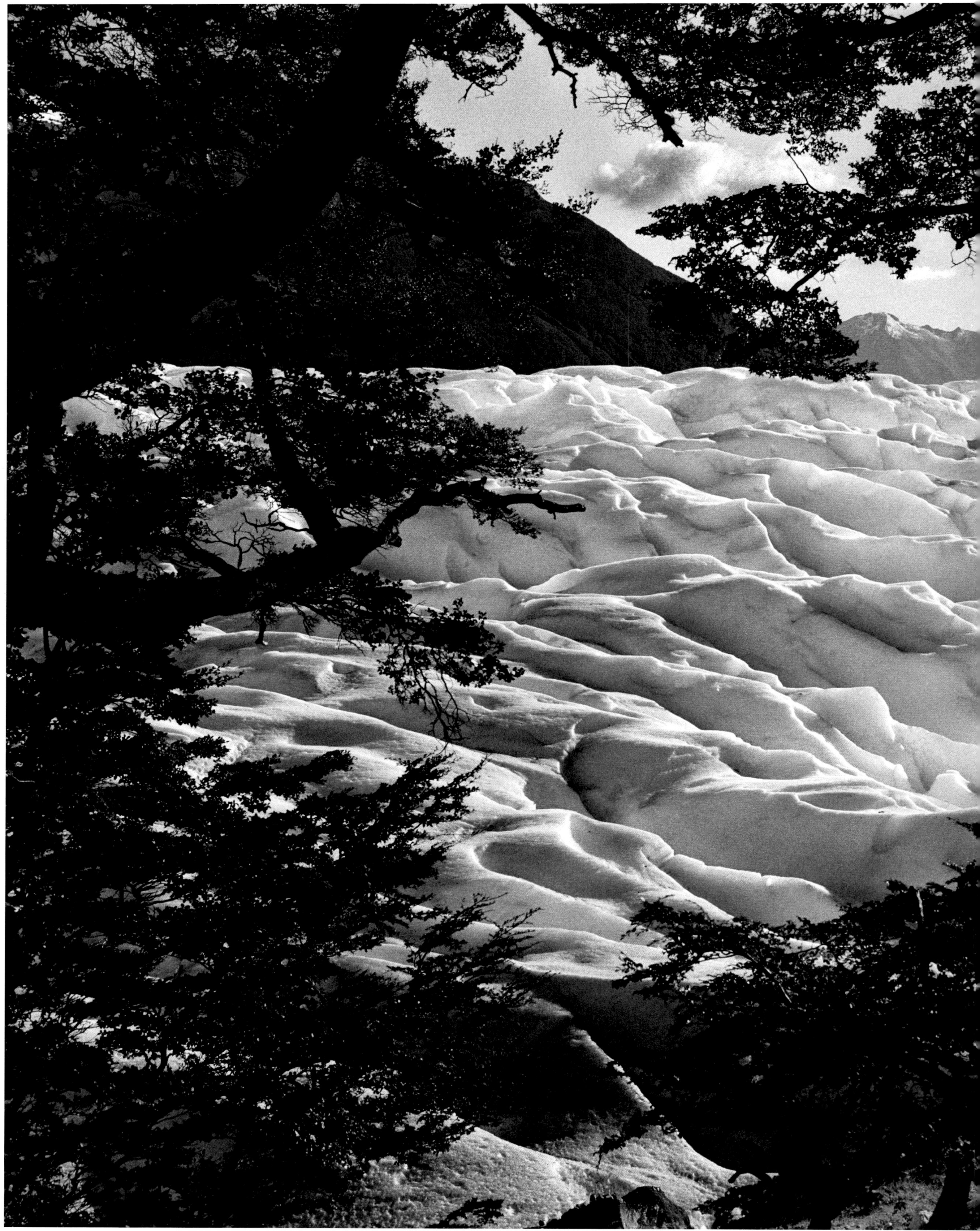

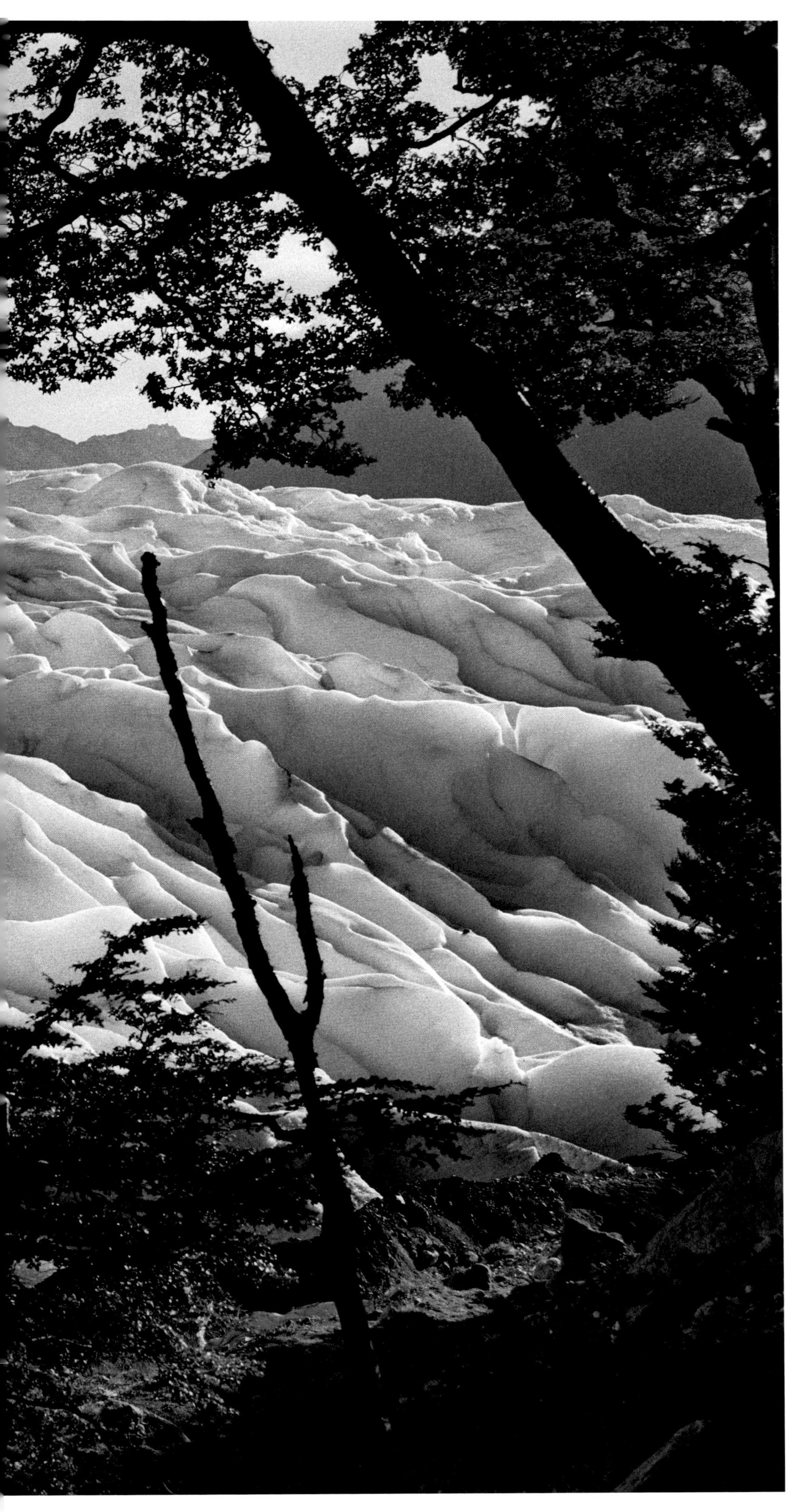

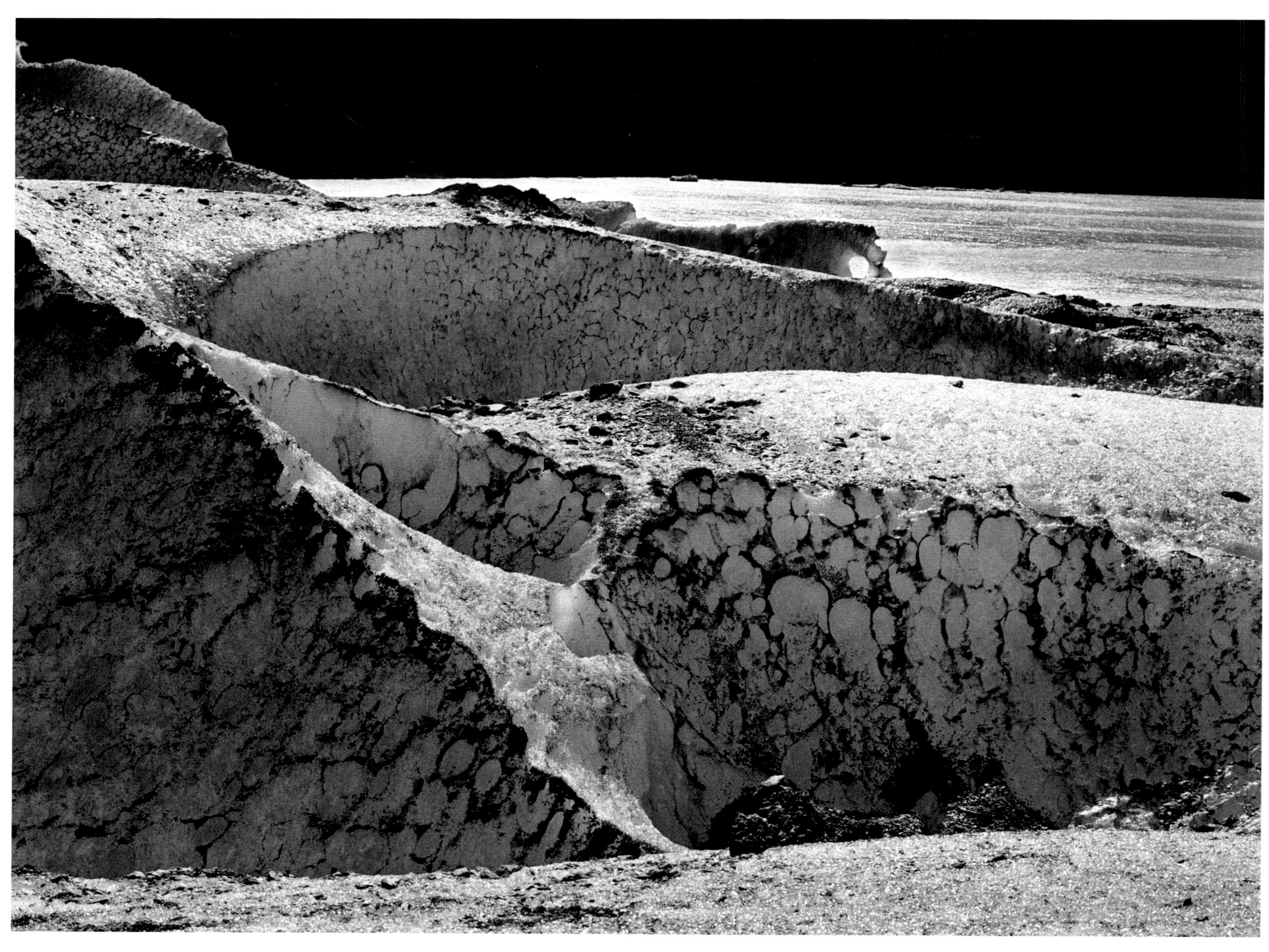

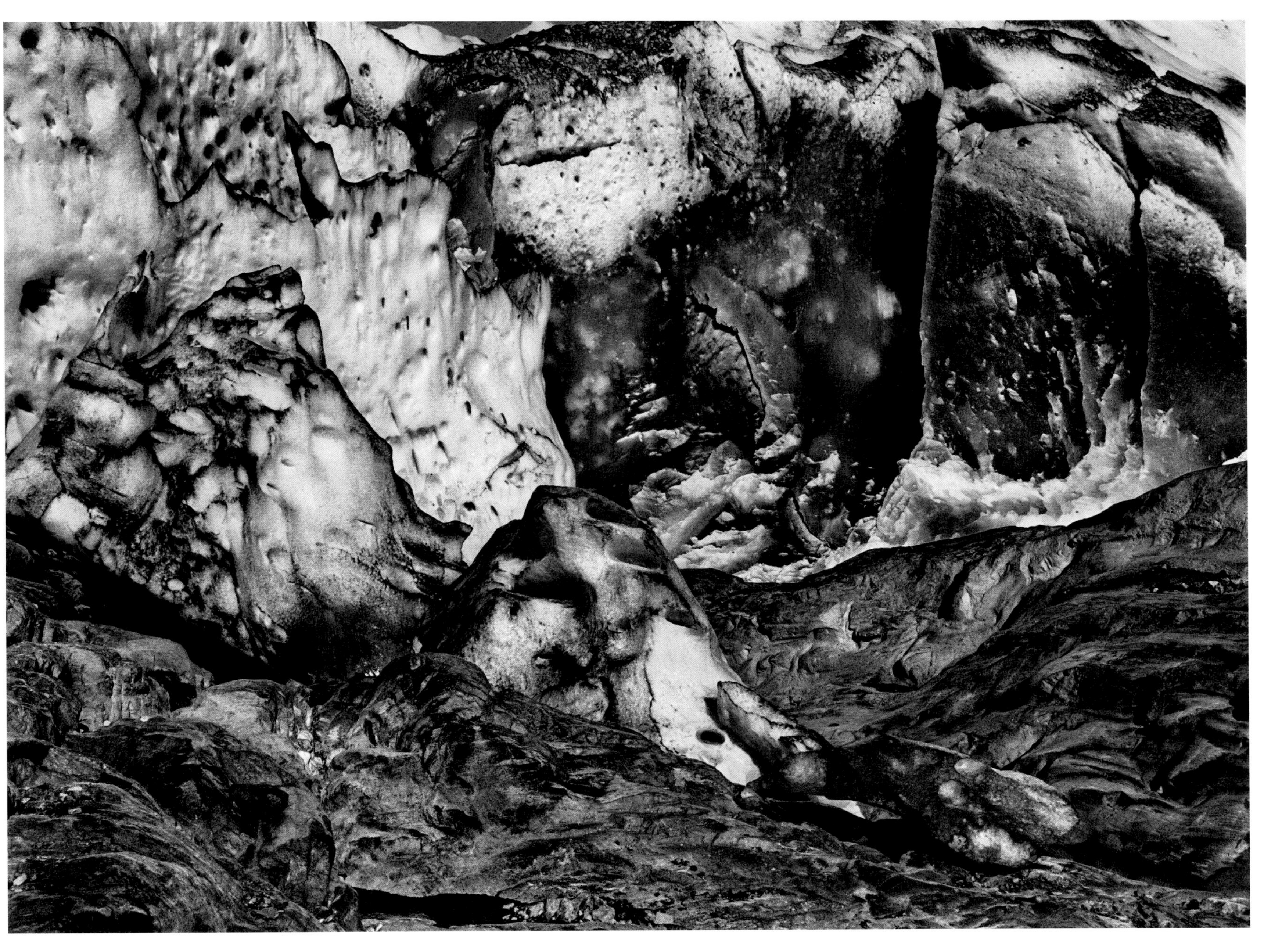

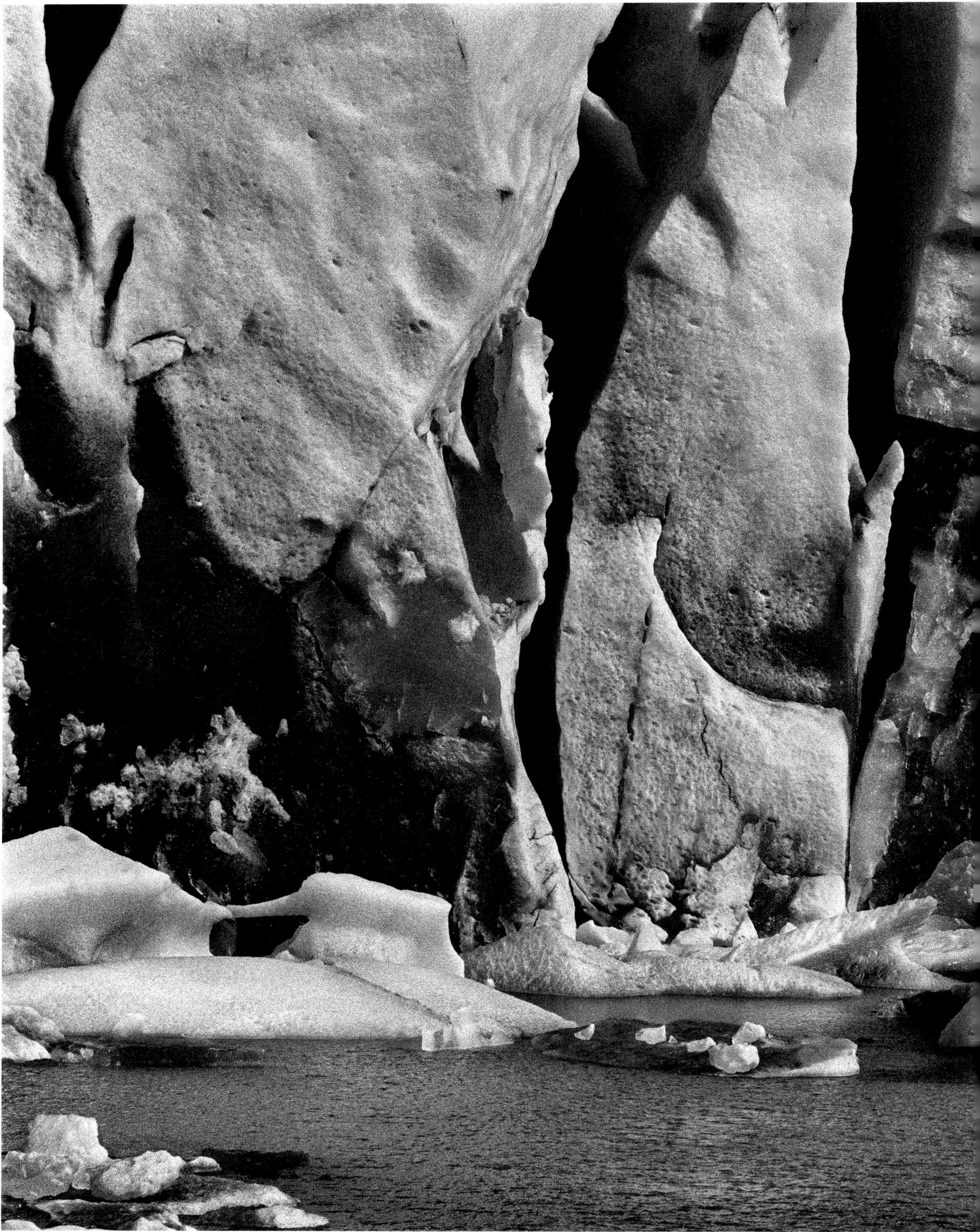

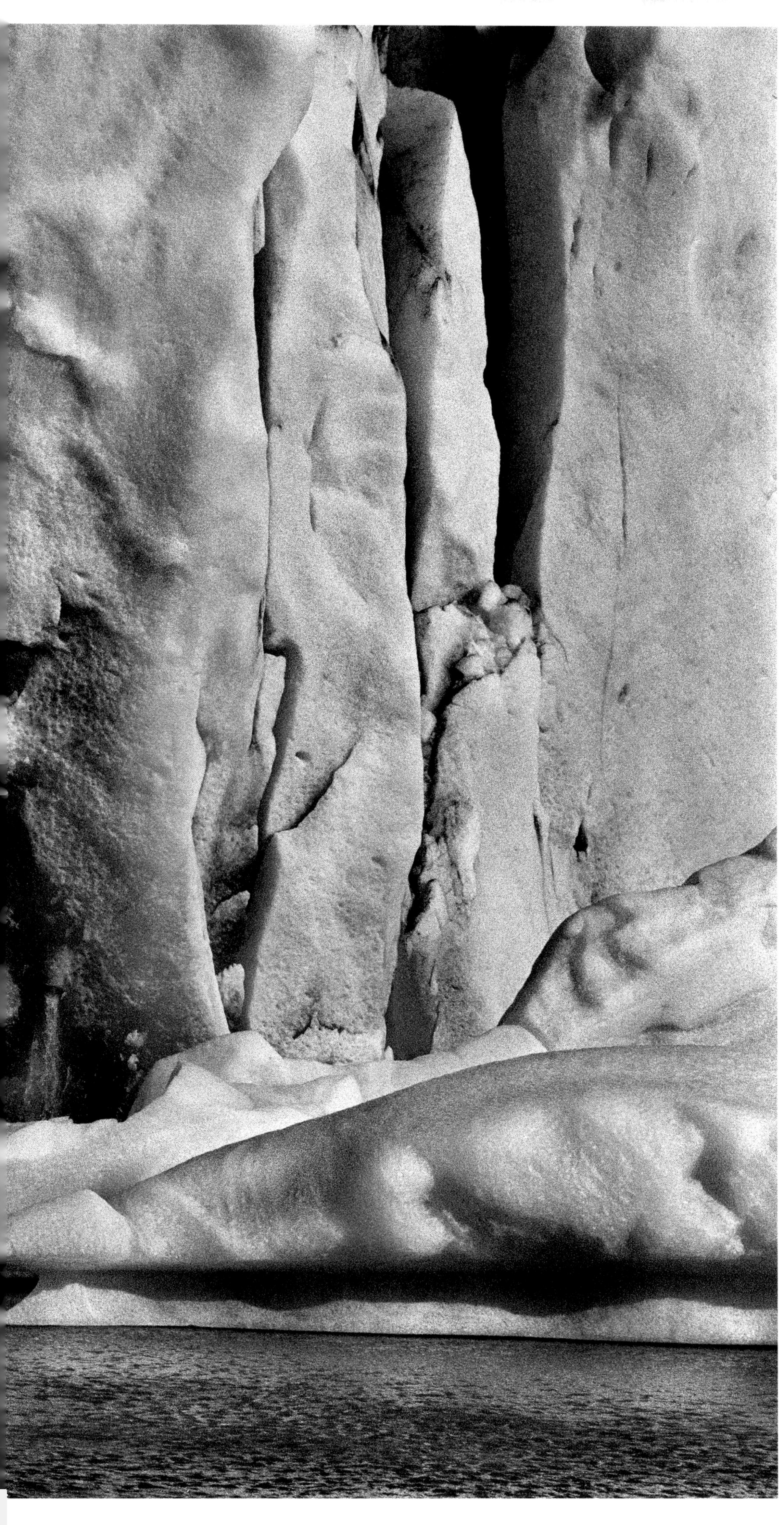

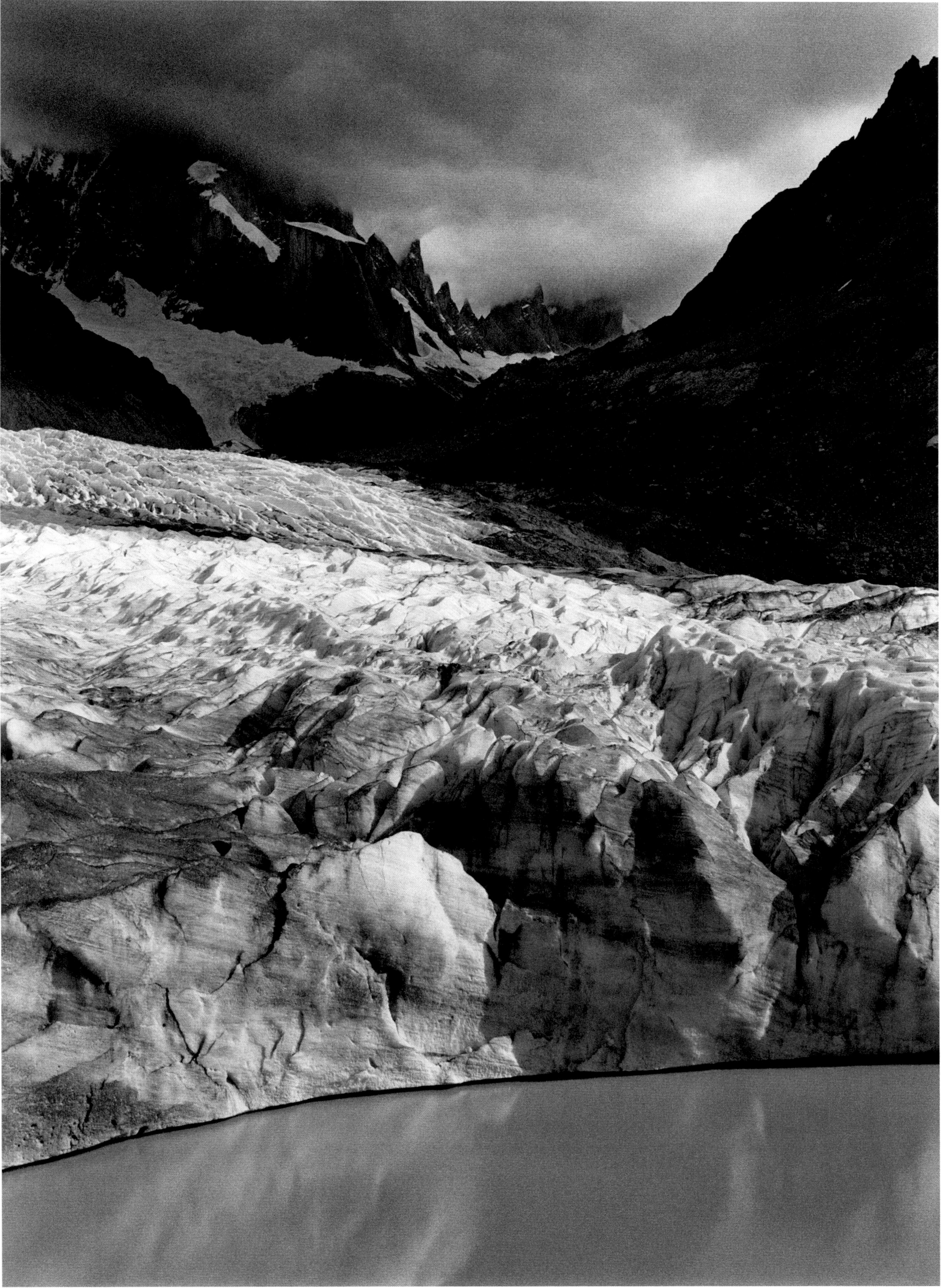

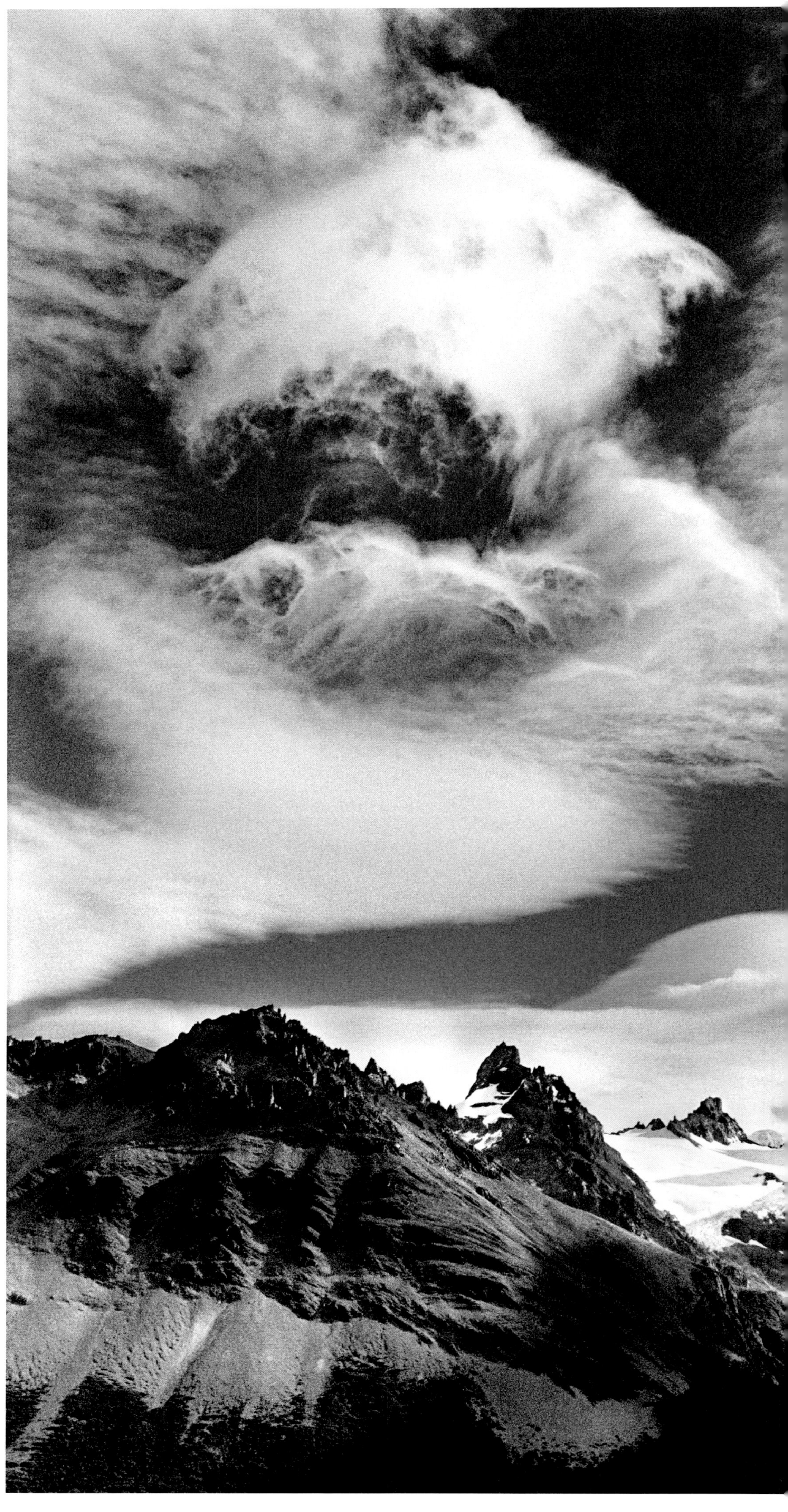

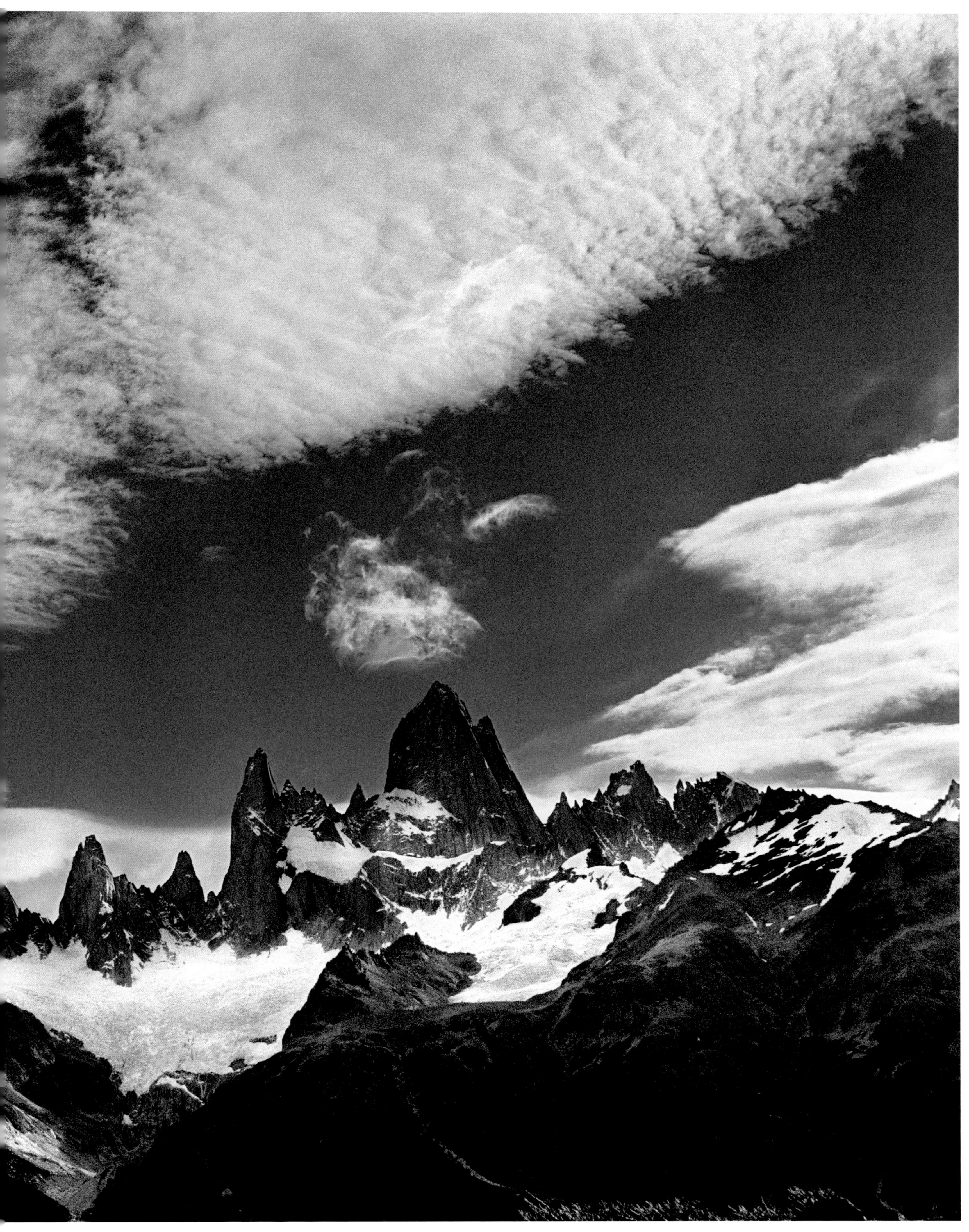

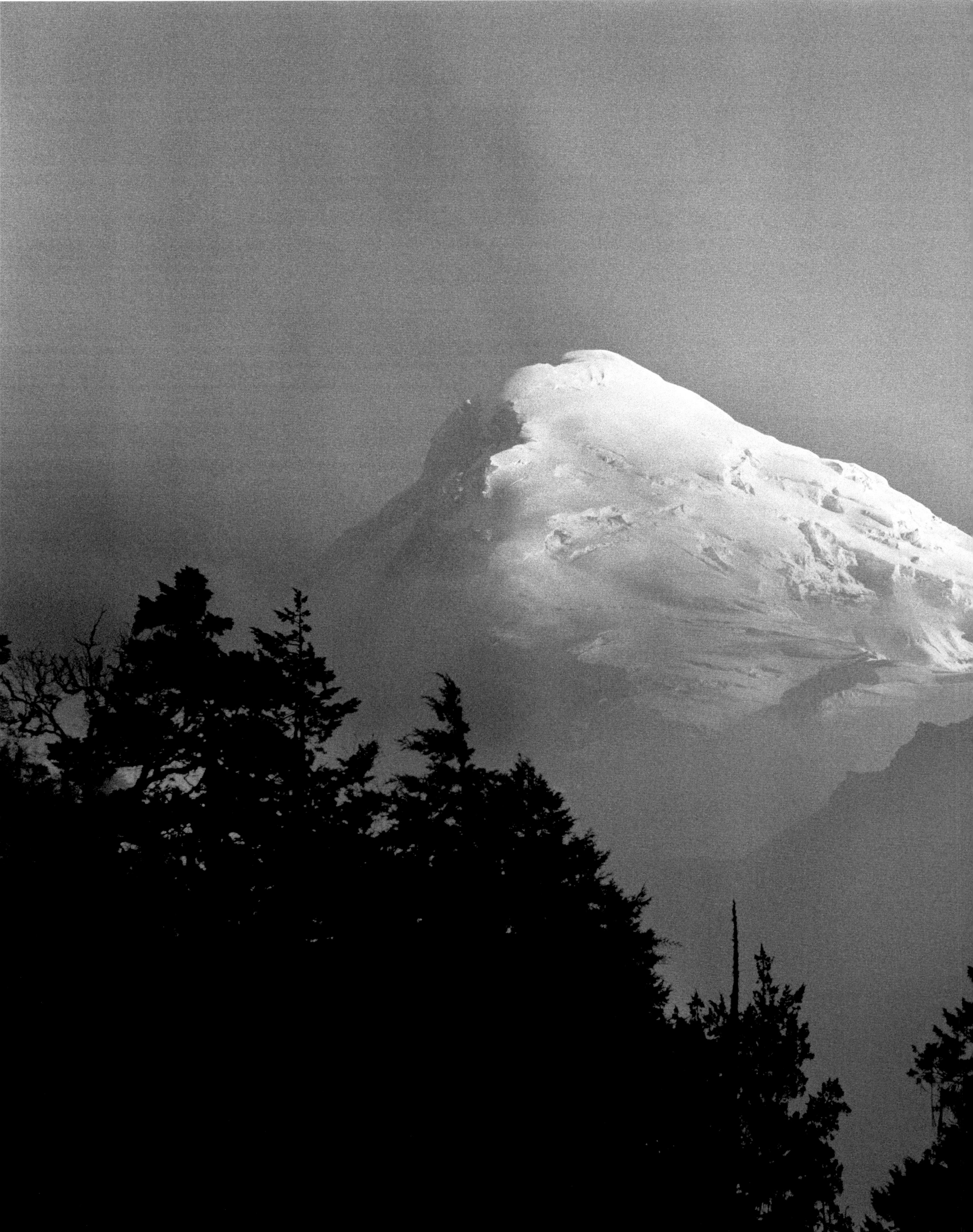

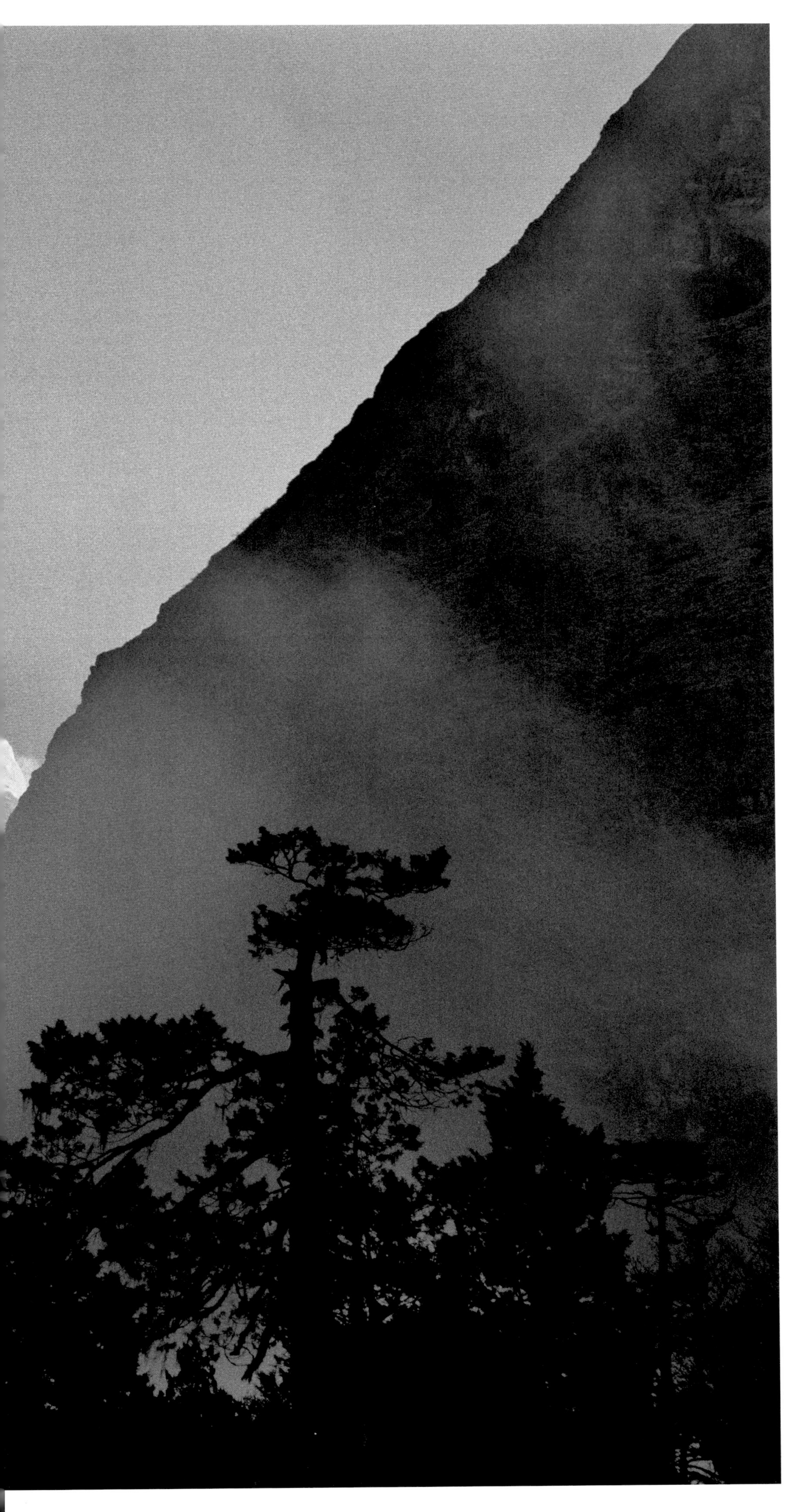

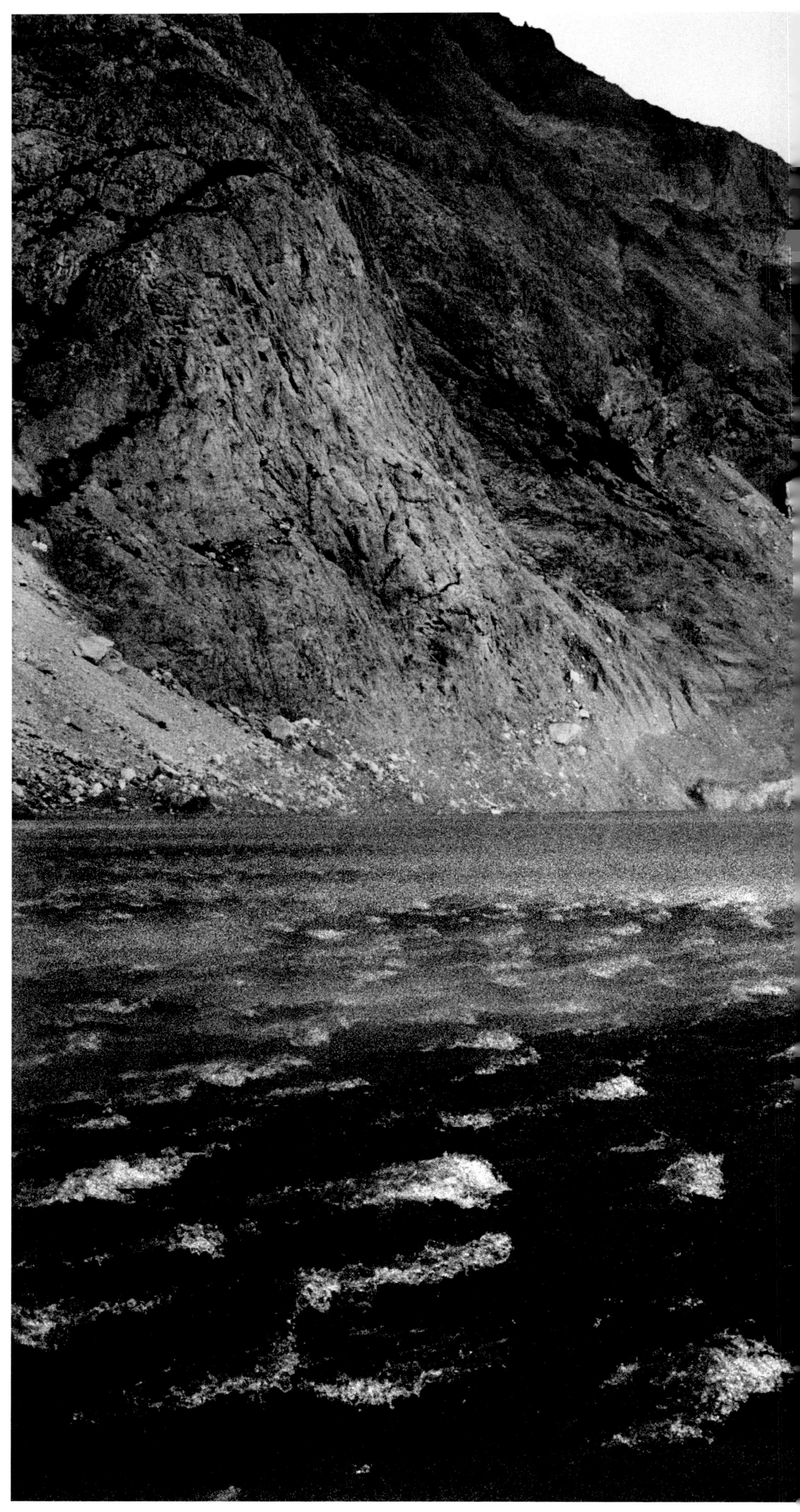

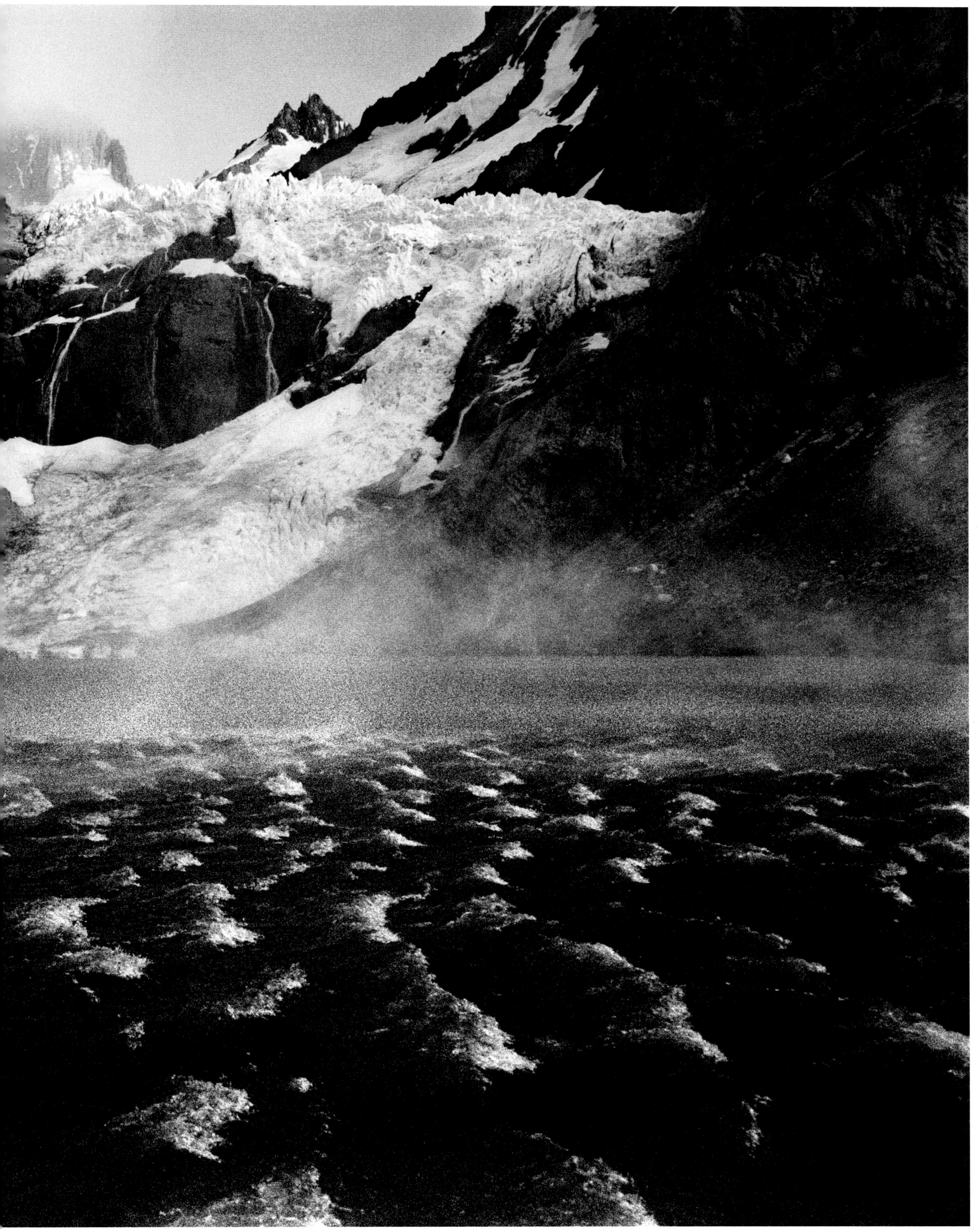

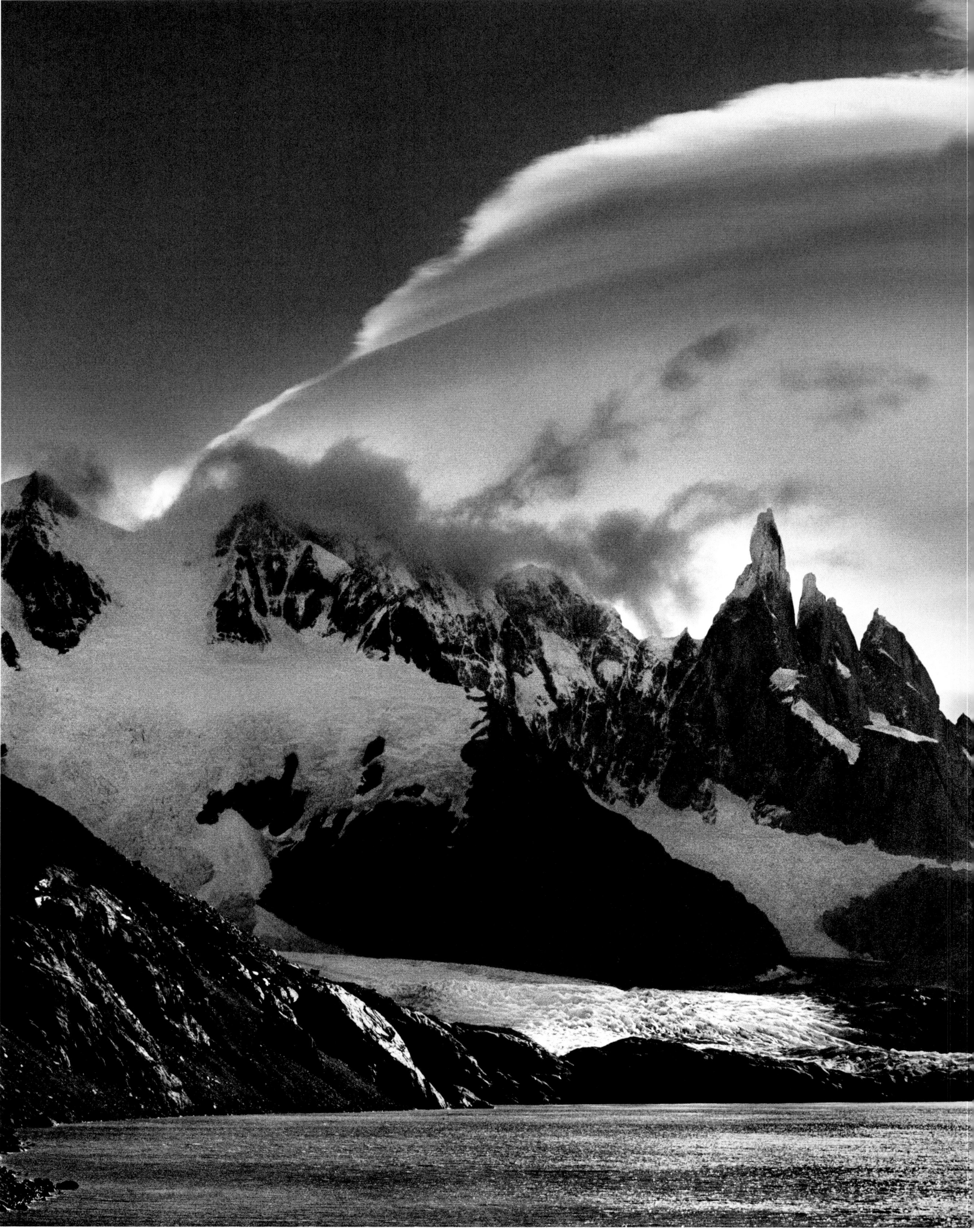

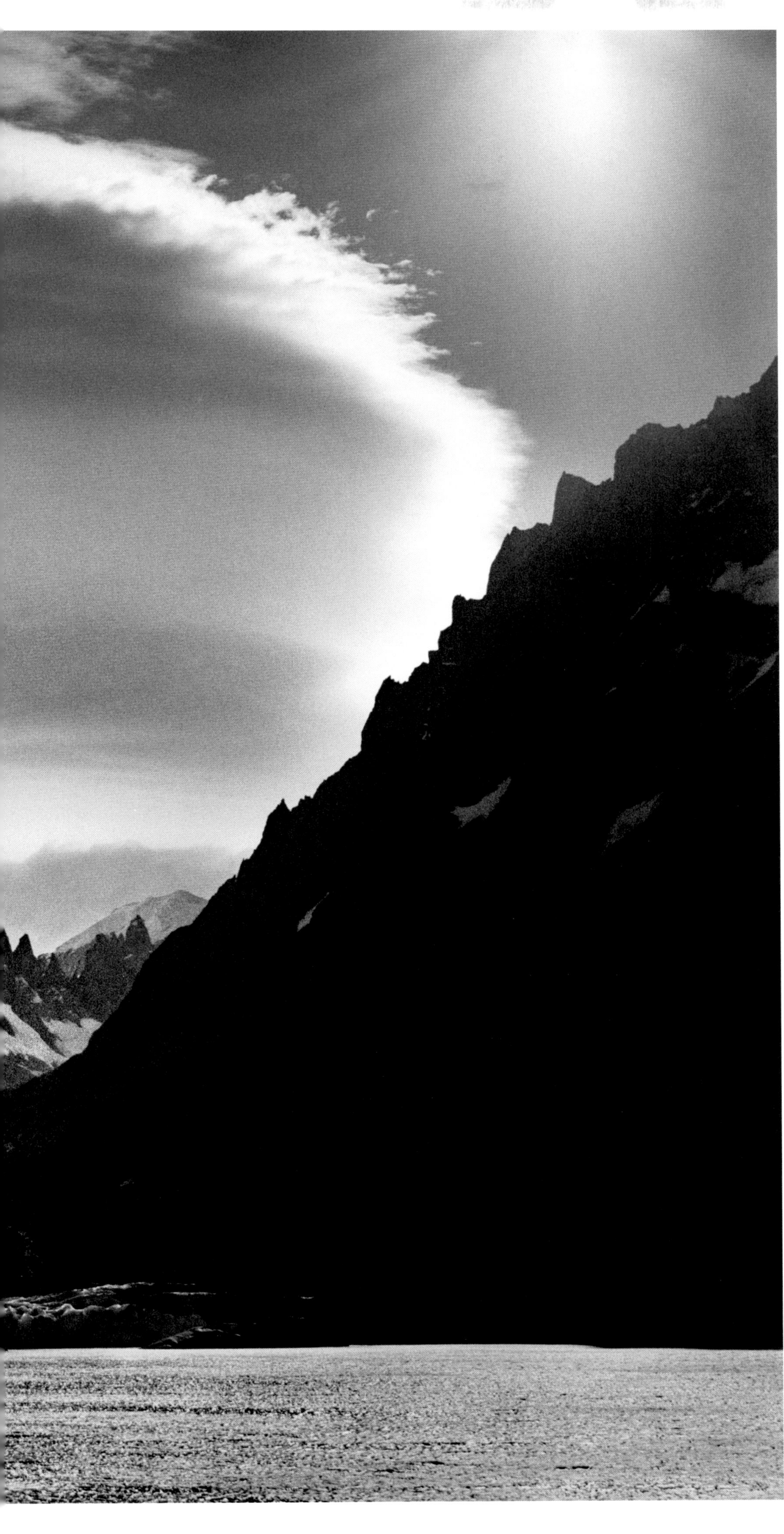

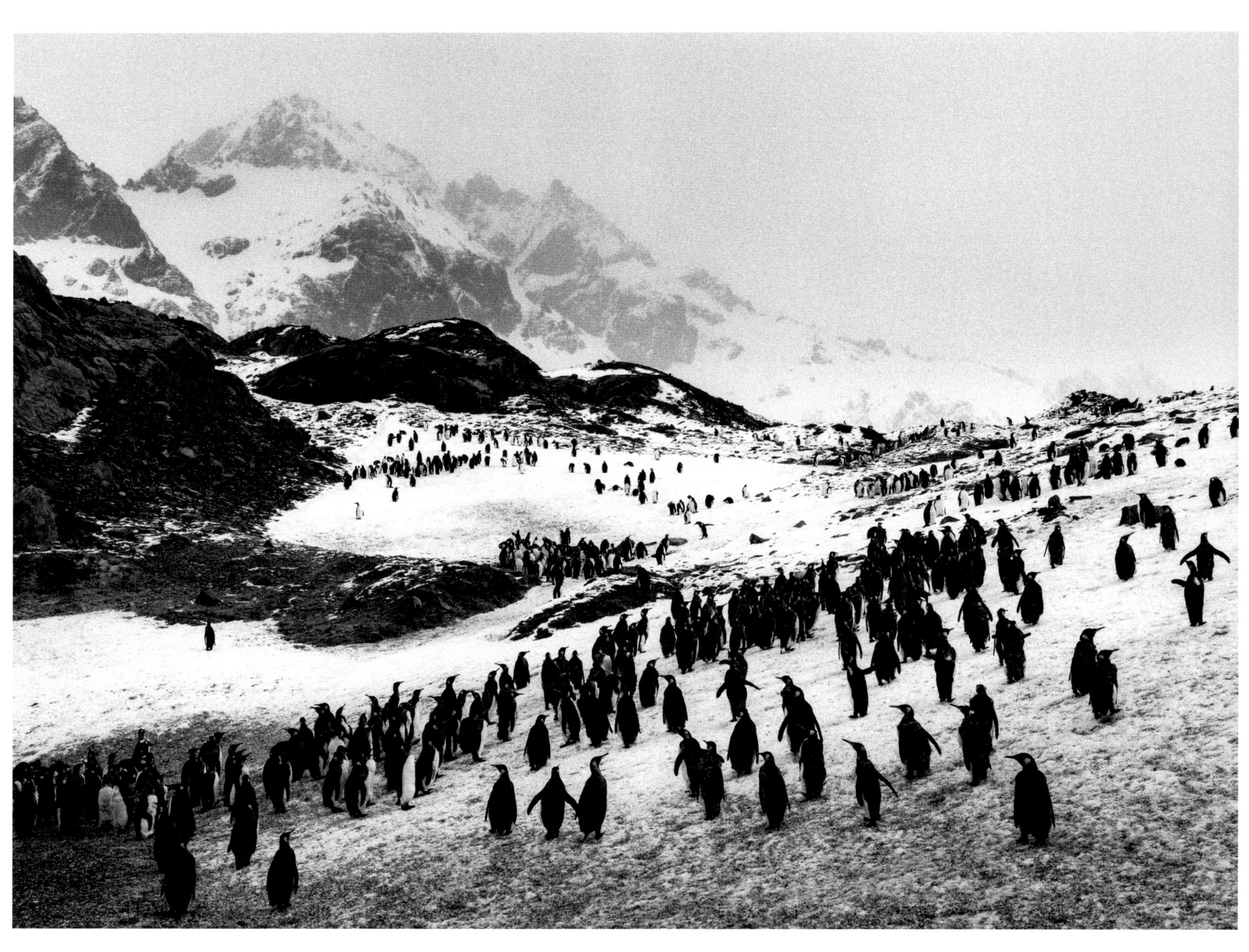

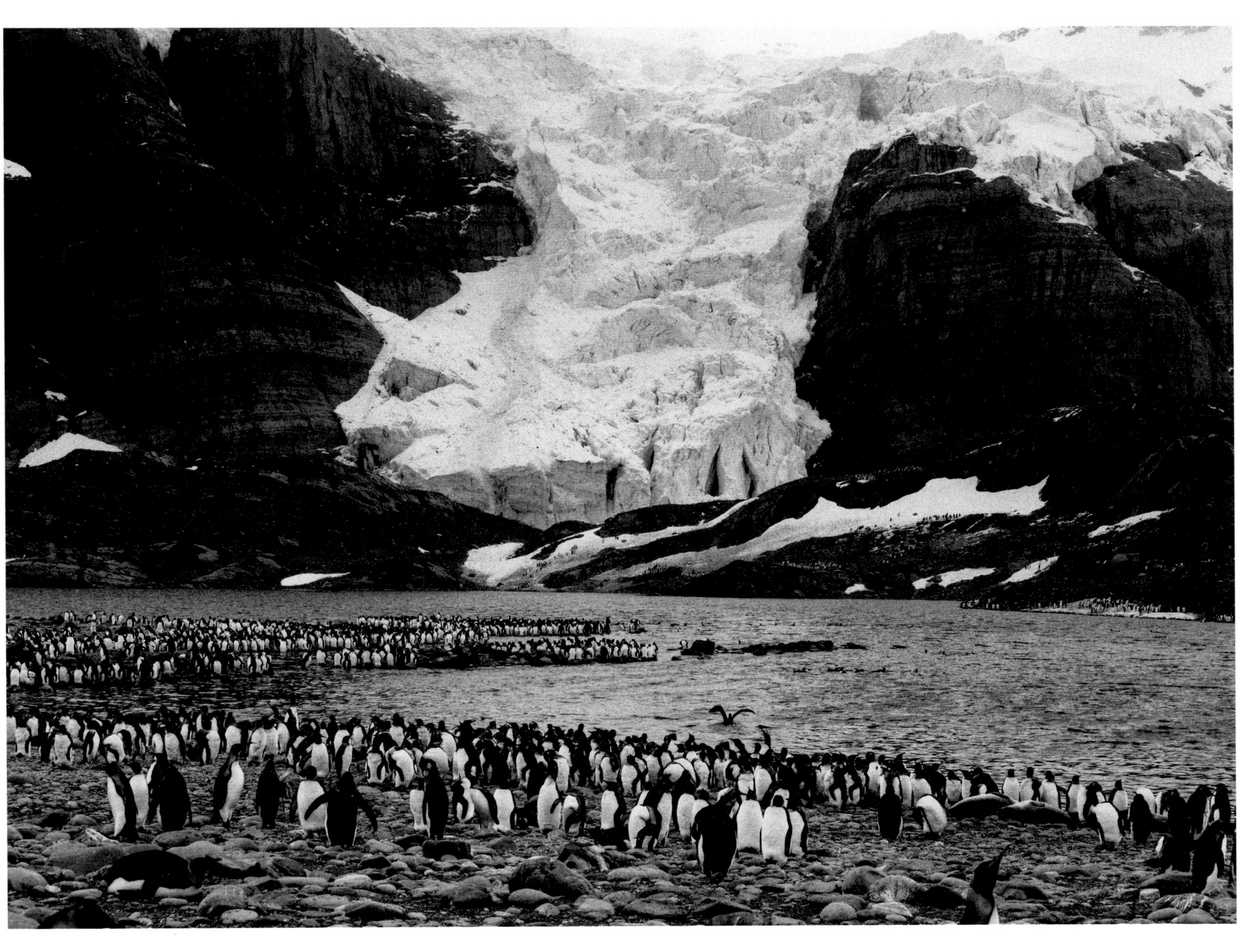

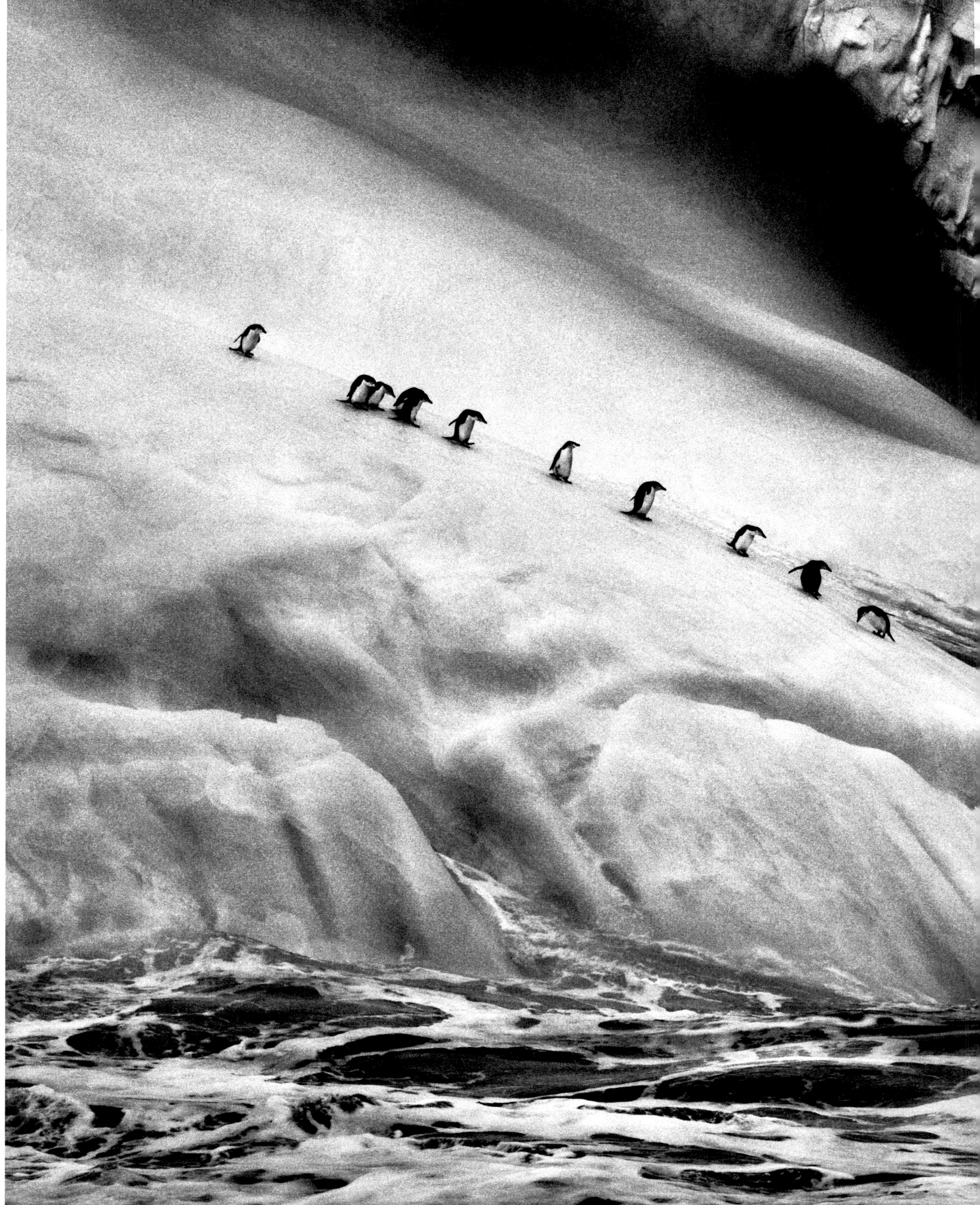

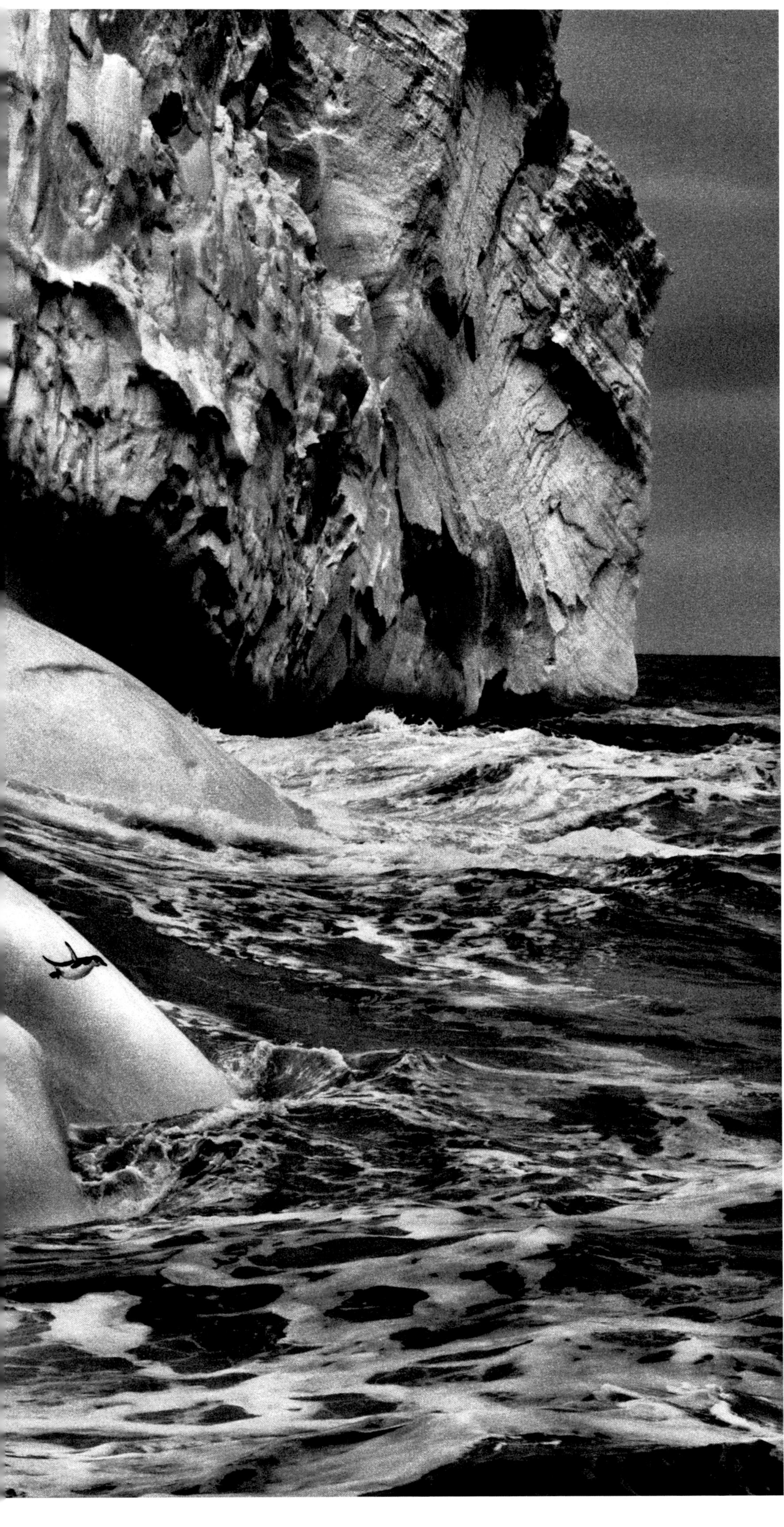

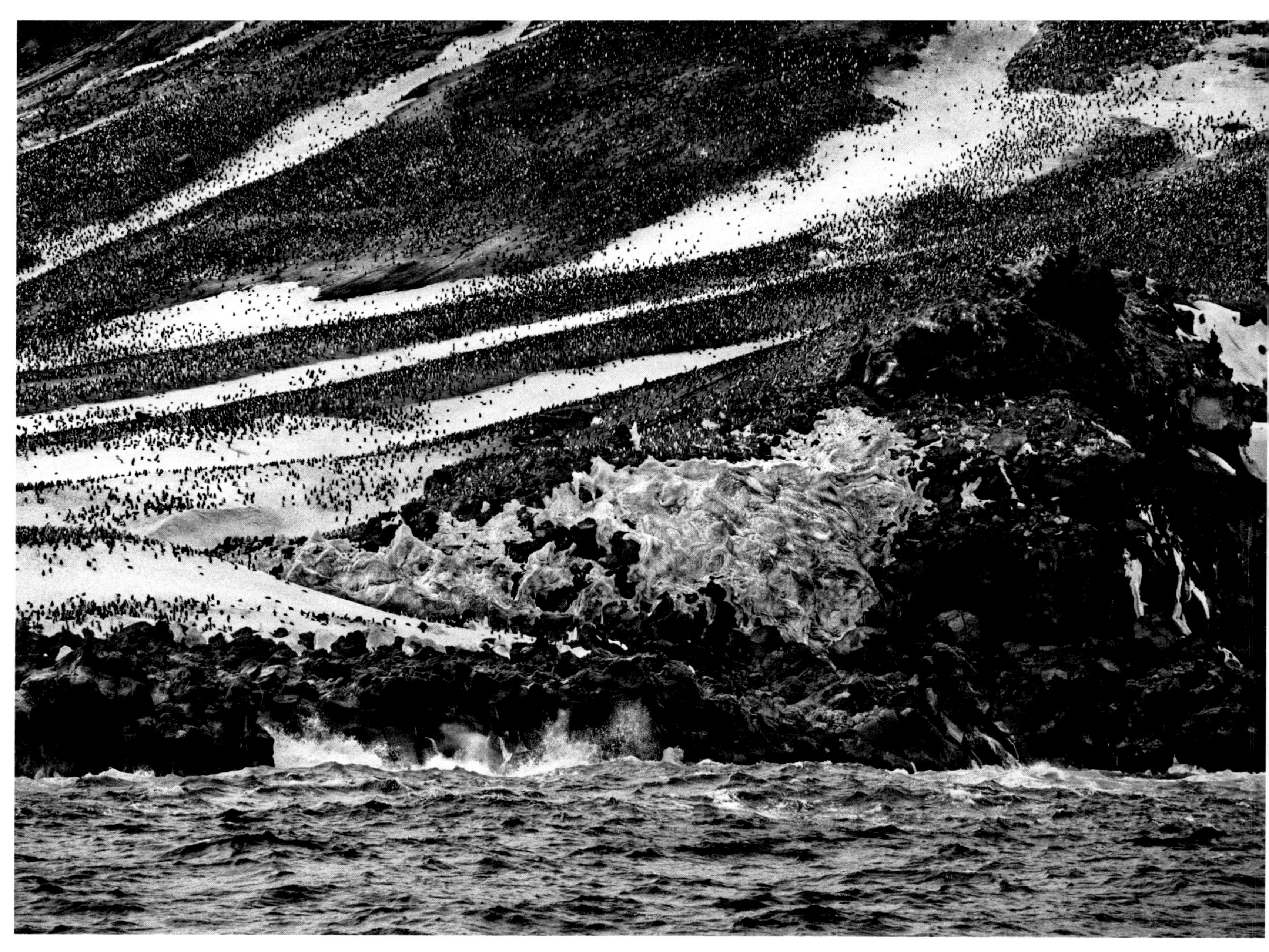

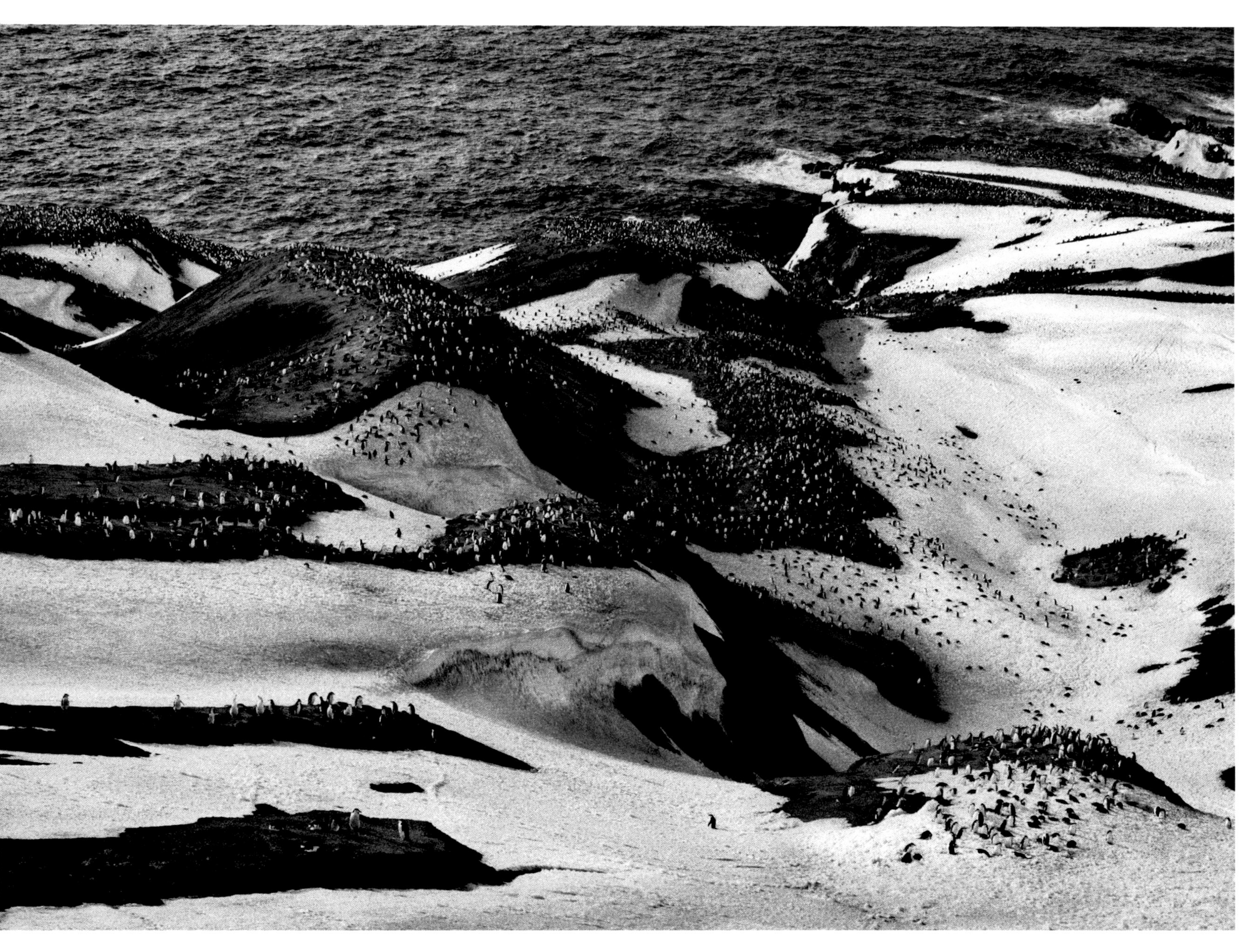

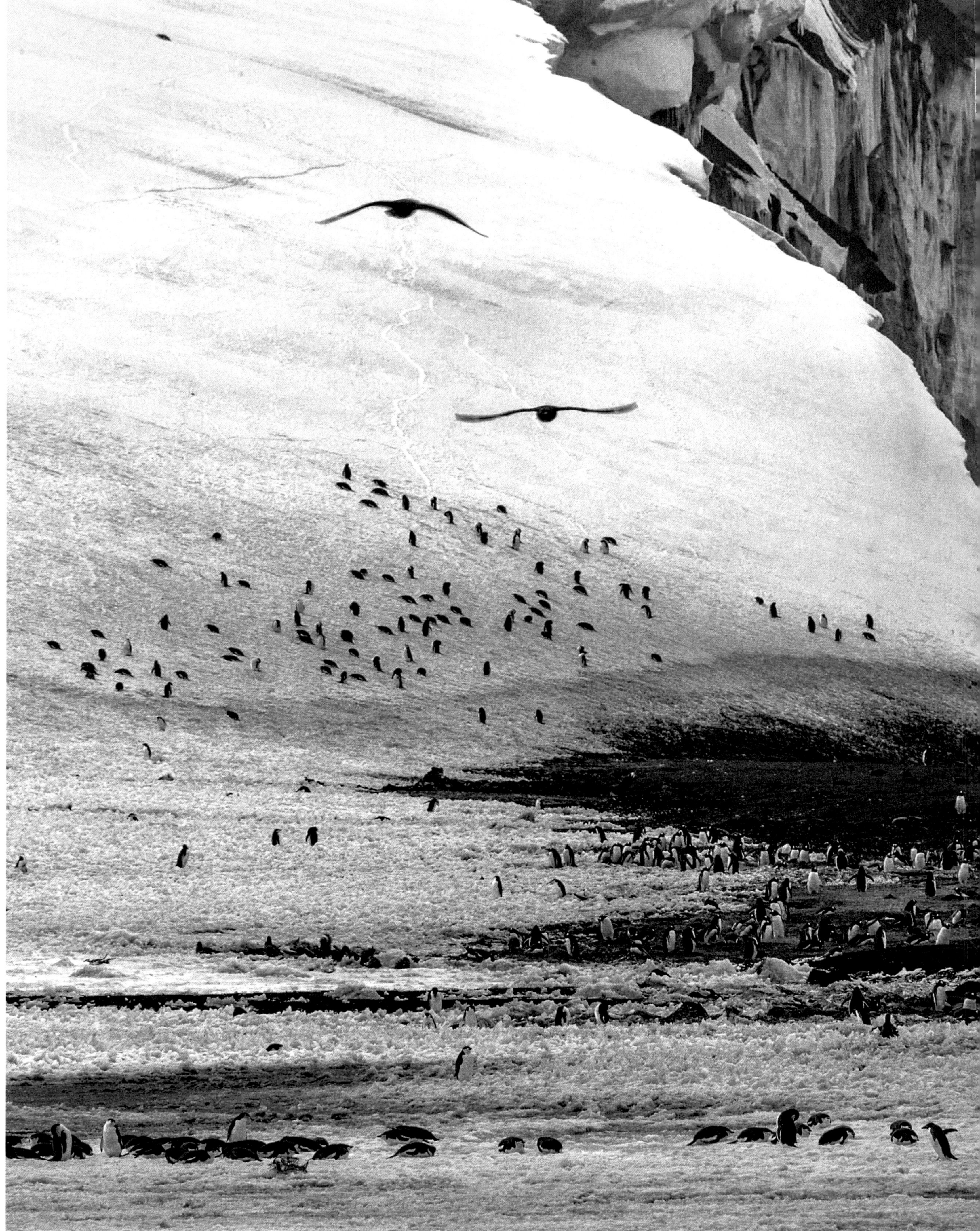

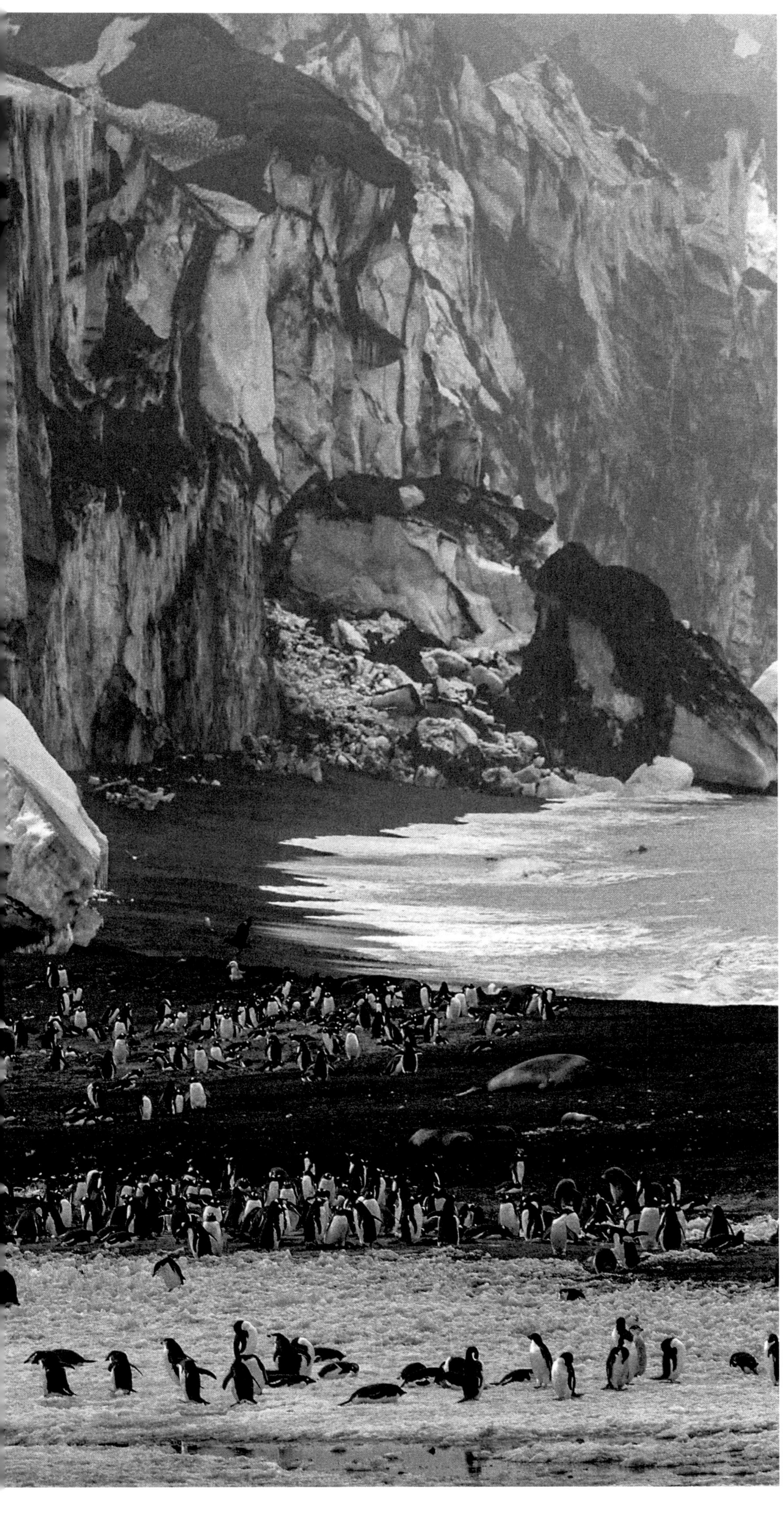

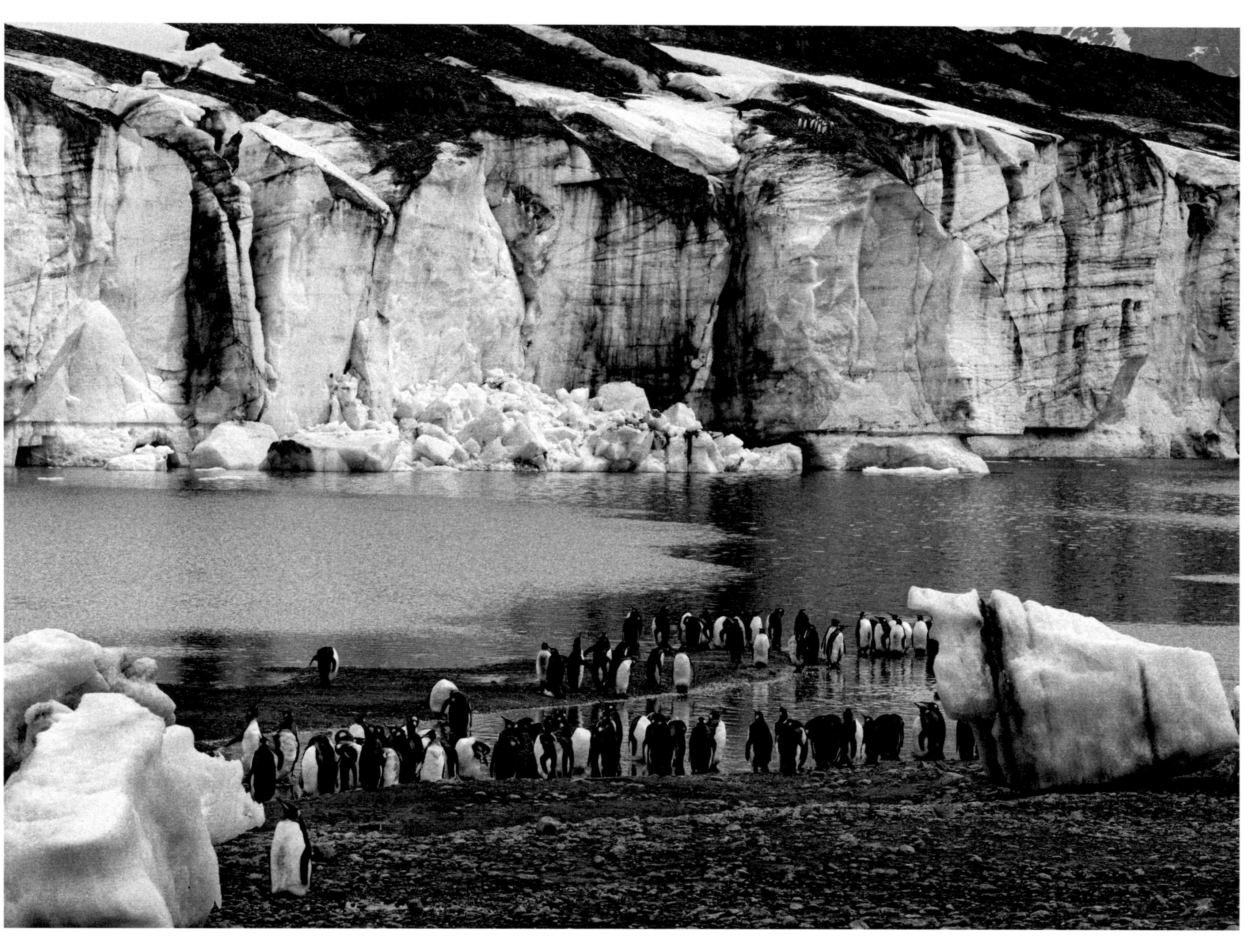

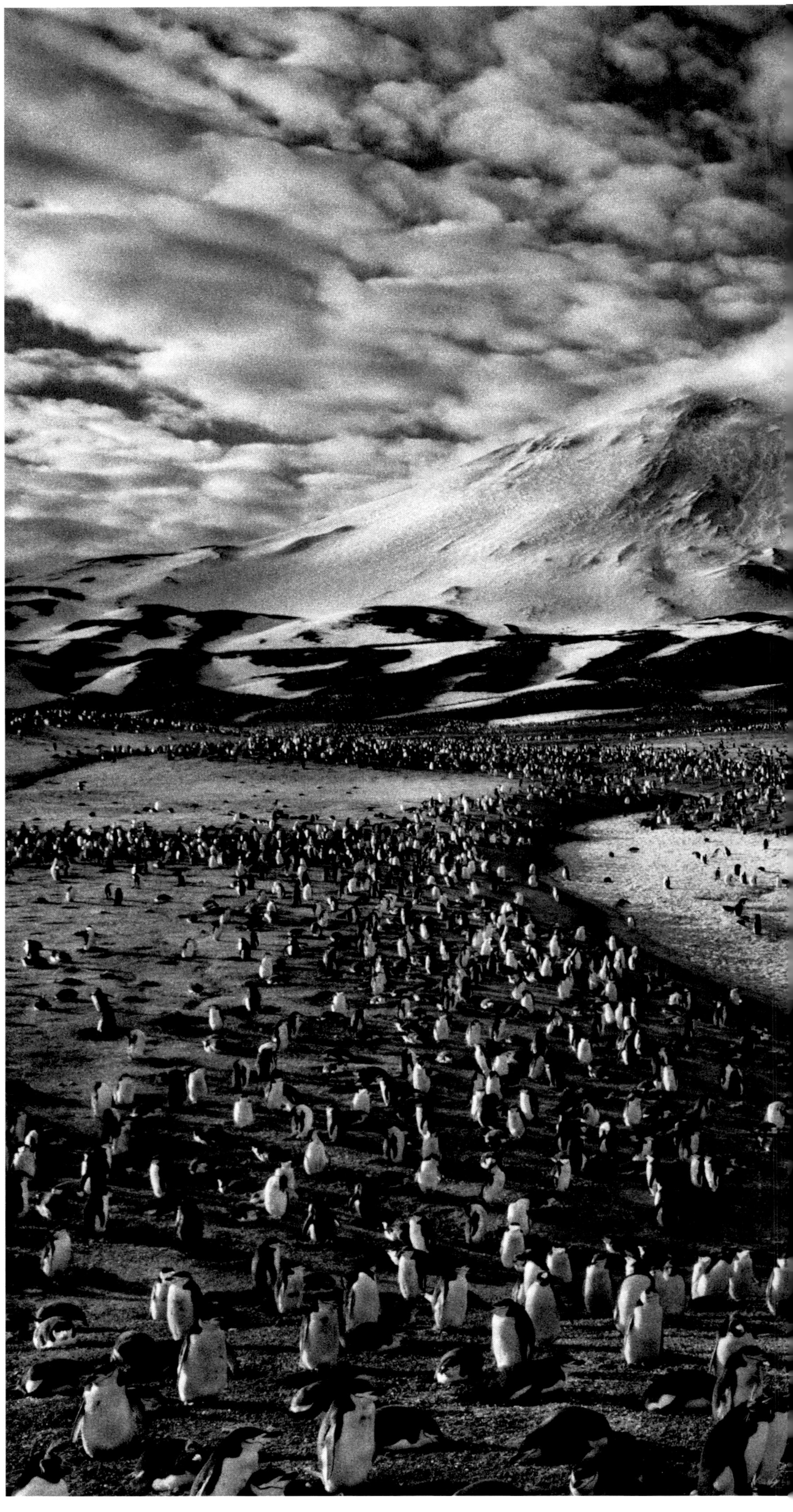

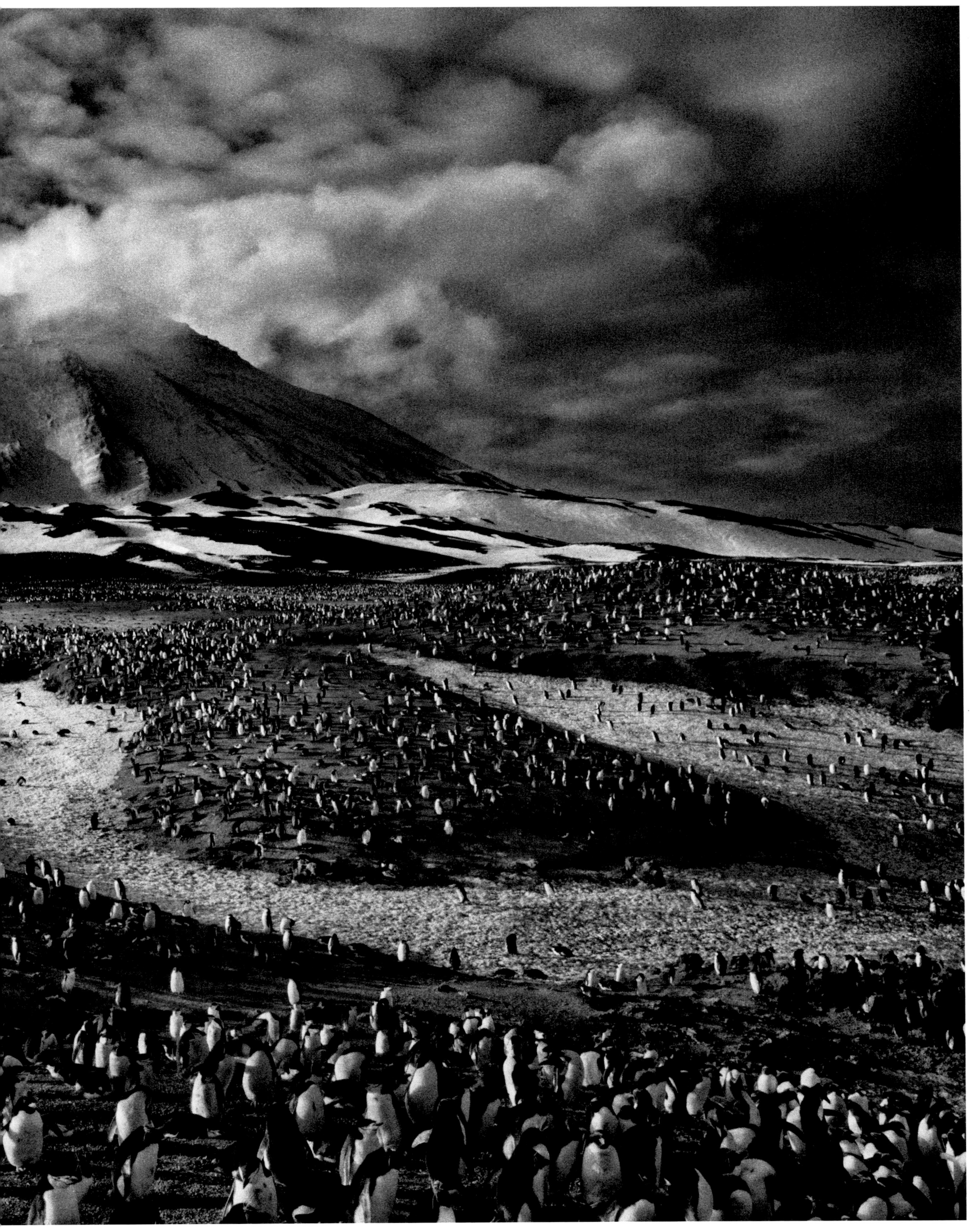

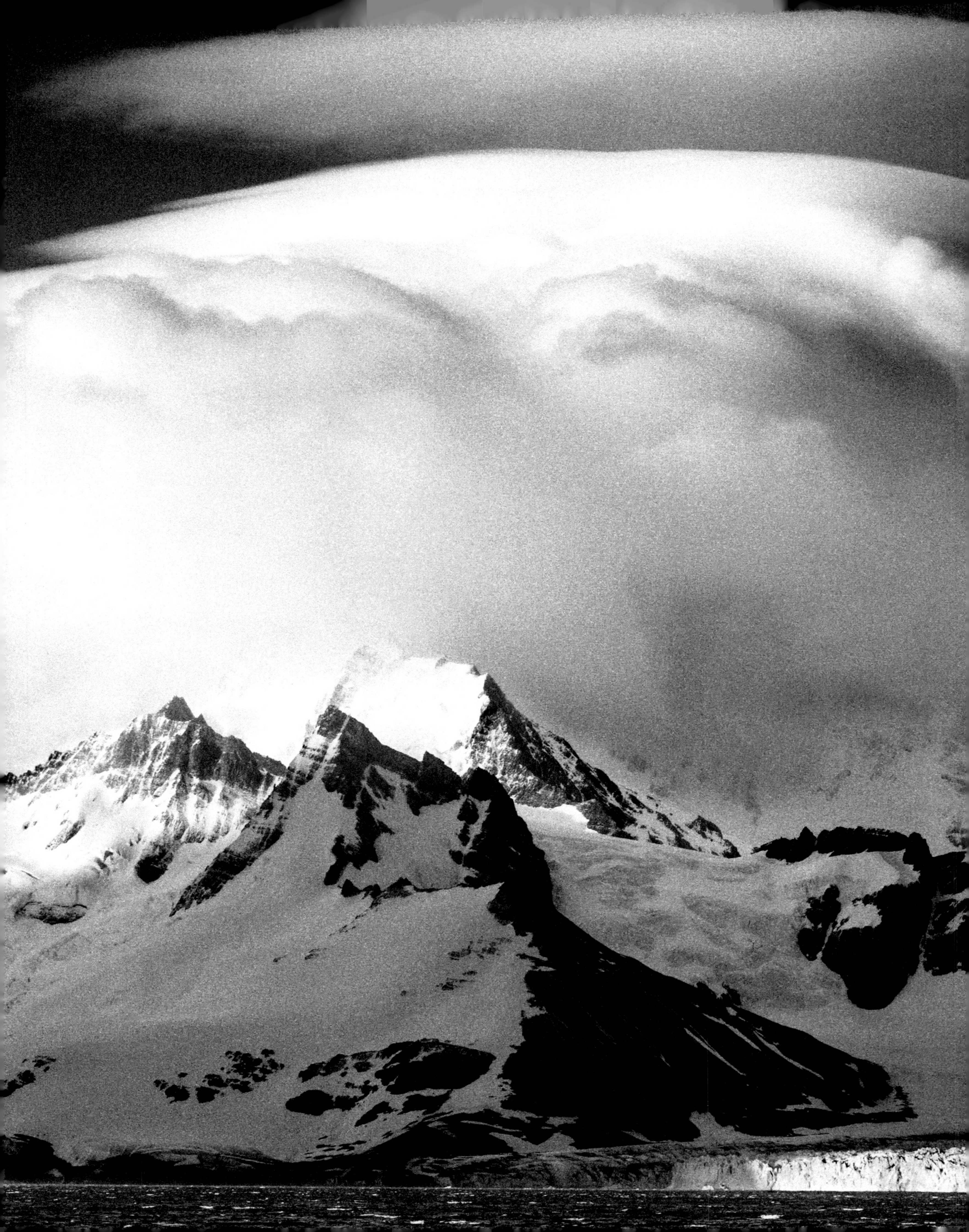

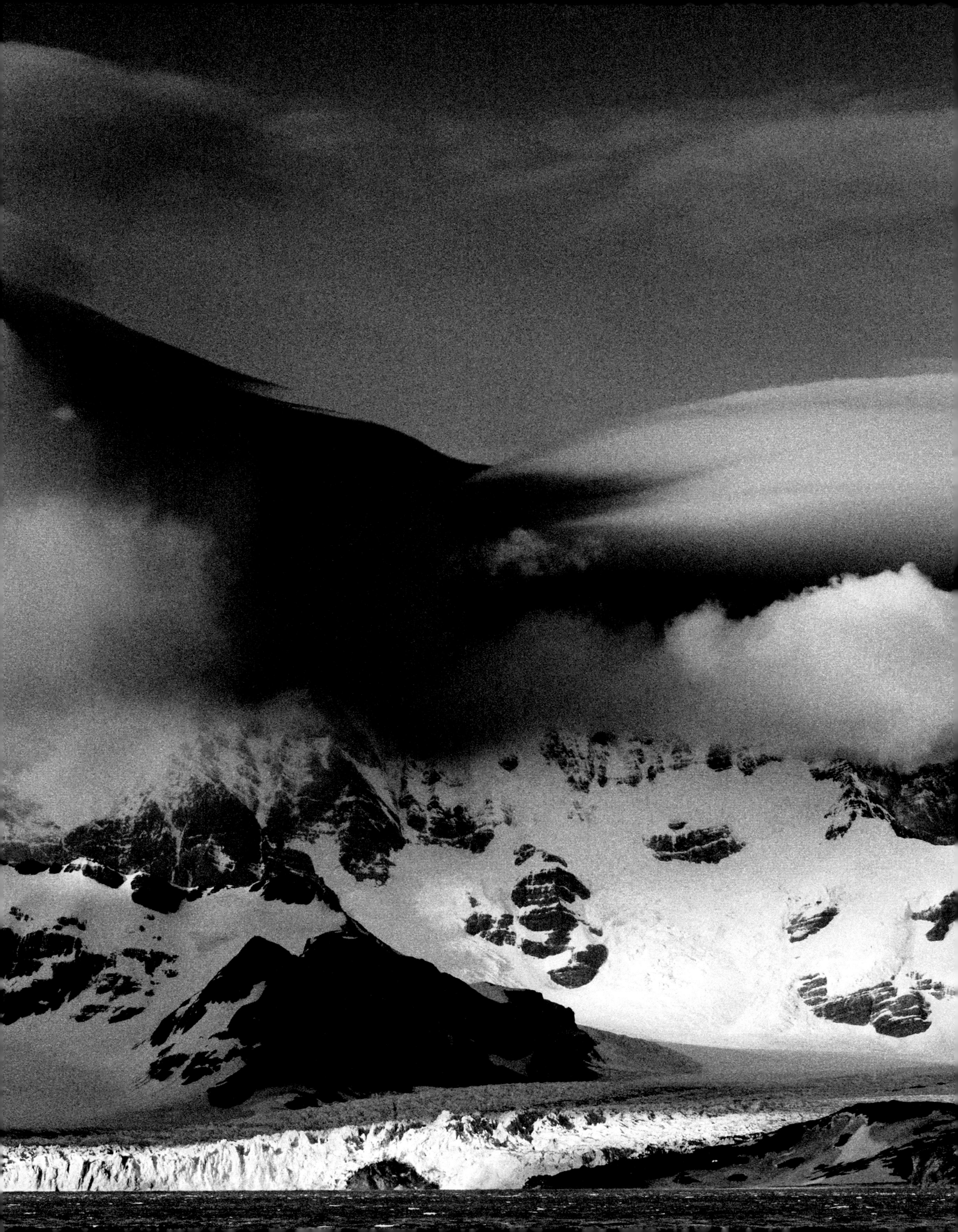

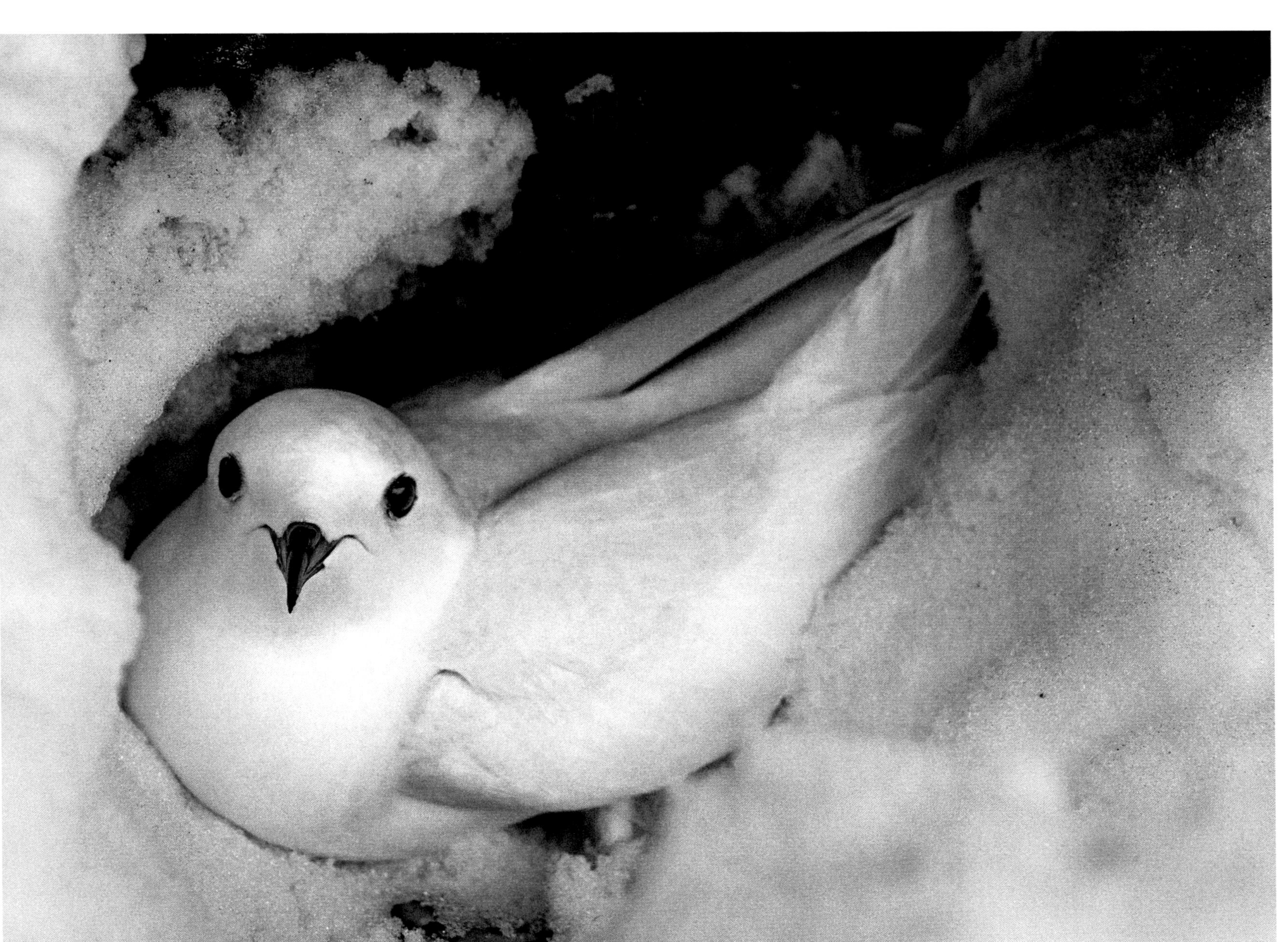

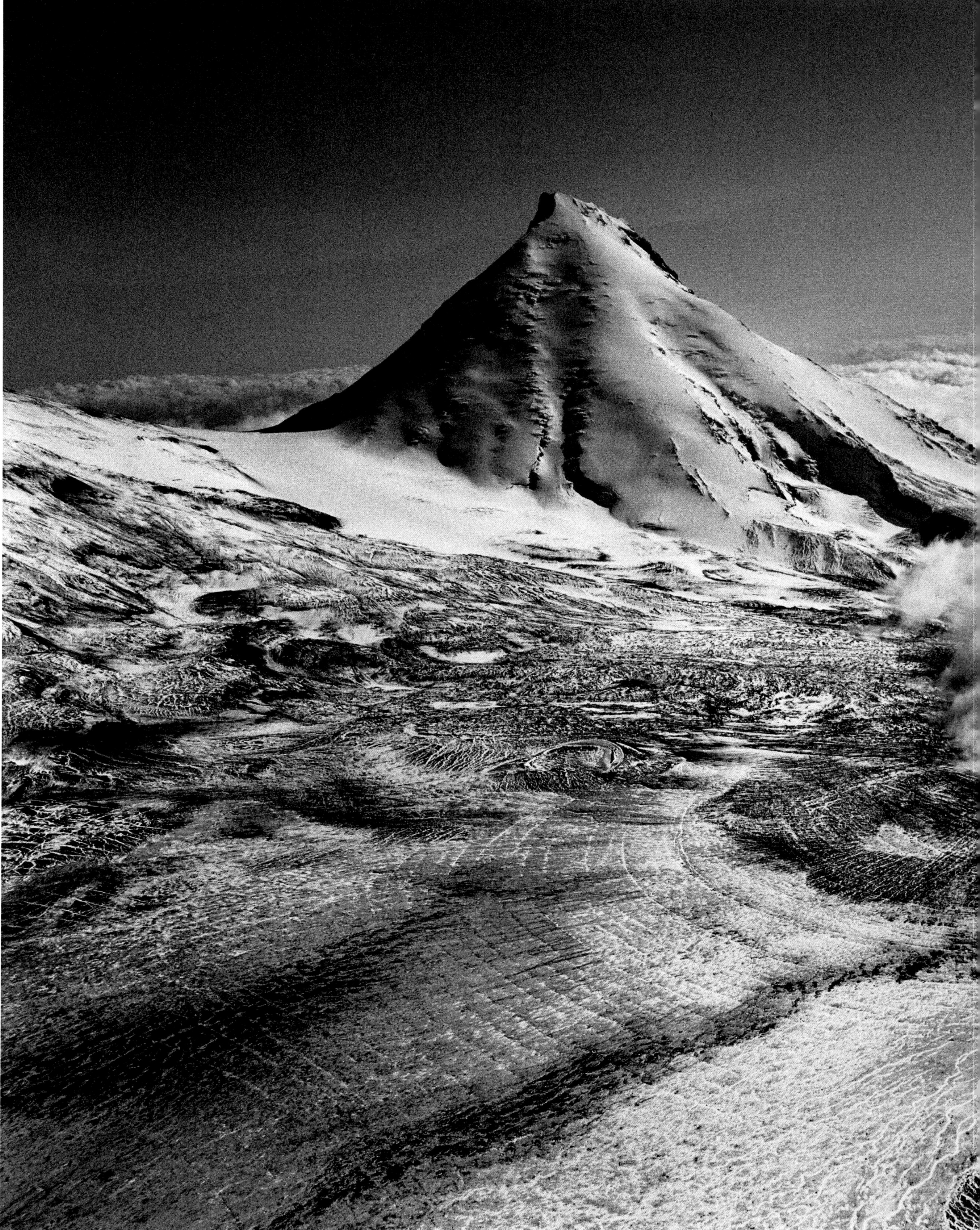

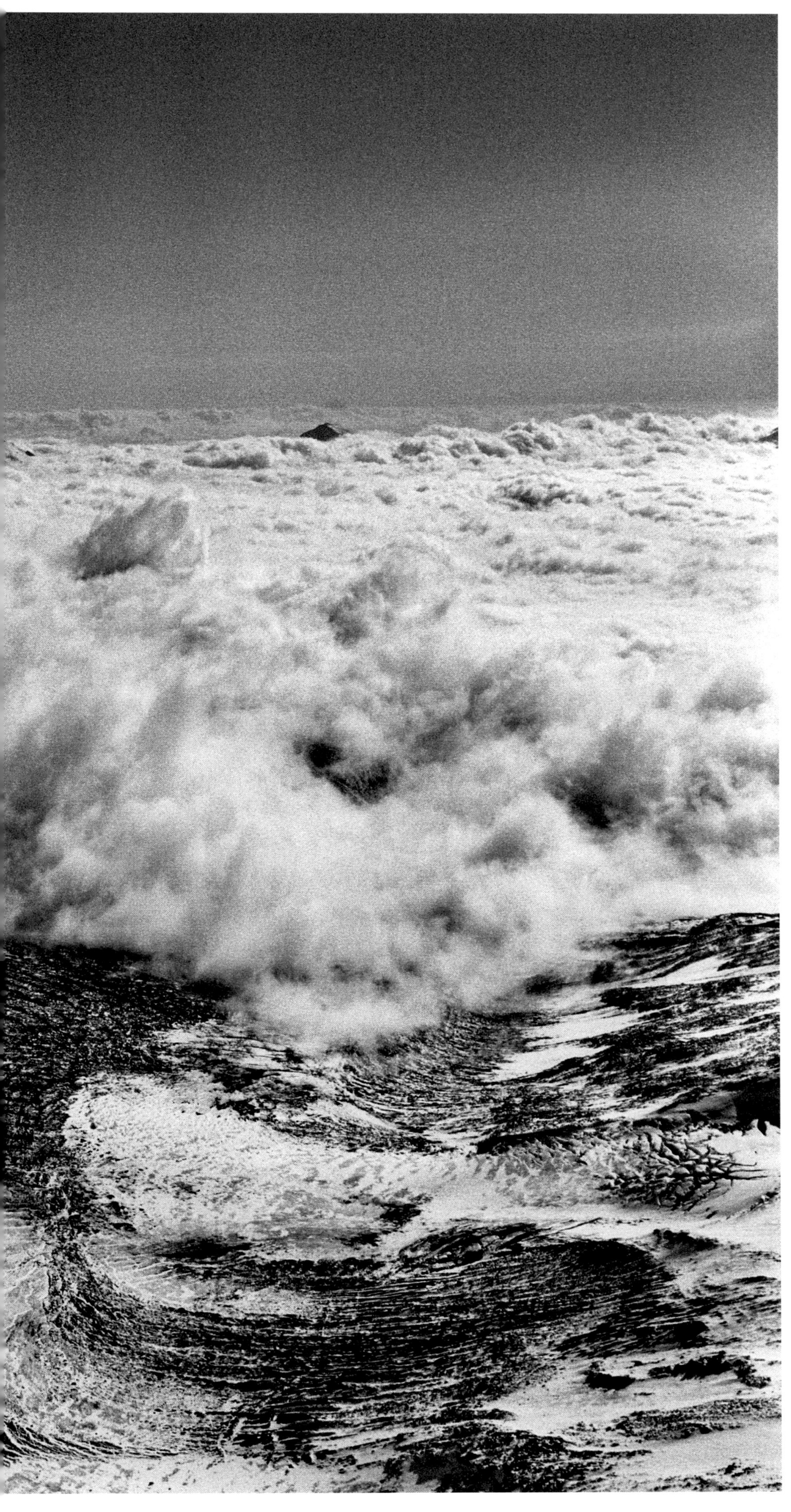

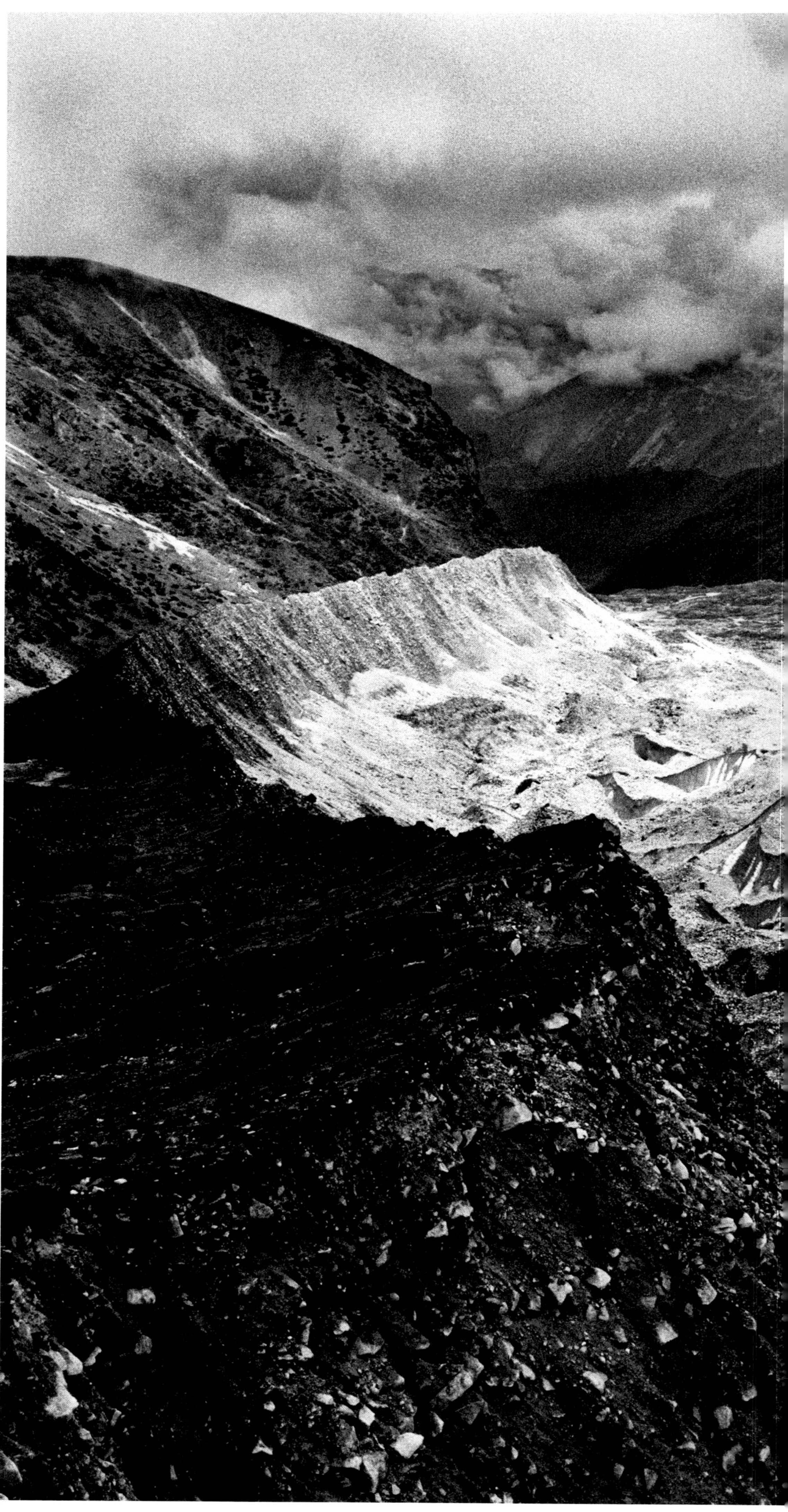

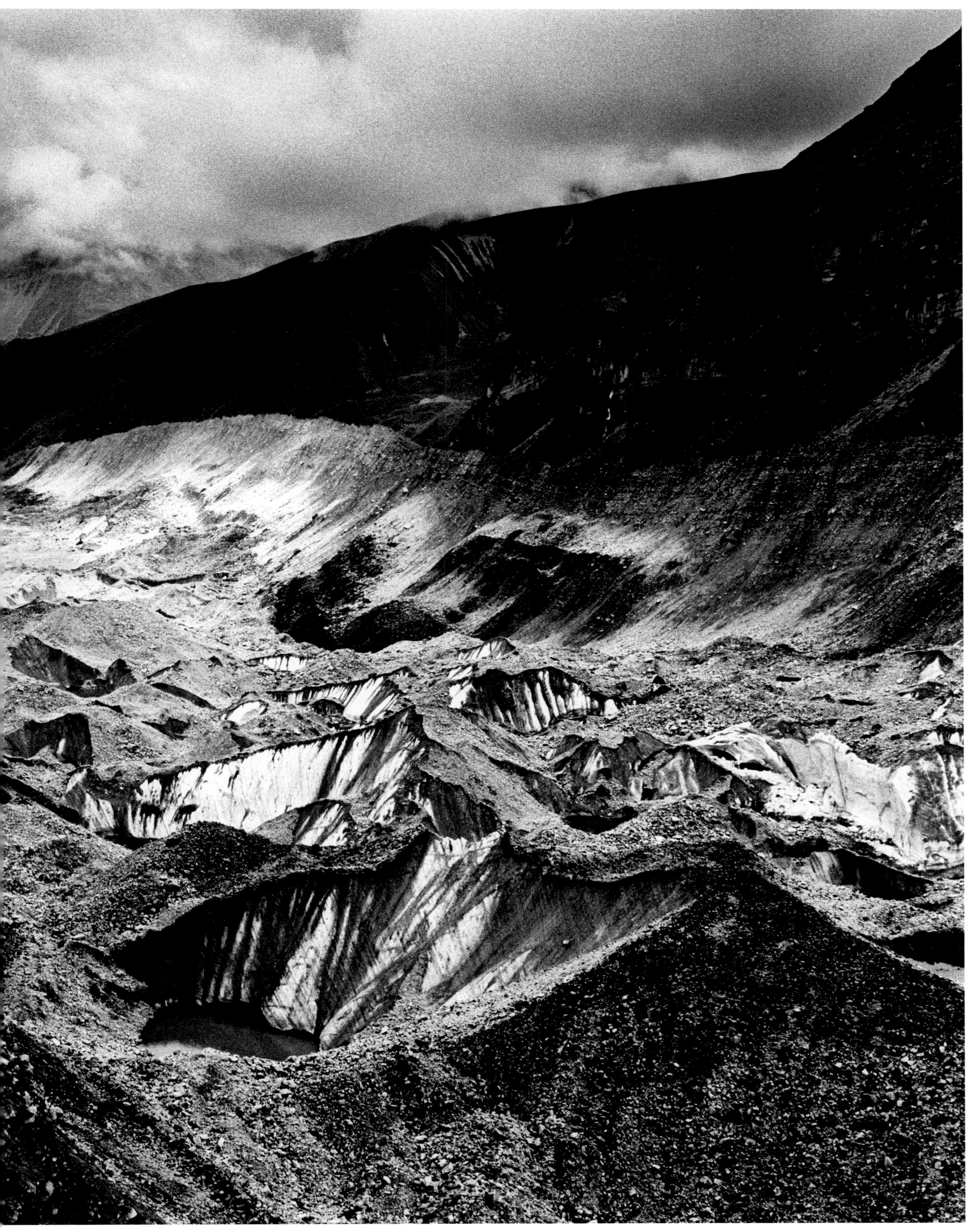

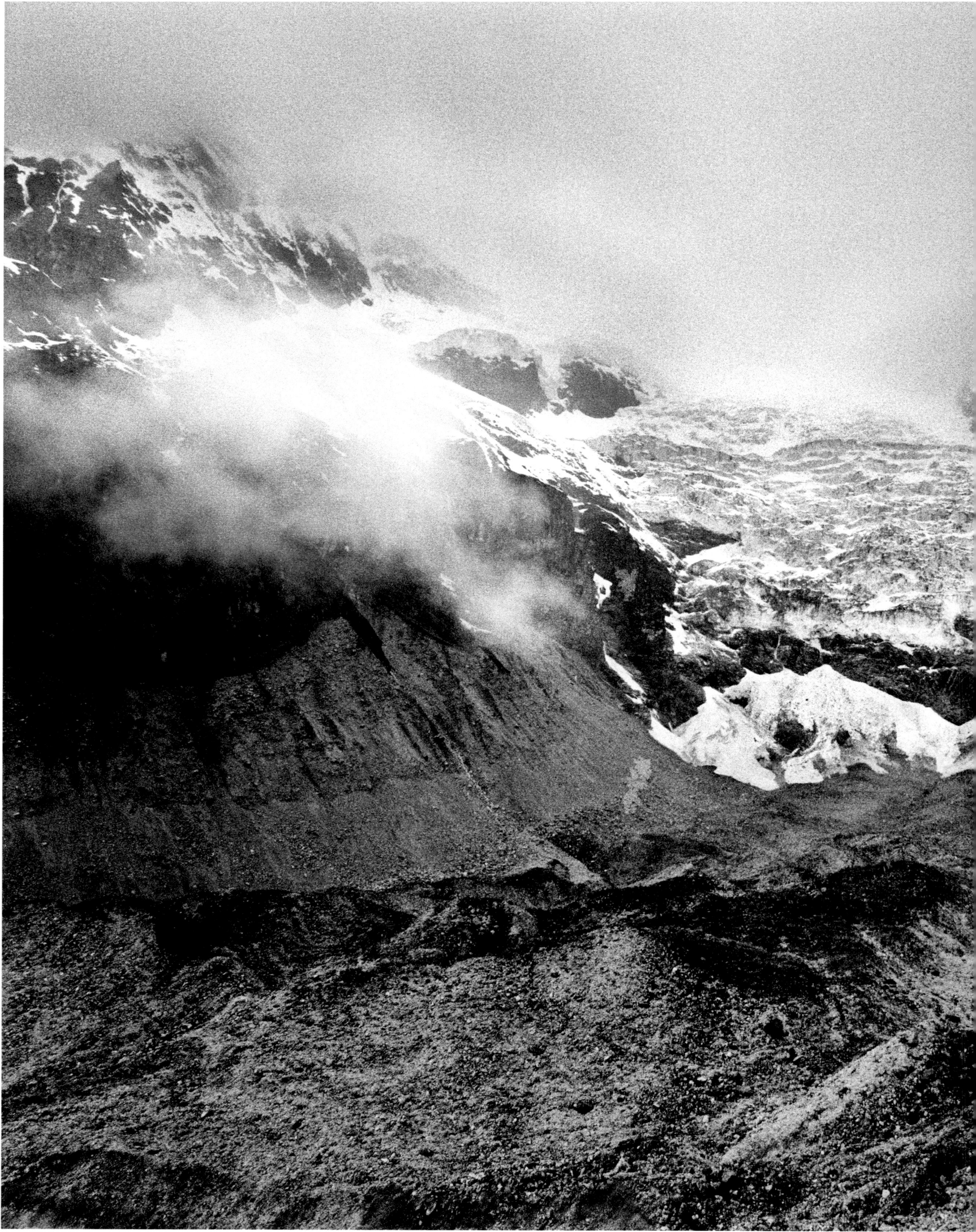

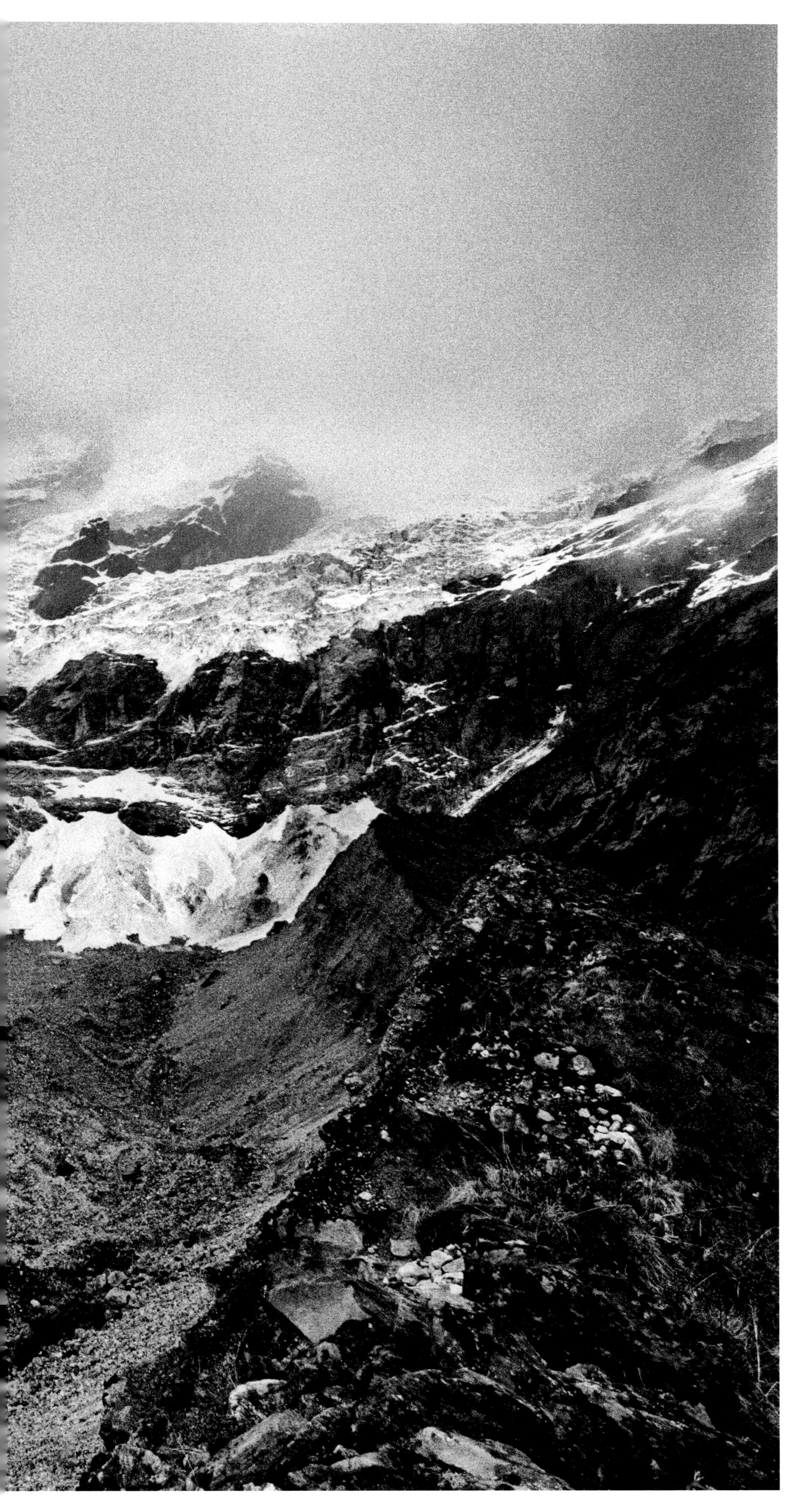

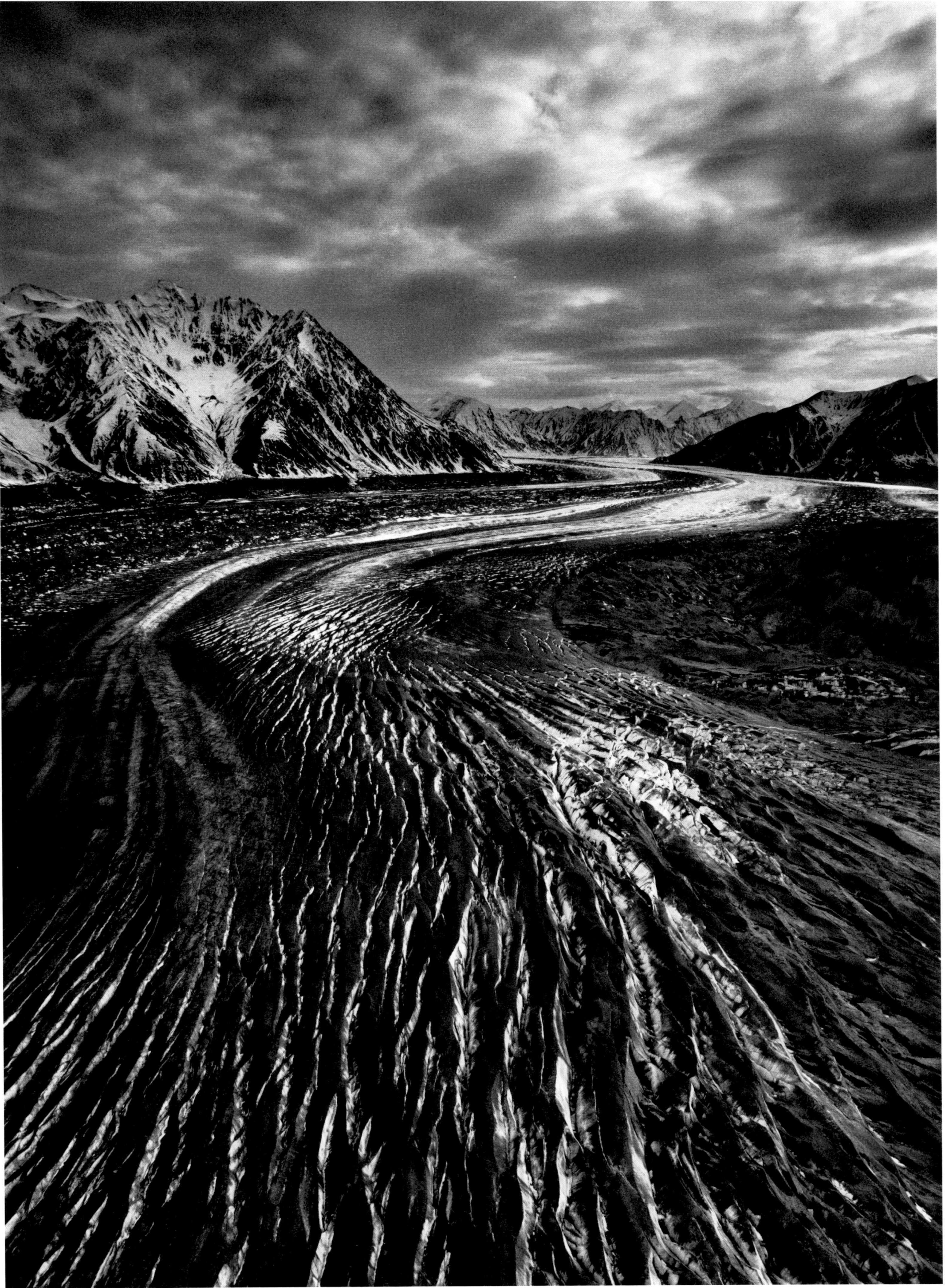

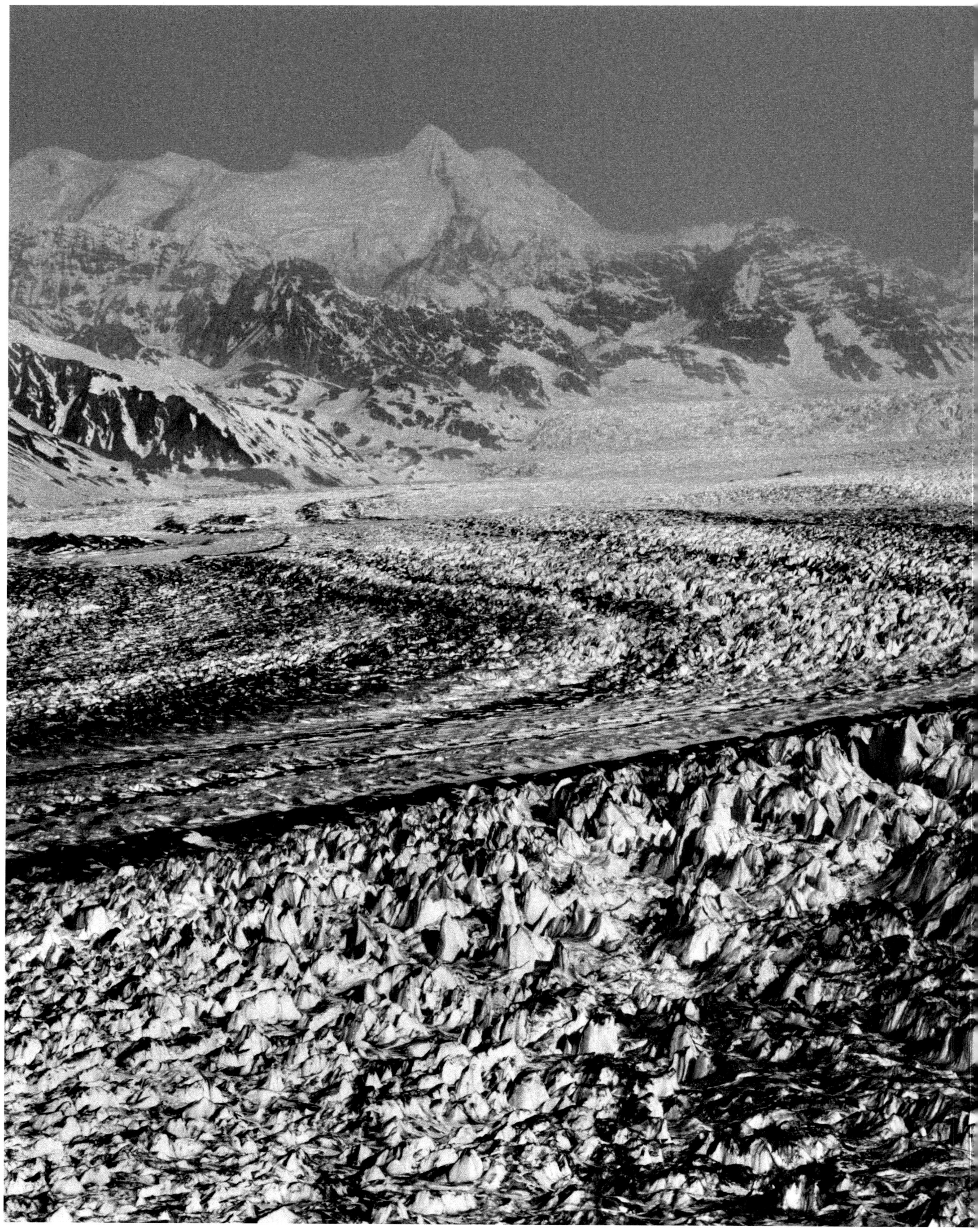

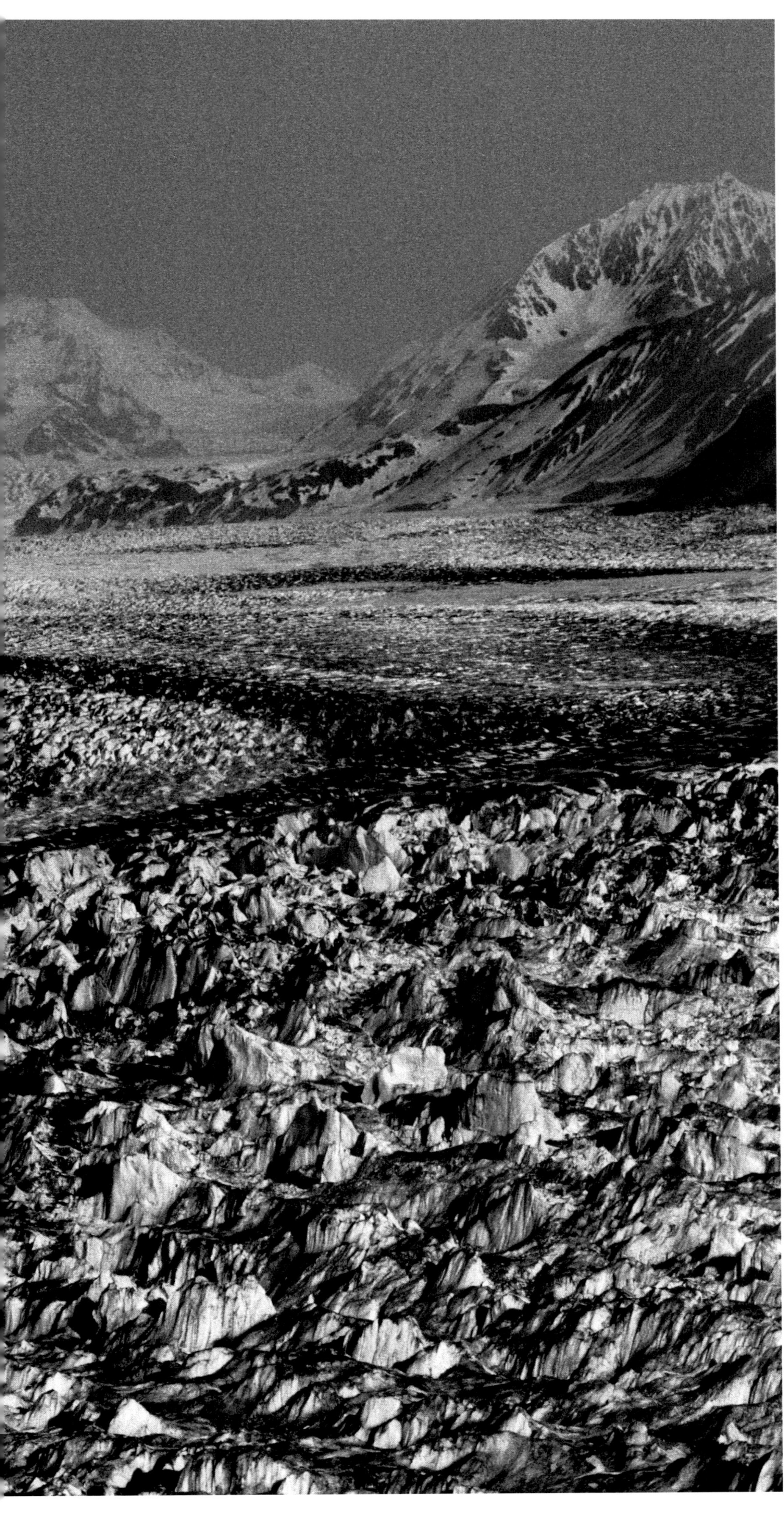

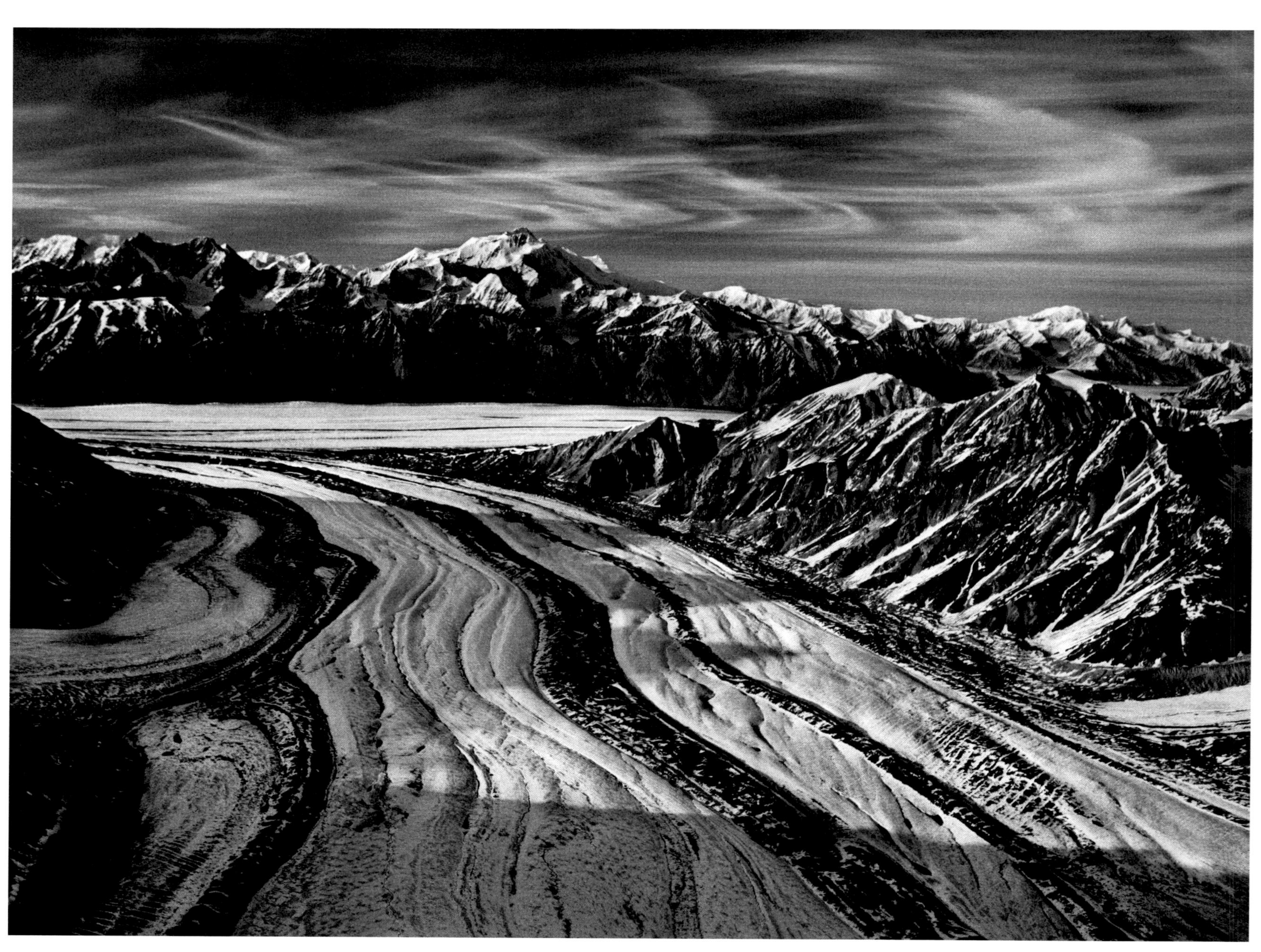

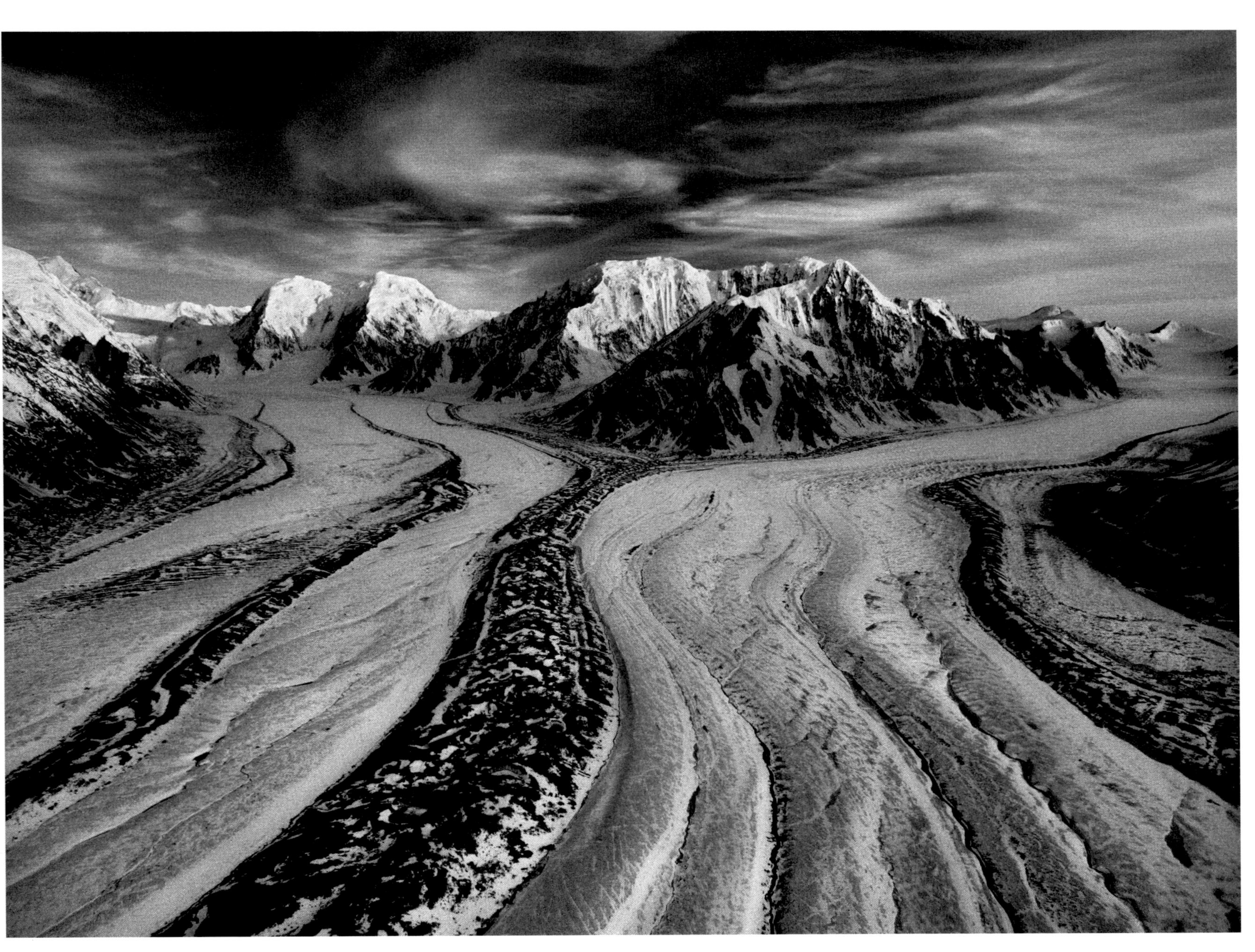

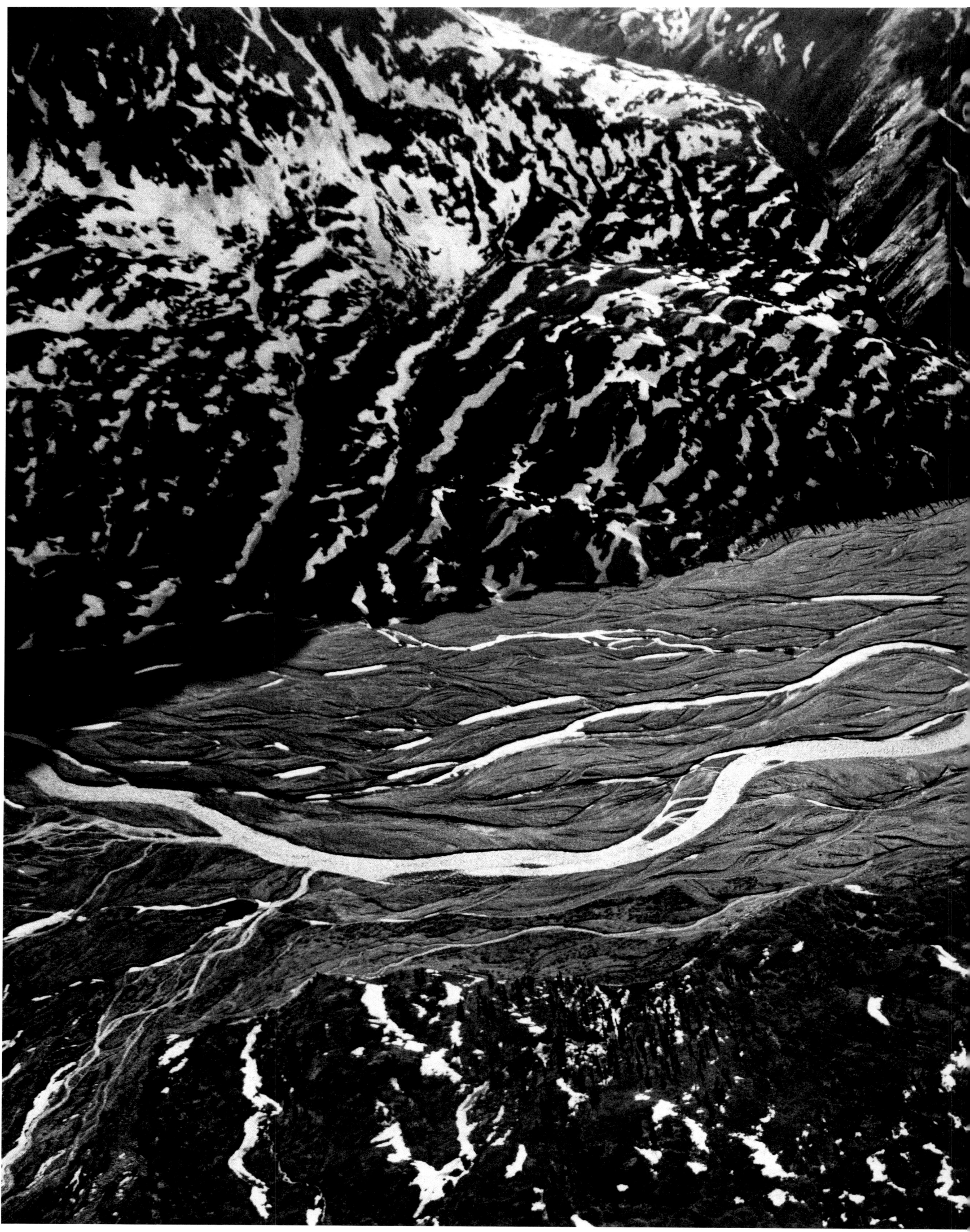

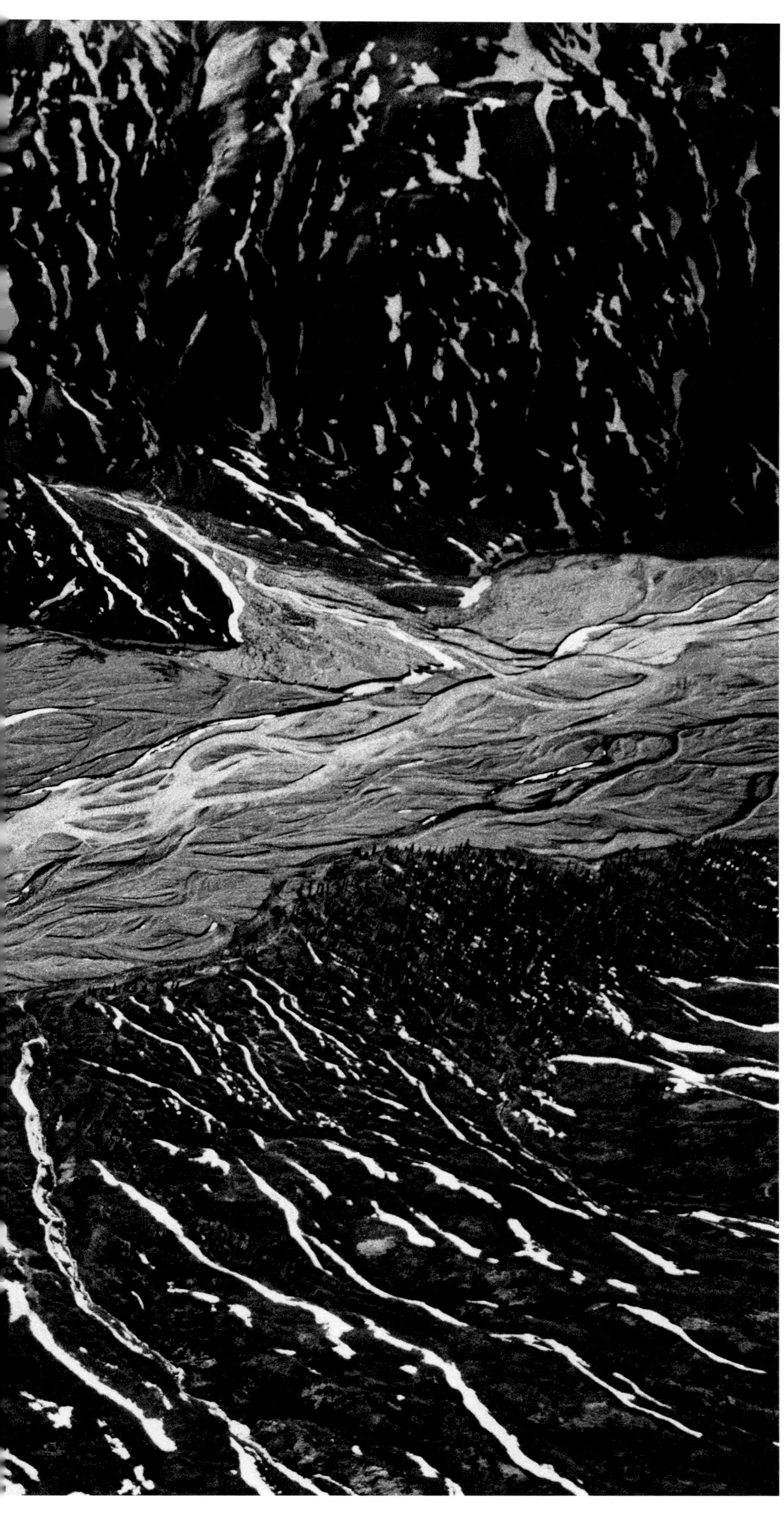

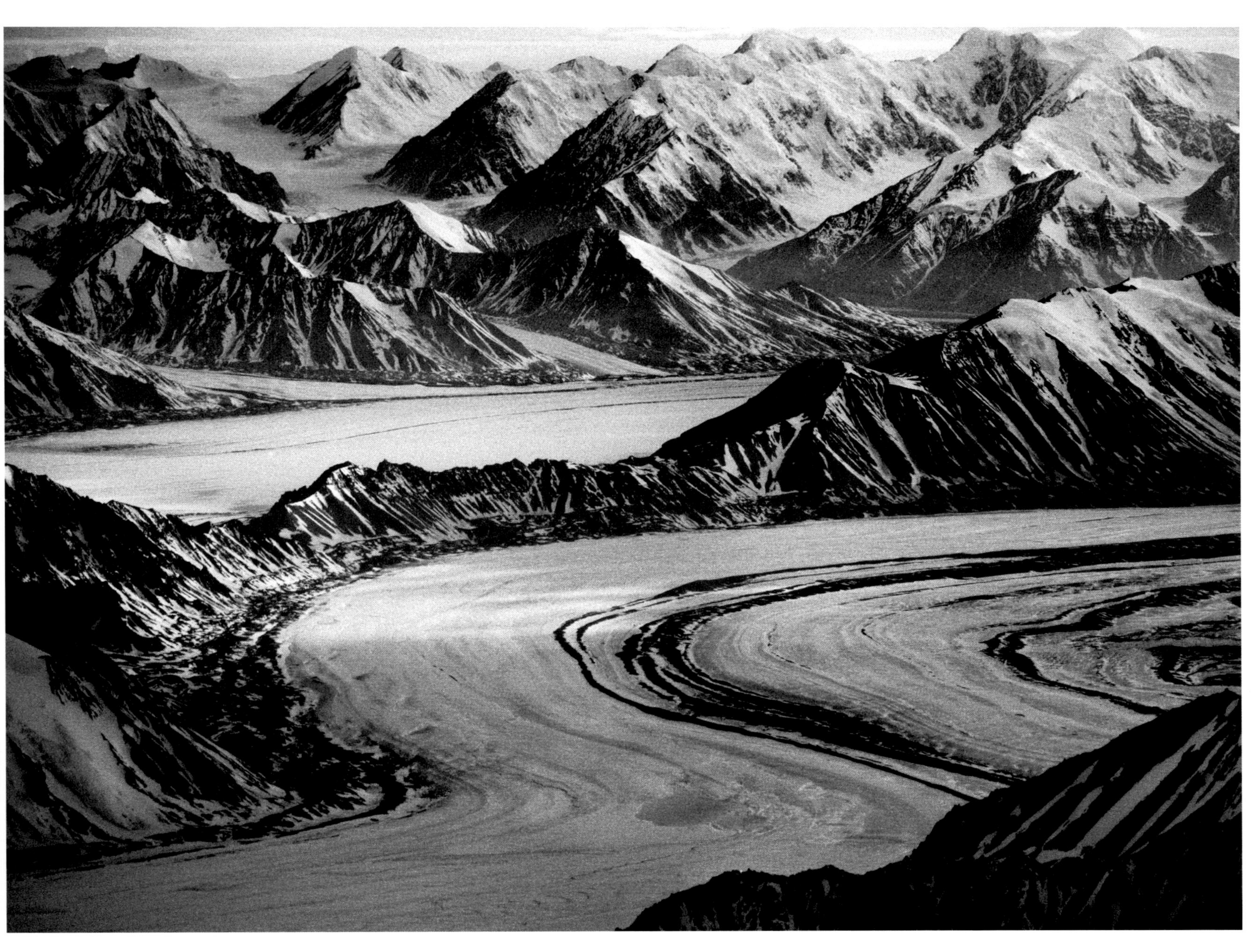

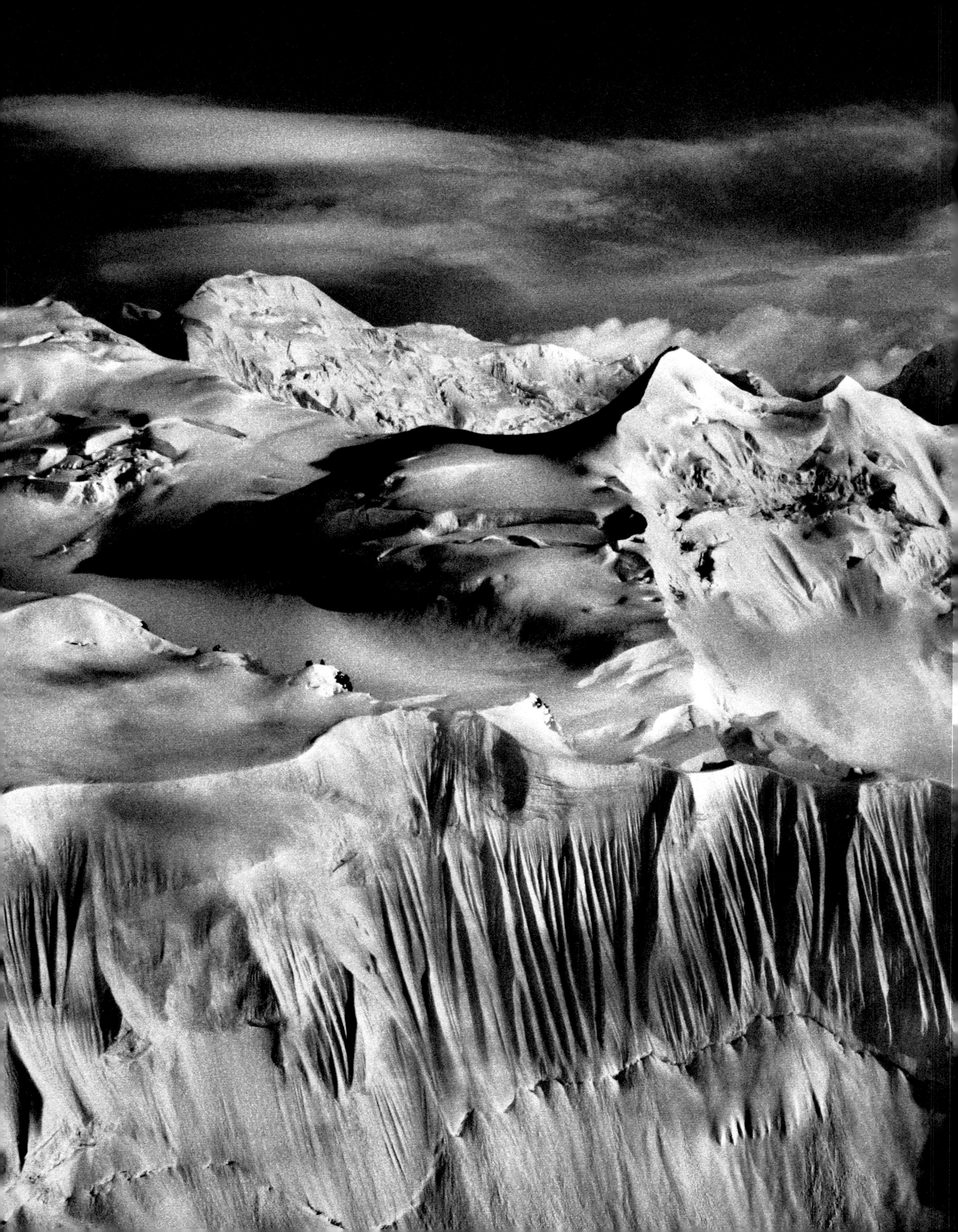

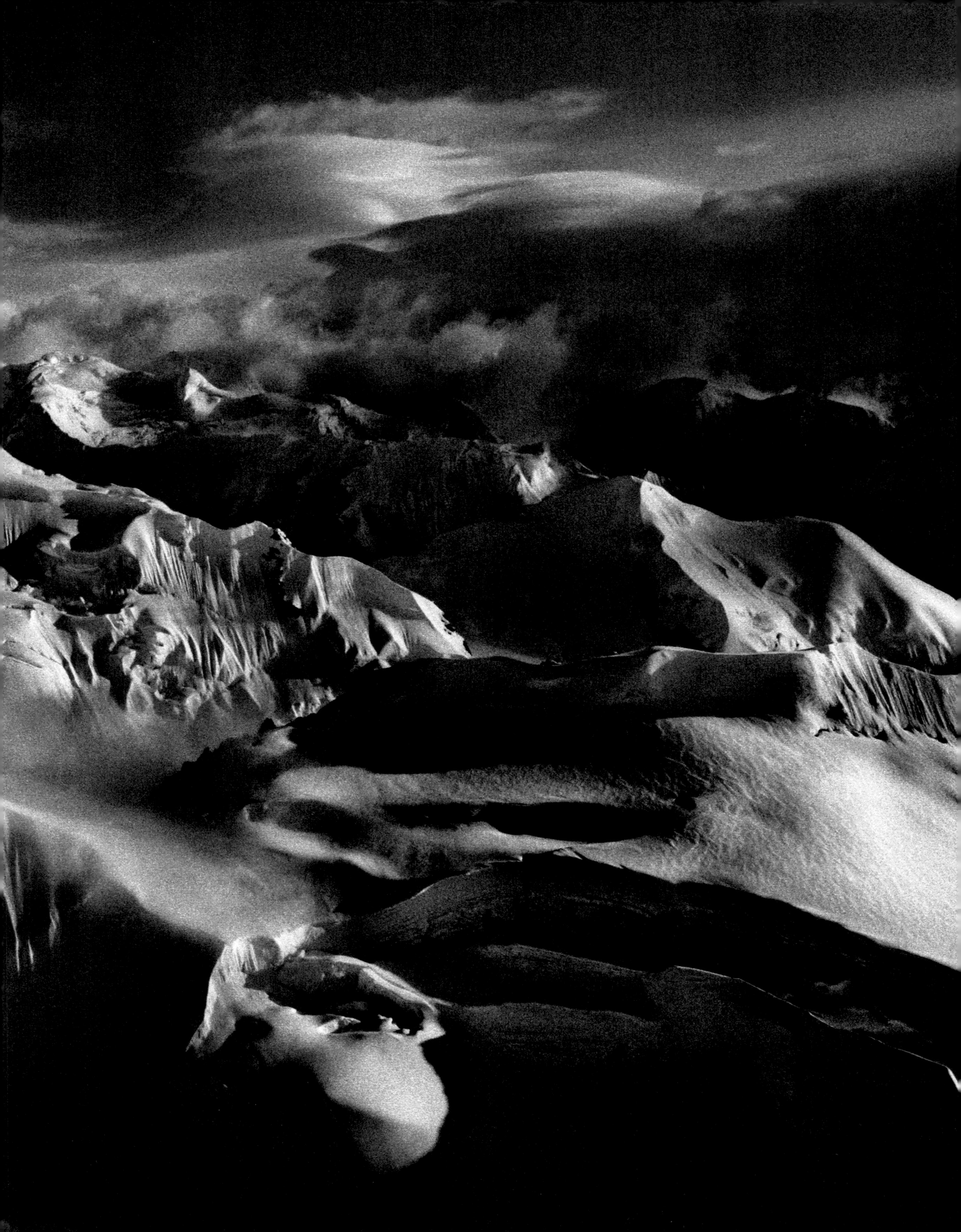

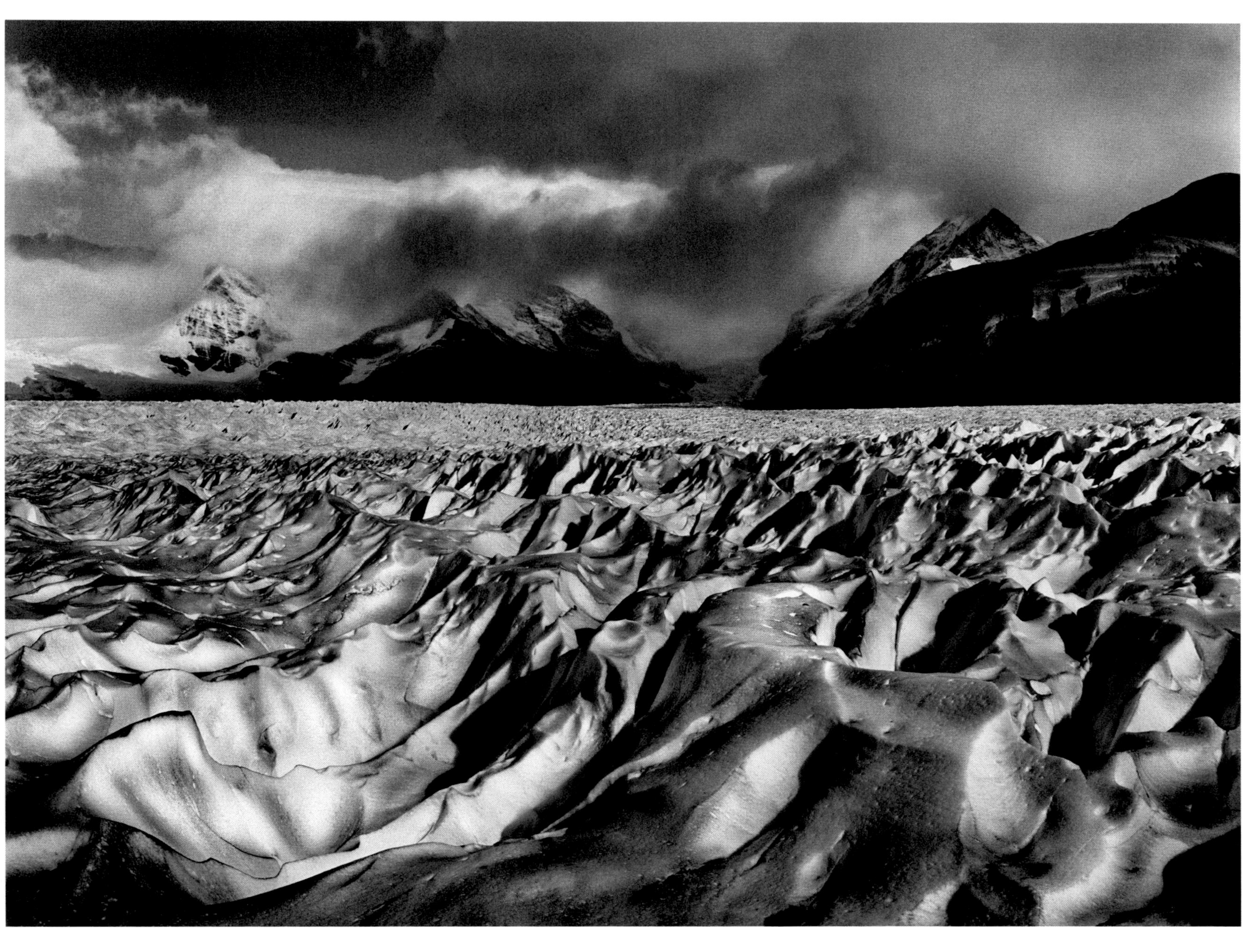

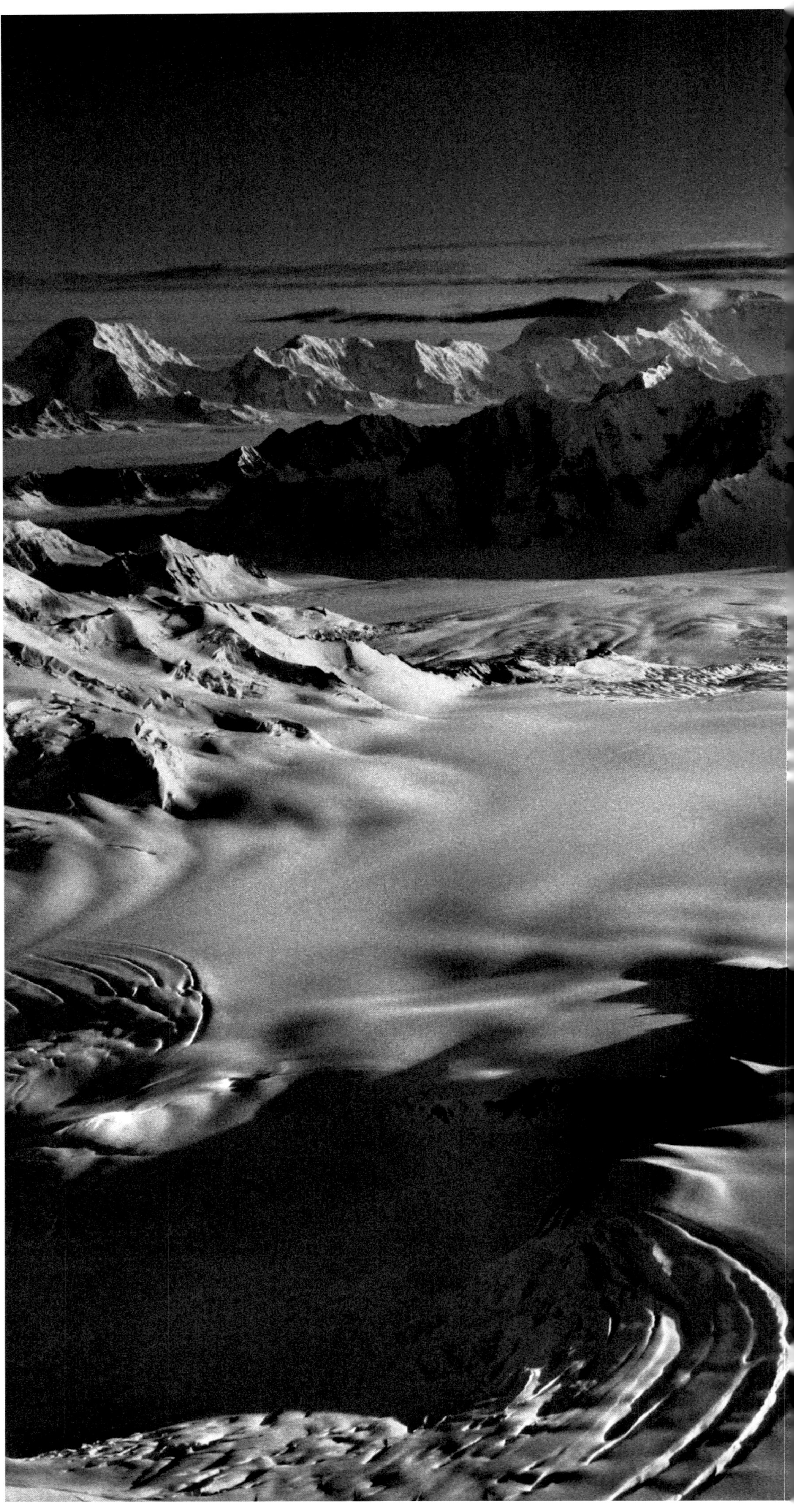

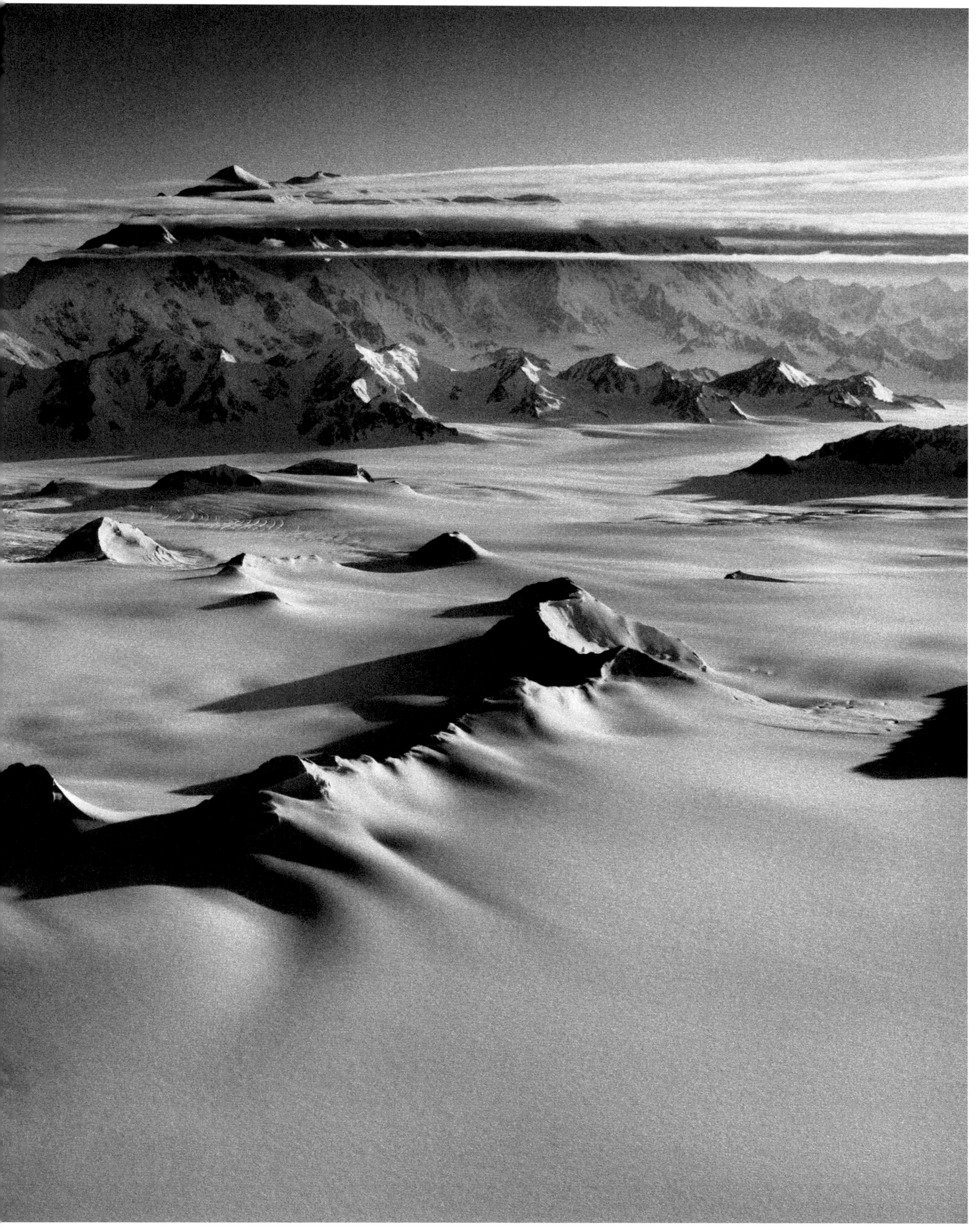

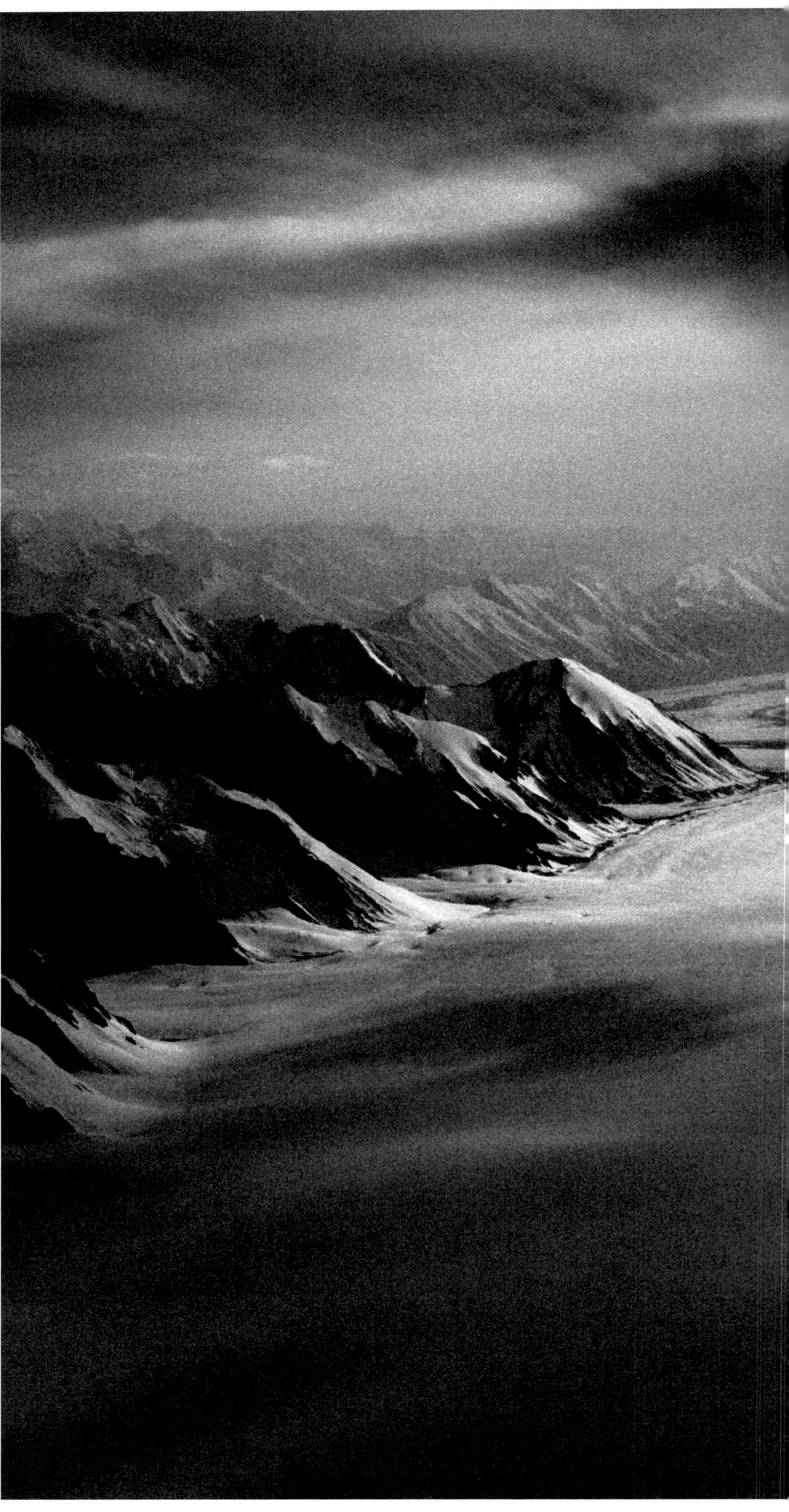

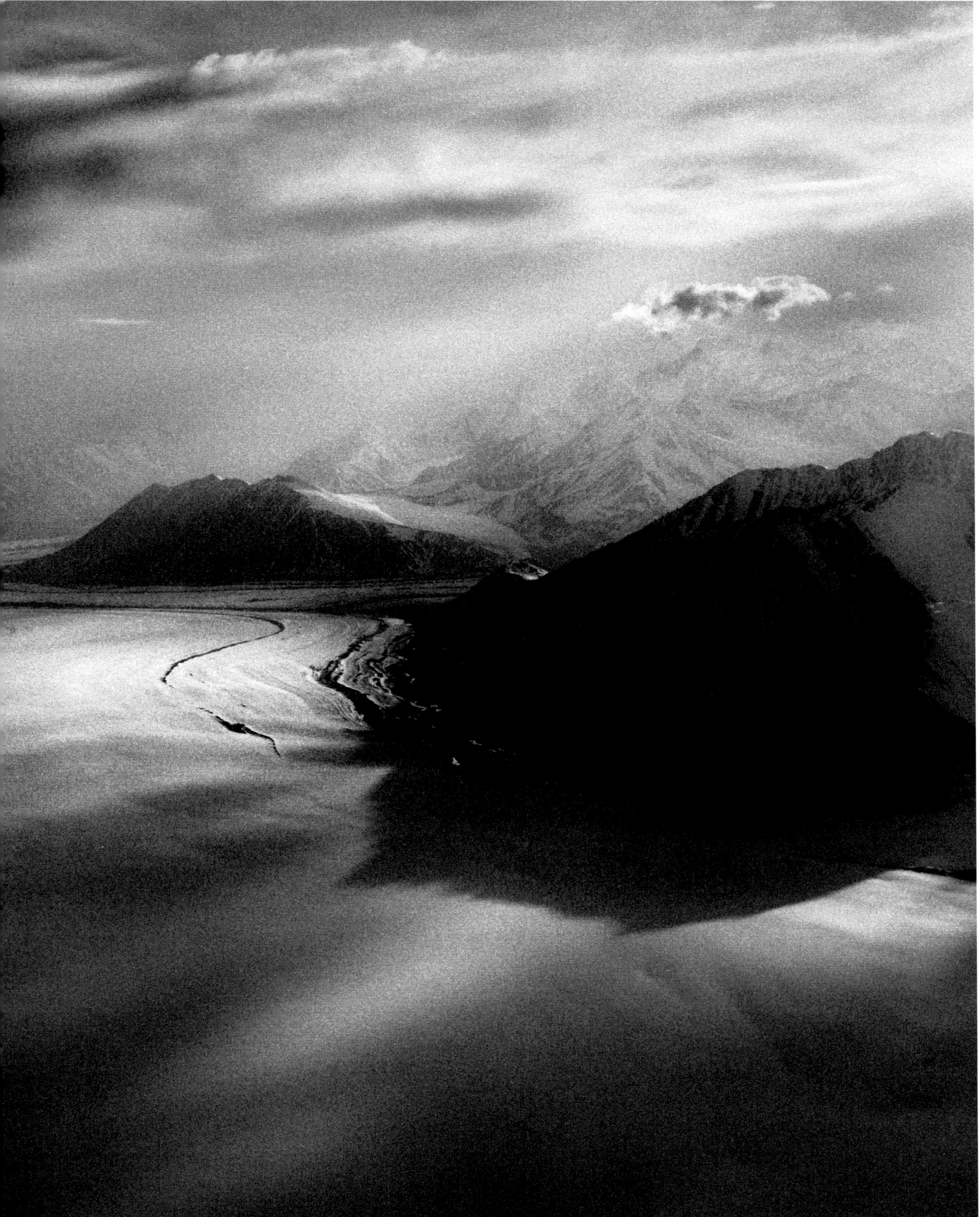

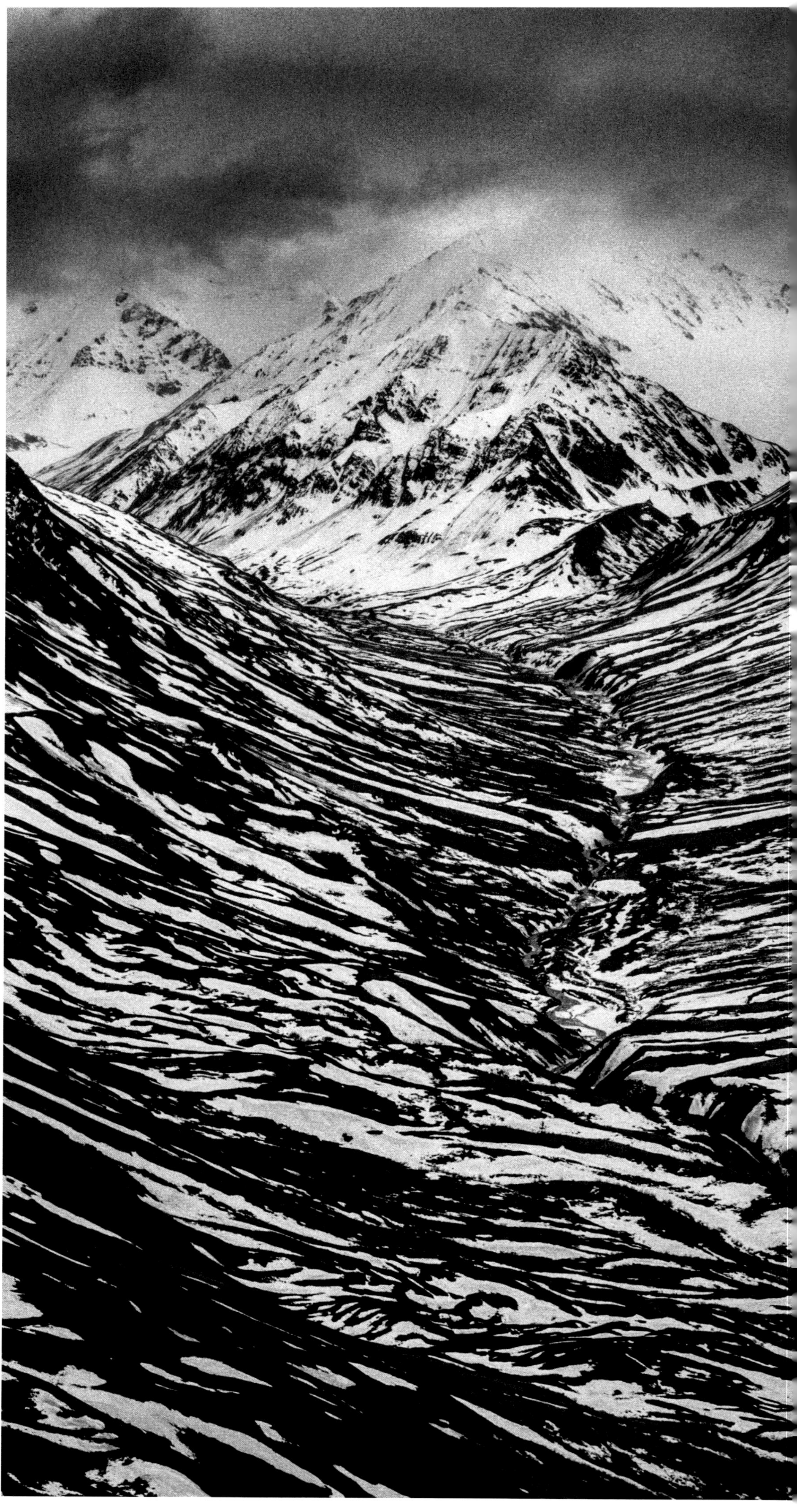

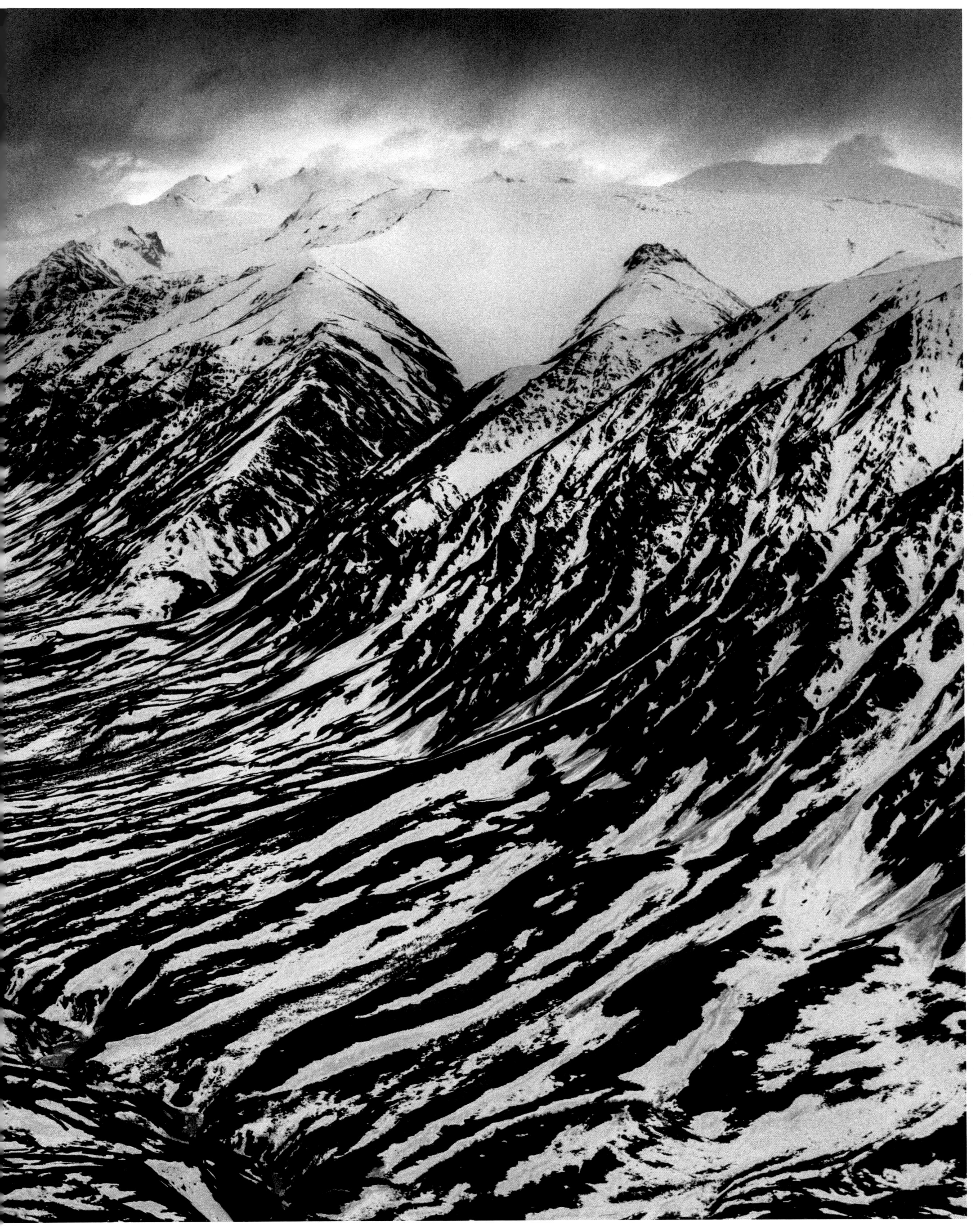

pp. 6–7 Kluane National Park and Reserve, Canada, 2011

pp. 12–13 Antarctic Peninsula, 2005

pp. 14–15 Antarctic Peninsula, 2005

p. 17 Antarctic Peninsula, 2005

pp. 18–19 Antarctic Peninsula, 2005

pp. 20–21 Antarctic Peninsula, 2005

pp. 22–23 Antarctic Peninsula, 2005

pp. 24–25 Antarctic Peninsula, 2005

p. 26 An ash-covered glacier near Candlemas Island volcano in the South Sandwich Islands, 2009

p. 27 An ash-covered glacier near the Baily Head volcano, Deception Island, Antarctic Peninsula, 2005

p. 29 An ash-covered glacier near the Baily Head volcano, Deception Island, Antarctic Peninsula, 2005

pp. 30–31 An ash-covered glacier near the Candlemas Island volcano, South Sandwich Islands, 2009

pp. 32–33 An ash-covered glacier near the Candlemas Island volcano, South Sandwich Islands, 2009

pp. 34–35 An ash-covered glacier near the Candlemas Island volcano, South Sandwich Islands, 2009

pp. 36–37 Enterprise Island, Antarctic Peninsula, 2005

pp. 38–39 Icebergs are huge blocks of ice that break off from a glacier and drift in the sea. Between Bristol Island and Bellingshausen Island, South Sandwich Islands, 2009

p. 40 Kluane National Park and Reserve, Canada, 2011

p. 41 Icebergs in the Weddell Sea, Antarctic Pensinsula, 2005

pp. 42–43 Icebergs between Bristol Island and Bellingshausen Island, South Sandwich Islands, 2009

p. 45 Icebergs in the Weddell Sea, Antarctic Peninsula, 2005

pp. 46–47 Icebergs in the Weddell Sea, Antarctic Peninsula, 2005

pp. 48–49 Icebergs in the Weddell Sea, Antarctic Peninsula, 2005

pp. 50–51 Antarctic Peninsula, 2005

p. 52 Antarctic Peninsula, 2005

p. 53 Antarctic Peninsula, 2005

pp. 54–55 A calving glacier, amidst a landscape that shows the effects of progressive erosion. Grey Glacier, Campo de Hielo, Torres del Paine National Park, Patagonia, Chile, 2007

pp. 56–57 A calving glacier, amidst a landscape that shows the effects of progressive erosion. Grey Glacier, Campo de Hielo, Torres del Paine National Park, Patagonia, Chile, 2007

pp. 58–59 The front of the Perito Moreno Glacier, Campo de Hielo, Patagonia, Argentina, 2007

p. 60 Perito Moreno Glacier, Campo de Hielo, Patagonia, Argentina, 2007

p. 61 Perito Moreno Glacier, Campo de Hielo, Patagonia, Argentina, 2007

pp. 62–63 Ice field of the Perito Moreno Glacier, Campo de Hielo, Patagonia, Argentina, 2007

p. 65 A condor above Perito Moreno Glacier, Campo de Hielo, Patagonia, Argentina, 2007

pp. 66–67 Perito Moreno Glacier, Campo de Hielo, Patagonia, Argentina, 2007

p. 68 Upsala Glacier, Campo de Hielo, Patagonia, Argentina, 2007

p. 69 Front of Viedma Glacier, Campo de Hielo, Patagonia, Argentina, 2007

pp. 70–71 Front of Upsala Glacier, Campo de Hielo, Patagonia, Argentina, 2007

p. 73 Tongue of Upsala Glacier, Campo de Hielo, Patagonia, Argentina, 2007

pp. 74–75 Glacier in the mountains at the base of Mount Fitz Roy, Patagonia, Argentina, 2007

pp. 76–77 Himalayas, Bhutan, 2006

pp. 78–79 Glaciers flowing into Lake Argentino, Patagonia, Argentina, 2007

pp. 80–81 A glacier at the foot of Cerro Torre, Torre Egger, and Punta Herron, peaks located in Patagonia on the border between Chile and Argentina, 2007

p. 82 Glaciers in South Georgia, 2009

p. 83 Glaciers in South Georgia, 2009

pp. 84–85 Icebergs are huge blocks of ice that break off from a glacier and drift in the sea. South Sandwich Islands, 2009

p. 86 Zavodovski Island, South Sandwich Islands, 2009

p. 87 Zavodovski Island, South Sandwich Islands, 2009

pp. 88–89 Glaciers in South Georgia, 2009

p. 91 South Georgia, 2009

pp. 92–93 Zavodovski Island, South Sandwich Islands, 2009

pp. 94–95 South Georgia, 2009

p. 97 Storm petrel on Bellingshausen Island, South Sandwich Islands, 2009

pp. 98–99 A glacier on the summit of the Klyuchevskaya Sopka volcano, Kamchatka, Russia, 2006

pp. 100–101 Moraine, a deposit of the rocky material moved by a glacier, left behind when the glacier's movement slows or stops. Himalayas, Bhutan, 2006

pp. 102–103 The moraine left behind by a moving glacier. Himalayas, Bhutan, 2006

p. 105 Kluane National Park and Reserve, Canada, 2011

pp. 106–107 Kluane National Park and Reserve, Canada, 2011

p. 108 Kluane National Park and Reserve, Canada, 2011

p. 109 Kluane National Park and Reserve, Canada, 2011

pp. 110–111 Ancient glacial moraine, Disappointment River, Kluane National Park and Reserve, Canada, 2011

p. 113 Kluane National Park and Reserve, Canada, 2011

pp. 114–115 Kluane National Park and Reserve, Canada, 2011

p. 117 Perito Moreno Glacier, Campo de Hielo, Patagonia, Argentina, 2007

pp. 118–119 Mount Logan, at 5,959 m, is the highest peak in Canada and the second highest in North America. Kluane National Park and Reserve, Canada, 2011

pp. 120–121 Kluane National Park and Reserve, Canada, 2011

pp. 122–123 A volcanic glacier, Bighorn Creek, Kluane National Park and Reserve, Canada, 2011

Lélia Wanick Salgado

Lélia Wanick Salgado, who comes from Vitória, Espírito Santo, Brazil, moved to Paris when she was young. She married Sebastião Salgado in 1967 and is the mother of their two children and grandmother of a boy and a girl. During her secondary education in Vitória, she studied piano at the conservatory for several years, learnt French at the Alliance Française, and in parallel studied painting in an artist's studio. In Paris, Lélia Wanick Salgado attended the Faculty of Architecture at the École Nationale Supérieure des Beaux-Arts and the Faculty of Urban Planning at the Université Paris 8, where she obtained her bachelor's and master's degrees. Her interest in photography began in the early 1970s and gradually blossomed. In the early 1980s, she worked with photography magazines before becoming director of Magnum's gallery in Paris, where she organised around twenty photography exhibitions. In 1987, Lélia Wanick Salgado set up her own organisation for exhibition design and conception/design of photo books, which remains the focus of her work today. She produced a series of photo books by Sebastião Salgado, the first of which was *Other Americas* in 1986. The eponymous exhibition that year, which she also curated, won the Jury Prize and the Audience Award at the Mois de La Photographie in Paris. In 1990, 1991, and 1992 she was artistic director of an international photography festival in Réunion. Lélia Wanick Salgado has designed and curated numerous exhibitions accompanying the books she conceived, such as *Workers: An Archaeology of the Industrial Age* (1993), *Earth* (1997), *Exodus* (based on photographs from *Migrations: Humanity in Transition* and *The Children: Refugees and Migrants*) (2000), *Africa* (2007), *Genesis* (2013), *The Scent of a Dream* (2015), *Kuwait: A Desert on Fire* (2016), *Gold* (2019), and *Amazônia* (2021). Over the years, Lélia Wanick Salgado has received awards and recognition for many of these books. The exhibitions she developed still travel to museums and galleries all over the world. In 1994, Lélia Wanick Salgado and Sebastião Salgado founded the Amazonas Images agency in Paris, dedicated exclusively to the photographer's work. Lélia Wanick Salgado is its director. It has now become the Salgado Studios. In the early 1990s, Lélia and Sebastião began working together on environmental remediation of part of the Atlantic Forest in Brazil. In 1998 they managed to have this land classified as a nature reserve, creating Instituto Terra, whose remit encompasses reforestation, environmental education, scientific research, and sustainable development. In 2010, the institute began work on a programme called 'Olhos d'Água' (Eyes of Water) dedicated to recovery, protection, and conservation of water resources in the Rio Doce river basin. In 2023, Lélia Wanick Salgado was awarded one of the most prestigious environmental prizes, the Gulbenkian Prize for Humanity, in recognition of her outstanding contribution to climate action and innovative solutions that inspire hope and possibility, as well as for all her work through Instituto Terra.

Sebastião Salgado

Sebastião Salgado was born in 1944 in Minas Gerais, Brazil, but moved to Paris in the late 1960s. In 1967 he married Lélia Deluiz Wanick, with whom he had two children and two grandchildren. An economist by training, he began his career as a photographer in 1973 in Paris; he worked with various photographic agencies until 1994, when he and Lélia Wanick Salgado founded Amazonas Images, an agency dedicated exclusively to his work. Today it is known as Salgado Studios. In the course of his photographic projects Salgado travelled to over a hundred countries; as well as being widely published in the international press, his work has been collected in books such as *Other Americas* (1986), *Sahel. L'homme en détresse* (1986), *Sahel. El fin del camino* (1988), *An Uncertain Grace* (1990), *Workers: An Archaeology of the Industrial Age* (1993), *Earth* (1997), *Migrations: Humanity in Transition* and *The Children: Refugees and Migrants* (2000), *Africa* (2007), *Genesis* (2013), *The Scent of a Dream* (2015), *Kuwait: A Desert on Fire* (2016), *Gold* (2019), and *Amazônia* (2021). Lélia Wanick Salgado handled planning and design of the books. Museums and galleries around the world have shown exhibitions based on his work and continue to present these shows. Lélia Wanick Salgado conceived most of the exhibitions in the role of curator. The year 2013 saw the publication of *From My Land to the Planet*, an account of Salgado's life and career written with French journalist Isabelle Francq. In 2014 the documentary *The Salt of the Earth* was released; co-directed by Wim Wenders and his son Juliano Ribeiro Salgado, it won the Special Jury Prize at the 2014 Cannes Film Festival in the Un Certain Regard section, as well as the César for best documentary in 2015. It was also nominated in the Best Documentary category at the 87th Academy Awards. Major awards received by Sebastião Salgado include the Primo Levi Prize (Italy); the Prince of Asturias Award for the Arts (Spain), the Peace Prize of the German Book Trade, and the Praemium Imperiale of the Japan Art Association, considered the Nobel Prize of the arts. He was made an honorary member of the American Academy of Arts and Sciences in the United States; in 2016 he became a member of the Académie des Beaux-Arts of the Institut de France and in 2019 was made an honorary member of the American Academy of Arts and Letters (New York). In 2021 he received an Honorary Doctor of Arts degree from Harvard University (Cambridge, MA). In the 1990s Sebastião and Lélia began working on environmental restoration of part of the Atlantic Forest in Brazil, in the Rio Doce valley, in the state of Minas Gerais. They rewilded a plot of land they own there, which became a nature reserve in 1998. In the same year they set up Instituto Terra to promote reforestation, conservation, and environmental education. Instituto Terra has since created a forest rich in numerous species of fauna and flora endemic to the Atlantic Forest. Sebastião Salgado died in Paris on 23 May 2025.

The poem 'The Glacier' by Primo Levi on page 5 was published in English in Primo Levi, *Collected Poems*, translated by Ruth Feldmann and Brian Swann (London, 1988).

Editorial direction: Curt Holtz
Editorial assistance: Marie Kuhn
Translation from Italian: Helen C. Ferguson
Copy-editing: Jonathan Fox
Design: Ginevra Costantini
Cover design: Sofarobotnik, Augsburg/Munich
Production management: Martina Effaga
Separations: DruckConcept, Berlin
Printing and binding: EBS, Verona, Italy

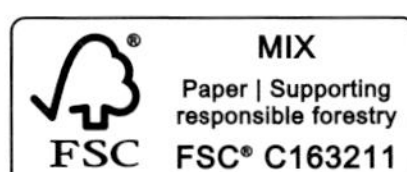

Penguin Random House Verlagsgruppe FSC® N001967

Printed in Italy

ISBN 978-3-7913-9403-9

www.prestel.com